Glencoe

Understanding Psychology

Reading Essentials and Study Guide

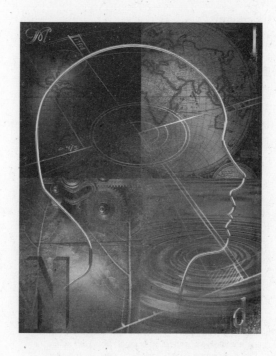

 **Glencoe McGraw-Hill**

New York, New York   Columbus, Ohio   Chicago, Illinois   Peoria, Illinois   Woodland Hills, California

To the Teacher

The **Reading Essentials and Study Guide** is designed to help students use recognized reading strategies to improve their reading-for-information skills. For each section of the student textbook, the students are alerted to key terms, asked to draw from prior knowledge, organize their thoughts with a graphic organizer, and then follow a process to read and understand the text. The **Reading Essentials and Study Guide** was prepared to help your students get more from their textbook by reading with purpose.

Customize Your Resources

No matter how you organize your teaching resources, Glencoe has what you need.

The **Teacher's Classroom Resources** for *Understanding Psychology* provides you with a wide variety of supplemental materials to enhance the classroom experience. The booklets are designed to open flat so that pages can be easily photocopied without removing them from their booklet. However, if you choose to create separate files, the pages are perforated for easy removal.

The individual booklets supplied in **Teacher's Classroom Resources** give you the flexibility to organize these resources in a combination that best suits your teaching style. Below are several alternatives.

- **Organize all resources by category**
  (all tests, all enrichment and extension activities,
  all cooperative learning activities, etc., filed separately)
- **Organize all resources by category and chapter**
  (all Chapter 1 activities, all Chapter 1 tests, etc.)
- **Organize resources sequentially by lesson**
  (activities, quizzes, readings, etc., for Chapter 1, Chapter 2, and so on)

Glencoe/McGraw-Hill

A Division of The McGraw-Hill Companies

Send all inquiries to:
Glencoe/McGraw-Hill
8787 Orion Place
Columbus, Ohio 43240

ISBN 0-07-830120-3

Printed in the United States of America

4 5 6 7 8 9 10 047 08 07 06

Contents

Study Guide 1-1

For use with textbook pages 7–13

Why Study Psychology?

Key Terms

physiological having to do with an organism's physical processes (page 7)

cognitive having to do with an organism's thinking and understanding (page 7)

psychology the scientific study of behavior that is tested through scientific research (page 9)

hypothesis an assumption or prediction about behavior that is tested through scientific research (page 11)

theory a set of assumptions used to explain phenomena and offered for scientific study (page 11)

basic science the pursuit of knowledge about natural phenomena for its own sake (page 11)

applied science discovering ways to use scientific findings to accomplish practical goals (page 11)

scientific method a general approach to gathering information and answering questions so that errors and biases are minimized (page 12)

Drawing From Experience

Why do people act and think the way they do? Why do people act differently in groups than they do when they are alone? How do we know what behavior is normal and abnormal? This section introduces the reasons to study psychology. It also explains the scientific basis of psychology.

Organizing Your Thoughts

Use the diagram below to help you take notes as you read the summaries that follow. Think about how each goal helps psychologists learn more about humans and animals.

Goals of Psychology			
1. _____	2. _____	3. _____	4. _____

Read to Learn

Introduction (page 7)

Physical needs such as food and sleep are known as **physiological** needs. **Cognitive** needs cannot be seen. They are needs that take place in our minds. Cognitive needs may be just as strong as physical needs. These two types of needs motivate human behavior.

5. List one physiological need and one cognitive need that you have had today.

_____

_____

Gaining Insight into Behavior (page 8)

Studying psychology will help you understand your own behavior. You will learn that you share behaviors with others. You will also learn that human behavior is very complex. Your behavior is unique to you. No one else behaves exactly like you do.

6. List a behavior of yours or of a friend that you would like to understand better.

_____

_____

Acquiring Practical Information (page 8)

Much of what you learn about psychology can be applied to your daily life. You will learn how to use rewards to get rid of an unwanted habit. You will learn how to improve your memory and study skills. You will also learn about the difficulties that people have in their lives and what psychology can do to help.

7. What would you like to learn about how humans behave or act?

_____

_____

Overview of Psychology (page 9)

Psychology is the scientific study of behavior. Psychologists study both human and animal behavior. Some psychologists study only behaviors that can be observed. Others study behavior that cannot be observed such as feelings, thoughts, and motives. All psychologists use the scientific method to study behavior. This method reduces the possibility of errors and bias. Since human behavior is so complex, simple explanations of behavior are not possible.

Psychologists have four goals in studying behavior. First, they seek to describe behavior. Second, they look for explanations of the behaviors. Psychologists propose a **hypothesis** to explain a behavior. They conduct research to test the hypothesis. From the research, they propose a **theory** to explain the behavior. Theories change as new research is completed.

The third goal of psychology is prediction. Using their research, psychologists try to predict how a human or animal will act in a certain situation. Finally, the fourth goal of psychology is to influence behavior. Some psychologists research behavior. They are doing **basic science**. Other psychologists view their work as **applied science**. They look for ways to use research to help people solve problems.

Some discoveries of basic science cannot be easily applied to real situations. For example, basic science found that children who lack stimulation are slow to develop. This information helps psychologists who are working with neglected children. It does not, however, tell psychologists what kind of stimulation is most helpful.

8. If you were a psychologist, would you want to discover how human behavior works or help someone resolve their personal problems? Why?

_____

_____

The Scientific Basis of Psychology (page 12)

Psychologists use the **scientific method**. The scientific method reduces errors and bias. Psychologists begin by asking a question or identifying a specific problem. They then propose a hypothesis to answer their questions. To test their hypothesis, psychologists collect data. There are many ways to collect data, including experiments, surveys, and case studies. After they collect their data, psychologists analyze their findings to see if their hypothesis was correct.

Early psychologists had to find ways to use the scientific method to study behavior. Wilhelm Wundt set up the first psychology laboratory. Wundt used scientific principles to study sensations and feelings. His technique was called introspection. He asked people to examine their own mental experiences. Although introspection is no longer used, the system of observing and analyzing behavior is an important part of the scientific study of behavior.

9. You have developed a hypothesis that gray and tan cars are more likely to be sideswiped than other colors of cars. How would you test this hypothesis?

_____

_____

_____

Study Guide 1-2

A Brief History of Psychology

For use with textbook pages 14–22

Key Terms

structuralist a psychologist who studied the basic elements that make up conscious mental experiences (page 16)

introspection a method of self-observation in which participants report on their thoughts and feelings (page 16)

functionalist a psychologist who studied the function (rather than the structure) of consciousness (page 16)

psychoanalyst a psychologist who studies how unconscious motives and conflicts determine human behavior (page 19)

behaviorist a psychologist who analyzes how organisms learn or modify their behavior based on their response to events in the environment (page 20)

humanist a psychologist who believes that each person has freedom in directing his or her future and achieving personal growth (page 20)

cognitivist a psychologist who focuses on how we process, store, and use information and how this information influences our thinking, language, problem solving, and creativity (page 20)

psychobiologist a psychologist who studies how physical and chemical changes in our bodies influence our behavior (page 21)

Drawing From Experience

People once believed the earth was flat. Have you ever believed something and later found it was not true? Did you change your belief? Scientists and psychologists revise theories as new information is learned.

In the last section, you learned reasons to study psychology. In this section you will study the history of psychology. You will also learn some of the modern approaches to understanding behavior.

Organizing Your Thoughts

Use the diagram on the next page to help you take notes as you read the summaries that follow. Think about how modern approaches to psychology use what the pioneers of psychology learned.

Historical Approaches	Modern Approaches
1. _____	5. _____
2. _____	6. _____
3. _____	7. _____
4. _____	8. _____
	9. _____
	10. _____

Read to Learn

Introduction (page 14)

Phrenology is the study of head shape and bumps on the skull. Phrenology is not really a science. It has been disproved. Phrenology, however, did help scientists recognize that the brain is responsible for our behavior.

11. If phrenology had been proven to be accurate, how might it have been used to predict human behavior?

_____

_____

_____

_____

_____

The Origins of Psychology (page 15)

Psychology has its roots in philosophy. The early Greeks were the first to study human behavior. They believed the heart was more important than the mind. Scientists, such as astronomers and physicists, began using formal scientific methods during the Renaissance. Their discoveries changed the way we look at the world.

One popular idea during the seventeenth century was *dualism*. It was the concept that the mind and body are separate. René Descartes disagreed. He believed that the mind controlled the body. He assumed that one influenced the other. Psychologists today still study how the mind and body work together.

12. Why do you think the Greeks thought the heart was more important than the mind?

_____

_____

_____

_____

Historical Approaches (page 15)

Not all psychologists agree. When psychology was a young science, different schools of psychology arose. Each offered its own explanation of human behavior. The **structuralists** studied the basic elements of human experience. Wilhelm Wundt founded this school. He used **introspection** to gather information. Introspection uses self-observation. From the observed behaviors, Wundt tried to map the processes of thought.

William James is considered the father of American psychology. He believed that everything we think and do helps humans survive. His school, the **functionalists**, studied how animals and people adapt to their environments.

Sir Francis Galton studied how heredity affects behavior. Heredity consists of the traits that we receive biologically from our parents. Galton studied traits by tracing ancestry. Psychologists today still study how heredity influences behavior.

The word *Gestalt* is German. It means "whole pattern." Gestalt psychology examines whole patterns. For example, when you look at a chair, you see it as the sum of its parts. You do not see it as four legs, seat, and back. You see the whole chair. Gestalt psychology still influences the study of sensation and perception.

13. Focus for one minute on exactly what you are doing. Write a complete description of your thought processes.

_____

_____

_____

_____

Contemporary Approaches (page 17)

Many of the ideas from historical approaches to psychology are still used today. Sigmund Freud studied the unconscious mind. He believed that much of our behavior results from conflicts we face. He encouraged his patients to use *free association* to help them to resolve their conflicts. He encouraged people to analyze their dreams. Freud was a **psychoanalyst**. His job was to listen and be

Reading Essentials and Study Guide

objective. He encouraged patients to work through their own problems. Most of Freud's research is based on case studies.

Ivan Pavlov examined how behaviors could be conditioned. He rang a tuning fork each time he fed a dog. Soon the dog began salivating whenever it heard the tuning fork. Pavlov trained the dog to respond to the tuning fork. Researchers have shown that conditioning works with humans also.

John B. Watson believed psychology should only study *observable* behaviors. He was a **behaviorist**. He believed that all behavior was the result of conditioning. Another behaviorist, B.F. Skinner, studied *reinforcement*. He believed that behavior is shaped by the rewards that we receive. Behavior that is rewarded will be repeated.

Humanists, like Abraham Maslow and Carl Rogers, disagree with behaviorists. They believe that human behavior is not controlled by outside events like rewards. They see behavior as internal and self-directed. They seek to find ways for each person to reach his or her full potential.

Cognitivists, like Jean Piaget and Noam Chomsky, focus on thinking, problem solving, and creativity. Their research has been directed toward understanding how we store, process, and use information.

Advances in technology have opened new avenues of research for psychologists. **Psychobiologists** use PET and CAT scans to study the brain. They link genetic factors to human behavior. They have been able to see what parts of the brain are active during sleep. They are demonstrating how the mind and body work together.

A new approach to psychology is called sociocultural psychology. It examines how cultural and ethnic similarities and differences influence behavior. For example, what you say when you sneeze is influenced by your culture. In some cultures, sneezes are good omens. In others, they may be viewed as bad omens. If your culture believed a sneeze was a bad omen, you would try hard not to sneeze. The United States has large immigrant populations. Each immigrant group has its own culture. Conflicts can arise when one culture holds different views from another culture. Sociocultural psychologists look for ways to resolve and minimize these conflicts.

14. How can social psychologists use other psychological approaches to help resolve cultural or ethnic conflicts?

_____

_____

_____

_____

Study Guide 1-3

Psychology as a Profession

For use with textbook pages 24–28

Key Terms

psychologist a scientist who studies the mind and behavior of humans and animals (page 25)

clinical psychologist a psychologist who diagnoses and treats people with emotional disturbances (page 25)

counseling psychologist a psychologist who usually helps people deal with problems of living (page 25)

psychiatry a branch of medicine that deals with mental, emotional, or behavioral disorders (page 25)

developmental psychologist a psychologist who studies the emotional, cognitive, biological, personal, and social changes that occur as an individual matures (page 26)

educational psychologist a psychologist who is concerned with helping students learn (page 26)

community psychologist a psychologist who may work in a mental health or social welfare agency operated by the government or private organization (page 26)

industrial/organizational psychologist a psychologist who uses psychological concepts to make the workplace a more satisfying environment for employees and managers (page 26)

experimental psychologist a psychologist who studies sensation, perception, learning, motivation, and emotion in carefully controlled laboratory conditions (page 28)

Drawing From Experience

What kinds of career choices are you considering? Does the idea of making discoveries about human behavior interest you? Do you like helping people? Perhaps a career in psychology is in your future.

In the last section, you learned about the different approaches to psychology. You also saw how psychology has evolved and how it continues to change. In this section, you will take a brief look at some of the specialties found in the profession of psychology.

Organizing Your Thoughts

Use the diagram on the next page to help you take notes as you read the summaries that follow. Think about the places in which you might encounter each of the specialties.

Specialty	Places in which they work:
1. clinical psychologist	
2. counseling psychologist	
3. developmental psychologist	
4. educational psychologist	
5. industrial/organizational psychologist	
6. environmental psychologist	
7. forensic psychologist	
8. health psychologist	
9. experimental psychologist	

Read to Learn

What Is a Psychologist? (page 25)

Psychologists are professionals trained to observe, analyze, and treat behavior. Most psychologists focus on a specific area of psychology. Psychologists earn advanced degrees and spend many years in training.

Psychology has many subfields. Clinical and counseling psychologists are the most numerous. **Clinical psychologists** treat abnormal behaviors. **Counseling psychologists** help people with everyday problems. For example, they can help people deal with the loss of a job.

Psychologists and psychiatrists both treat behavioral problems. **Psychiatrists**, however, have medical degrees. They can prescribe medicine. Psychologists often refer patients to psychiatrists.

Developmental psychologists look at the ways in which people develop over their lifetimes. Development includes physical, emotional, cognitive, and social areas. **Educational psychologists** explore intelligence, memory, and problem solving. They work closely with educators to develop new instructional tools. **Community psychologists** often work for government agencies. They design, run, or evaluate mental health clinics. Many businesses employ **industrial/organizational psychologists**. These professionals help boost worker productivity. They may develop training programs and ways to improve working conditions.

Environmental psychologists study how changes in the environment affect human behavior. For example, government agencies may consult with environmental psychologists to develop ways to help victims of natural disasters. Forensic psychologists work with attorneys and police officers. They develop profiles of criminal offenders. Health psychologists search for connections between psychological and physical health. **Experimental psychologists** conduct research, usually in a laboratory. Other psychologists use their research.

The largest professional organization for psychologists is the American Psychological Association, or APA. It has 53 sections. Each section represents a specialty that is recognized by the profession.

10. Which psychologists practice basic science? Applied science? Both types of science?

_____

_____

_____

_____

_____

_____

_____

_____

_____

_____

_____

_____

_____

Study Guide 2-1

For use with textbook pages 35–41

What Is Research?

Key Terms

sample the small group of participants, out of the total number available, that a researcher studies (page 36)

naturalistic observation research method in which the psychologist observes the participant in a natural setting without interfering (page 37)

case study research method that involves an intensive investigation of one or more participants (page 37)

survey research method in which information is obtained by asking many individuals a fixed set of questions (page 38)

longitudinal study research method in which data is collected about a group of participants over a number years to assess how certain characteristics change and remain the same during development (page 38)

cross-sectional study research method in which data is collected from groups of participants of different ages and compared so that conclusions can be drawn about differences due to age (page 38)

correlation the measure of a relationship between two variables or sets of data (page 39)

hypothesis an educated guess about the relationship between two variables (page 40)

variable any factor that is capable of change (page 40)

experimental group the group of participants to which an independent variable is applied (page 40)

control group the group of participants that is treated in the same way as the experimental group except that the experimental treatment (the independent variable) is not applied (page 40)

Drawing From Experience

Have you ever wondered how pollsters can predict who is going to win an election? Have you ever considered how advertisers determine that 9 out of 10 people prefer a certain brand? This section explains the various research methods that psychologists use. It also discusses why psychologists choose a certain method.

Organizing Your Thoughts

Use the diagram on the next page to help you take notes as you read the summaries that follow. Think about why each type of research is useful to psychologists.

	Naturalistic Observation	Case Studies	Surveys	Longitudinal Studies	Cross-Sectional Studies	Correlations	Experiments
Description	1.	2.	3.	4.	5.	6.	7.
Example	8.	9.	10.	11.	12.	13.	14.

Read to Learn

Introduction (page 35)

Jane Goodall observed the behavior of chimpanzees. She used naturalistic observation and case studies to conduct her research. To develop theories, psychologists must gather useful information. Like other scientists, they have developed many methods for gathering and analyzing the information they need.

15. How do the methods used by psychologists to gather information differ from everyday information-gathering methods?

_____

Pre-Research Decisions (page 36)

Researchers begin by asking a question. They then make a guess about the answer to their question. This guess is called a **hypothesis**. Then researchers gather evidence to see if their hypothesis is correct. There are many ways to gather information. Researchers might conduct an experiment. They might use case studies. They might use another method of gathering information. The method they use depends upon the question they are trying to answer.

When psychologists study a group of people, the entire group is called a *population*. Psychologists cannot always investigate every member of a population. For example, if psychologists want to know what American high school students think about college, they cannot ask every student in the country. Instead they will study a small group of students who represent all of the students in the country. This small group is called a **sample**.

If psychologists choose their samples carefully, they can get an answer that can be applied to the entire population. To find the correct answer, a sample must be representative of the entire population. For example, if you are studying the average height of American men, you would not study only basketball players.

There are two ways to get samples that represent an entire population. One way is to collect a *random sample*. Random samples give every person in the population an equal chance of being chosen. The second way to get a sample is to collect a *stratified sample*. To collect a stratified sample, psychologists divide the population into subgroups. They then pick out the people they want in the sample. They try to pick people so that every subgroup in the population is represented proportionately.

16. Each week a list is published of the most popular television programs from the previous week. The survey gathers information from a few thousand homes across America. What type of sample is used?

_____

Methods of Research (page 37)

Psychologists use many different methods to gather information. To study how people and animals behave in daily life, psychologists use **naturalistic observation**. They watch people or animals in their natural settings without interfering. To acquire detailed information about individuals or groups, psychologists use **case studies**. Case studies do not prove anything about people not studied. They do, however, provide much information psychologists can use to develop experiments. To gather data about the behaviors, attitudes, and experiences of large numbers of people, psychologists use **surveys**. Surveys include interviews, questionnaires, or a combination of the two.

To study how behavior changes over time, psychologists use **longitudinal studies**. They study the same group of people over a long period of time. Longitudinal studies can take too long to conduct. Another way to study changes in behavior over time is to use **cross-sectional studies**. In a cross-sectional study, psychologists study people of different ages.

Often, psychologists want to study the relationship between two sets of observations. This type of study is known as a **correlation**. Correlations compare two things or two sets of data. If a positive correlation exists, the increase (or decrease) in one thing is matched by an increase (or decrease) of the other. For example, people with high IQ scores tend to have high grades as well. If a negative correlation exists, an increase in one thing is matched by a decrease in the other—or vice versa. For example, the more hours you practice tennis, the fewer double faults you have. A correlation simply describes the relationship. It does not prove that one event caused the other.

Many psychologists use experiments to conduct research. Experiments begin with a **hypothesis**. Psychologists then identify the things that are likely to be changed by the experiment. These are called **variables**. An *independent variable* is something researchers change during the experiment. A *dependent variable* is something that changes on its own in response to changes in the independent variable.

Participants in an experiment are divided into two groups called the **experimental group** and the **control group**. The experimental group is exposed to the independent variable. The control group is not exposed to the independent variable. The experimenter then compares the results from the two groups. Other researchers then repeat the experiment and try to replicate the results to make sure no errors were made in the original experiment. Psychologists must meet certain ethical standards in their research. The American Psychological Association (APA) publishes ethical guidelines for researchers to follow.

17. What research method would you use to find out how many people noticed a company's new billboard?

_____

Study Guide 2-2

Problems and Solutions in Research

For use with textbook pages 42–45

Key Terms

self-fulfilling prophecy a situation in which a researcher's expectations influence the researcher's own behavior, and thereby influence the participant's behavior (page 42)

single-blind experiment an experiment in which the participants are unaware of which participants received the treatment (page 43)

double-blind experiment an experiment in which neither the experimenter nor the participants know which participants received which treatment (page 43)

placebo effect a change in a participant's illness or behavior that results from a belief that the treatment will have an effect, rather than the actual treatment (page 45)

Drawing From Experience

Have you ever believed strongly that something would happen? Have you ever acted to make sure that something happens? In the last section, you read about the methods psychologists use to conduct research. In this section, you will read about problems that can happen with research.

Organizing Your Thoughts

Use the diagram below to help you take notes as you read the summaries that follow. Think about kinds of problems researchers face and the techniques they use to avoid them.

Problems Researchers Face	Possible Solutions
Self-fulfilling prophecies	1.
Deceiving participants	2.
Placebo effect	3.

Read to Learn

Introduction (page 42)

When researchers test a hypothesis they expect certain results. If they are not careful, their body language or facial expressions may give the participants clues as to how to behave. This is called a **self-fulfilling prophecy**. Researchers get the results they expect because their behavior tells participants what to do.

4. Describe a time when your behavior influenced the behavior of someone else.

_____

Avoiding Self-Fulfilling Prophecies (page 43)

Researchers have developed ways to avoid self-fulfilling prophecies. They may use a single-blind experiment or a double-blind experiment. In a **single-blind experiment**, the participants do not know if they have received the treatment. For a study on the effects of tranquilizers, for example, the participants do not know if they took the tranquilizer or a placebo. The placebo would be a pill that looks like the tranquilizer, but has no medical effects. The researcher knows which participants received the tranquilizer and which received the placebo. When the participants describe the effects of the tranquilizer, the researcher can determine whether the participants' expectations have shaped their responses.

In a **double-blind experiment**, neither the participant nor the researcher knows who is receiving the treatment. This avoids any chance of a self-fulfilling prophecy. Researchers cannot give away information that they do not have.

5. How may a participant's expectations affect the results of an experiment?

_____

The Milgram Experiment (page 44)

Stanley Milgram conducted a famous single-blind experiment. He tested whether people would shock a person simply because an authority figure told them to do it. It was a single-blind experiment because Milgram knew the real purpose of the experiment but the participants did not. Although Milgram's experiment supported his hypothesis, many researchers considered his methods unethical. Before experimenting on people today, the American Psychological Association requires its members to give a plan to its Human Participants Committee for approval.

6. Why do you think some psychologists considered Milgram's experiment unethical?

_____

The Placebo Effect (page 45)

When researchers study drugs they must consider the **placebo effect**. This is a change in behavior due to the belief that the treatment will be effective. In one experiment three groups were studied. One group was told they were receiving a tranquilizer. The second group was told that they were receiving an energizing drug. The control group did not receive any drugs at all. More than half the people in the experimental groups reported benefits from the drugs. All the drugs used in the experiment, however, were placebos. Participants' reactions were due to their expectations, not to actual effects.

7. Why do you think the placebo effect works?

_____

Study Guide 2-3

Statistical Evaluation

For use with textbook pages 47–54

Key Terms

statistics the branch of mathematics concerned with summarizing and making meaningful inferences from collections of data (page 48)

descriptive statistics the listing and summarizing of data in a practical, efficient way (page 48)

frequency distribution an arrangement of data that indicates how often a particular score or observation occurs (page 49)

normal curve a graph of frequency distribution shaped like a symmetrical, bell-shaped curve; a graph of normal distribution (page 51)

central tendency a number that describes something about the "average" score of a distribution (page 51)

variance a measure of difference or spread (page 52)

standard deviation a measure of variability that describes an average distance of every score from the mean (page 52)

correlation coefficient a statistic that describes the direction and strength of the relationship between two sets of variables (page 52)

inferential statistics numerical methods used to determine whether research data support a hypothesis or whether results were due to chance (page 53)

Drawing From Experience

Have you ever played on a sports team? What type of statistics did the team keep? What did the statistics tell the coaches about the team members' performances?

In the last section, you explored how to overcome common research problems. In this section, you will learn how researchers organize and evaluate their results. These tools are known as **statistics**.

Organizing Your Thoughts

Use the diagram at the top of the next page to help you take notes as you read the summaries that follow. Think about the type of information that you learn from each type of statistic.

Types of Distributions	Measures of Central Tendency	Measures of Variance
1.	3.	6.
2.	4.	7.
	5.	8.

Read to Learn

Introduction (page 47)

Psychologists try to collect meaningful data. They then have to organize and evaluate the data correctly. To organize and evaluate the data, psychologists use **statistics**.

9. How can statistics help you evaluate a hypothesis?

_____

_____

_____

Descriptive Statistics (page 48)

Descriptive statistics list and summarize data in useful ways. Tools include tables and graphs. One descriptive statistic is a **frequency distribution**. This table arranges data so that the researcher can quickly see which response was given most often. Percentages may be calculated from the table. For example, a student collects data about the number of hours spent watching TV the night before a big test. The frequency distribution shows that 3 participants watched TV for one hour. Since there were 15 participants, 20 percent of the students surveyed watched TV for one hour on the night before the big test.

Frequency information can also be displayed as a *histogram* or a frequency polygon. A histogram is similar to a bar graph. A frequency polygon plots points by participant and frequency. The points on the graph are then connected to form an irregular shape.

When very large amounts of data are collected, a graph of frequency distribution may produce a bell-shaped curve. This kind of curve is called a **normal curve**. A normal curve is symmetrical. The largest frequency is at the center of the curve.

Three methods psychologists use to summarize information are the *mean*, the *median*, and the *mode*. These are the measures of **central tendency**. They describe something about the average score of a distribution. The mode is the most frequent score. The median is the middle score. It is determined by listing all the scores from lowest to highest. The median score has an equal number of lower and higher scores. The mean is the mathematical average. To find the mean, you add all the scores then divide by the total number of scores you added.

Distributions vary in ways other than averages. They also vary in how spread out they are. Measures of variance tell how wide or tall the distribution is. Three common measures of **variance** are the range, the **standard deviation**, and the **correlation coefficient**. The range is the difference between the highest and lowest scores. The standard deviation uses all the data points in its calculation. It is a measure of the distance of each score from the mean. The correlation coefficient describes the strength of the relationship between two sets of data. A *positive correlation* means that as one variable increases, the other variable also increases. A *negative correlation* indicates that as one variable increases, the other variable decreases.

10. What do each of the following measure: mean, median, mode, correlation coefficient, and range?

_____

_____

_____

_____

Inferential Statistics (page 53)

Psychologists use **inferential statistics** to make generalizations about sets of data. These statistics tell whether the research supports the hypothesis or is simply due to random chance. Probability is the chance that a particular outcome will occur. For example, the chance of a coin landing heads up is 50 percent. This 50 percent chance is the same every time you toss the coin.

Researchers use measures of statistical significance to determine if the results occurred because of chance. These complex tools help researchers rule out the possibility that their results were due to chance. For sets of data that are normally distributed, the researcher uses statistics to verify that their data distribution is not far away from the distribution of a normal curve.

11. Toss a coin 10 times and record the results. What do your results indicate about the likely results of the next toss? Are the results likely due to chance or due to an unfair coin?

_____

_____

_____

_____

Study Guide 3-1

Physical, Perceptual, and Language Development

For use with textbook pages 61–68

Key Terms

developmental psychology the study of changes that occur as an individual matures (page 61)

grasping reflex an infant's clinging response to a touch on the palm of his or her hand (page 62)

rooting reflex an infant's response in turning toward the source of touching that occurs anywhere around his or her mouth (page 62)

maturation the internally programmed growth of a child (page 64)

telegraphic speech the kind of verbal utterances in which words are left out, but the meaning is usually clear (page 67)

Drawing From Experience

Do you remember anything from when you were a baby? How have you changed since then? When did you learn to crawl, stand, and walk? How did you learn to talk?

This section discusses human development. You will learn how infants develop skills in stages as their bodies mature. You will see how they learn to walk, speak, and perceive the world.

Organizing Your Thoughts

Use the diagram below to help you take notes as you read the summaries that follow. Think about how infants learn new skills as their bodies grow. Next to each skill, write the age when children normally learn that skill.

Skill	Months	Skill	Months
1. Raise head		**7.** Pull self to standing position	
2. Roll over		**8.** Walk holding on to furniture	
3. Smile		**9.** Crawl	
4. Sit with support		**10.** Stand alone	
5. Grasp objects		**11.** Walk	
6. Sit without support			

Read to Learn

Introduction (page 61)

You have changed a lot since you were a baby. You learned more in early childhood than you ever will again. People grow and develop in stages throughout their lives. **Developmental psychology** is the study of changes that occur as a person matures.

12. What types of growth do developmental psychologists study?

_____

Nature and Nurture (page 62)

Developmental psychologists study the question of nature versus nurture. Nature refers to our genes (heredity). Nurture refers to what we have learned and experienced. Psychologists want to know how much of development results from heredity (nature) and how much is learned (nurture). Usually both nature and nurture influence behavior.

13. In what ways do you behave like your father or mother? Do you think you inherited this behavior or learned it from them?

_____

Newborns (page 62)

Most infants are born with certain inborn, automatic movements called reflexes. The **grasping reflex** is an infant's clinging response to a touch on the palm of the hand. For example, infants can grasp a finger so strongly that they can be lifted into the air. The **rooting reflex** is an infant's response to a touch near the mouth. The infant turns toward the source of the touch.

How can psychologists study infants who cannot speak or understand questions? They do this by stimulating them in different ways. Then they study the responses infants make, such as cry, smile, or show surprise or fear. From these responses, psychologists learn how infants see the world.

14. Have you ever given a cookie to an infant? Did the infant smile? What do you think this response says about the infant's feelings about cookies?

_____

Physical Development (page 63)

Within two years, infants change into children who can walk, talk, and feed themselves. These changes are the result of both maturation and learning. **Maturation** is the internally programmed growth of a child. It is like a plant that shoots up and unfolds according to a built-in plan. Children normally develop according to a general schedule. For example, they begin to lift their heads at about 3 months of age. They can grasp objects at about 5 to 6 months. Children can only do such skills when their bodies are physically ready. This is called *maturational readiness*.

Psychologists developed a timetable for maturation by observing thousands of children. They recorded the ages at which infants first began to smile, sit up, crawl, and walk. They discovered that each child is different. On average, infants start to walk at 12 to 13 months, but some are ready at 9 months. Others are not ready until 18 months.

15. If your child didn't start walking until 14 months, would you be concerned? Why or why not?

_____

Perceptual Development (page 65)

Infants are born with perception skills. For example, experiments showed that infants have depth perception. Using glass with a shelf below it, researchers created a visual cliff. They learned that infants can perceive a dropoff, because the infants responded with fear to the dropoff.

16. Why do very young infants seem unafraid of the visual cliff, when crawling infants are afraid?

_____

The Development of Language (page 66)

Both language and thought use symbols. Children begin to think about things before they can speak. For example, 1-year-old children will look for a toy that has disappeared. They know in their minds that the toy exists, even if they cannot see it.

Chimpanzees can be taught to "talk" using sign language or special typewriters. By "talking" in this way, chimps are using words as symbols. Chimps, however, cannot put words together to form sentences like humans can. The rules for organizing words into sentences are called *grammar*. Grammar is what makes the sentence "The rhinoceros roared at the boy" mean the same as "The boy was roared at by the rhinoceros." Learning language involves several steps. First, children must learn words. Then they must give the words meaning. Finally, they must learn grammar.

Infants begin to babble sounds in their first year. Late in their first year, children begin to imitate the speech of their parents, brothers, and sisters. In their second year, children begin using sounds as symbols. The sounds may be incomplete words, but they have meaning for the child. For example, the child may use the sound "ba" to represent the object "ball."

Children can join words into two-word phrases by the end of their second year. At age 2, though, a child's grammar is not like an adult's. At this age, children use **telegraphic speech**. They leave out words, but the meaning is usually clear. For example, a child might say "Where my apple?" By the age of 4 or 5, children know several thousand words.

17. If a child says "Daddy *goed* yesterday," why is this a "good" error?

_____

Study Guide 3-2

For use with textbook pages 70–77

Cognitive and Emotional Development

Key Terms

schema a conceptual framework a person uses to make sense of the world (page 71)

assimilation the process of fitting objects and experiences into one's schemas (page 71)

accommodation the adjustment of one's schemas to include newly observed events and experiences (page 71)

object permanence a child's realization that an object exists even when he or she cannot see or touch it (page 72)

representational thought the intellectual ability of a child to picture something in his or her mind (page 72)

conservation the principle that a given quantity does not change when its appearance is changed (page 73)

egocentric a young child's inability to understand another person's perspective (page 73)

imprinting inherited tendencies or responses that are displayed by newborn animals when they encounter new stimuli in their environment (page 75)

critical period a specific time in development when certain skills or abilities are most easily learned (page 75)

Drawing From Experience

Why can't young children grasp the rules of a simple game like hide-and-seek? Why do infants seem to forget about toys when they are out of view? How do emotional bonds form between mother and child?

In the last section, you read about physical, perceptual, and language development. In this section you will read about two other types of human development: cognitive (intelligence) and emotional development.

Organizing Your Thoughts

Use the diagram at the top of the next page to help you take notes as you read the summaries that follow. Think about the key steps in cognitive and emotional development. Draw a line to match each principle on the left with its example on the right.

Principle	Example
1. object permanence	**A.** A gosling sees a man soon after birth and follows the man wherever he goes.
2. representational thought	**B.** A child is able to solve a math word problem.
3. conservation	**C.** A child sees another child throw a temper tantrum. The next day, the child imitates the tantrum.
4. formal operations stage	**D.** When water is poured from one jar to another, a child no longer thinks the amount of water has changed.
5. imprinting	**E.** When a child sees you hide her ball, she looks for it in the last place she saw you put it.

Read to Learn

Introduction (page 70)

Children think differently from adults in many ways. Children form their own ideas about how the world works.

6. Describe something that you believed as a child that you would never believe now, as a young adult.

_____

_____

_____

Cognitive Development (page 70)

Intelligence is the ability to understand. According to psychologist Jean Piaget, intelligence develops gradually as a child grows. A 4-year-old cannot understand things a 7-year-old grasps easily. After years of studying children, Piaget concluded that young children think in a different way than older children and adults. As children's intelligence grows, the amount of information they know increases. Also, the way they think changes.

A **schema** is a mental representation of the world. Each of us constructs schemas in our minds. We try to understand new things by applying our schemas to them. This process is called **assimilation**. For example, an infant has stacked blocks before. He has a "stacking schema." He then finds a new block. He can assimilate or fit this new object into his stacking schema. But what happens if the infant finds an open box? He finds that the stacking schema does not work. When he tries to stack, the block falls into the open box. Now the infant must adjust his schema to accommodate the new object.

Accommodation means adjusting one's schemas to include newly observed events and experiences. Together, accommodation and assimilation make intelligence grow. When new things do not fit existing schemas, we must create new schemas. This causes us to understand things in new ways.

Infants' views of the world are limited to what they can see, touch, or taste. They cannot picture or think about things in their minds. When a young infant's toy is hidden, she acts as if it no longer exists. She does not look for it. But at 7 to 12 months, this changes. When the child sees you hide the toy under a blanket, she will look for it there. If you then hide it behind your back, the child will continue looking under the blanket. Later, at age 18 to 24 months, the child will have learned to look in the last place she saw you put it. She knows the toy must be somewhere. This is an important step in intellectual development. The child understands that an object exists even when she cannot see or touch it. This is called **object permanence**. Achieving object permanence is evidence that the child can now picture (or represent) things in her mind. This is called **representational thought**.

Between the ages of 5 and 7, most children begin to achieve **conservation**. This means that they understand that the amount of something does not change when its appearance changes. For example, imagine you have two identical short, wide jars filled with water. You pour the contents of one jar into a tall, thin jar. A child under 5 will say that the tall jar contains more water than the short one. If you pour the water back into the short jar to show the amount has not changed, the child will still insist that the tall jar contained more water. By age 7, however, the child will tell you that the tall jar contains the same amount of water as the short one. The principle of conservation is closely related to the idea of egocentrism. Young children are **egocentric**. This means that they cannot understand someone else's viewpoint.

Everyone goes through four stages of cognitive development in the same order but not necessarily at the same ages. In the *sensorimotor* stage, infants understand the world mostly through their body and senses. In the *preoperational stage*, they begin to use mental images or symbols to understand things. Children begin to use reason in the *concrete operations stage*, but have trouble with abstract ideas. In the *formal operations stage* the person is able to solve abstract problems.

7. Suppose you show a child two identical pencils. You put them together so that the child can see that they are the same length. The child agrees that they are the same length. Then you move the pencils apart so that one pencil sticks out further, and ask which is longer. The child still says they are the same length. What principle has the child demonstrated?

_____

_____

_____

Emotional Development (page 74)

While children are learning to use their bodies to think, and to express themselves, they are also developing emotionally. They become attached to specific people and care about what these people think and feel.

Konrad Lorenz discovered that goslings become attached to their mothers in a sudden learning process called **imprinting**. A few hours after hatching, the goslings will follow the first thing they see that moves. Usually, it is their mother. Even if the first thing they see is a human, they will treat that person like their mother from then on. A **critical period** is a time in development when certain skills or abilities are most easily learned. For geese, this period occurs just after birth. Whatever goslings learn during this period makes a deep impression. However, a gosling will correct its imprinted response when later exposed to its mother.

Psychologist Harry Harlow raised baby monkeys with two substitute mothers. One mother was made of soft cloth and the other was made of wire. He discovered that the young monkeys became strongly attached to the cloth mother, whether she gave food or not. They ignored the wire mother. When frightened, the babies would run to the cloth mother, not the wire one. Harlow concluded that monkeys cling to their mothers because of the need for touching, which he called contact comfort.

Human infants become attached to their mothers at about 6 months of age. This attachment is especially strong between ages 6 months and 3 years. At 3 years of age, children have reached the stage where they can imagine their mother and feel a relationship with her, even when she is absent.

A 1-year-old child may display *stranger anxiety* when she is near a stranger, even when the mother is present. *Separation anxiety* occurs whenever the child is suddenly separated from the mother.

Researchers have identified four patterns of attachment. Infants who demonstrate *secure attachment* welcome the mother back when she leaves and are not angry at her. In *avoidance attachment*, infants avoid or ignore the mother when she leaves or returns. Infants with *resistance attachment* are not upset when the mother leaves but reject her or act angry when she returns. Infants with *disorganized attachment* behave inconsistently. They may not be upset when the mother leaves but they avoid her when she returns. This attachment seems to be the least secure type of attachment.

8. Why is imprinting important to the survival of baby geese?

_____

_____

_____

_____

_____

Study Guide 3-3

Parenting Styles and Social Development

For use with textbook pages 78–86

Key Terms

authoritarian family parents attempt to control, shape, and evaluate the behavior and attitudes of their children and adolescents in accordance with a set code of conduct (page 79)

democratic/authoritative family children and adolescents participate in decisions affecting their lives (page 79)

permissive/laissez-faire family children and adolescents have the final say; parents are less controlling and have a nonpunishing, accepting attitude toward children (page 79)

socialization the process of learning the rules of behavior of the culture within which an individual is born and will live (page 81)

identification the process by which a child adopts the values and principles of the same-sex parent (page 82)

sublimation the process of redirecting sexual impulses into learning tasks (page 82)

role taking children's play that involves assuming adult roles, thus enabling the child to experience different points of view (page 84)

Drawing From Experience

How would you describe your parents' style of parenting? How do you think their style influenced your personality?

In the last section, you learned how intelligence and emotional bonds develop. In this section, you will read about different parenting styles and how children learn society's rules of behavior.

Organizing Your Thoughts

Use the diagram at the top of the next page to help you take notes as you read the summaries that follow. Think about the different theories of social development. Record the name of the theory that goes with each main idea presented.

Main Idea	Theory of Social Development
1. Children learn right from wrong as they learn to control their powerful sexual and aggressive impulses.	**1.**
2. Social approval is important to development. Development is a lifelong interactive process.	**2.**
3. Social development is a matter of conditioning and imitation.	**3.**
4. Social development is the result of children trying to make sense of their experiences and the world around them.	**4.**

Read to Learn

Introduction (page 78)

Children learn how to behave in their society from their parents, from other people around them, and from their own experiences. The process of learning the rules of behavior in a culture is called **socialization**.

5. What are some experiences that taught you right from wrong?

_____

_____

_____

Parenting Styles (page 79)

The parent-child relationship influences the way children seek independence and resolve conflicts. In **authoritarian families**, parents are the bosses. They set the rules and expect children to follow them without question. In **democratic** or **authoritative families**, children participate in the decisions that affect their lives. Parents listen to the children's reasons for wanting to do something. The parents, however, still have the right to say no. In **permissive** or **laissez-faire families**, children have the final say. Parents may try to guide the children. They often, however, give in to the children's wishes. They may even give up their parenting responsibilities. They may set no rules and simply ignore the children.

Studies show that children who grow up in democratic/authoritative families are more confident than are other young people. This results from two behaviors of the parents. The parents establish limits on the child and respond to the child with warmth and support. Children of democratic families are also likely to want to make their own decisions.

6. How would families with each parenting style set a curfew for teens?

_____

_____

_____

Child Abuse (page 80)

Child abuse includes physical or mental injury, sexual abuse, neglect, or mistreatment of children by adult caregivers. Many abusive parents were themselves mistreated as children. Also, overburdened and stressed parents are more likely to abuse their children.

Parent education for abusive parents helps them to learn better ways to deal with their children. Also, community resources and support systems can help reduce abuse.

Abuse can rob children of their childhood. It can cause them to lose trust and feel guilty. These feelings can lead to emotional problems, such as depression and low self-esteem. Every state and most counties offer protective services to children.

7. Why do you think child abuse often goes unreported?

_____

_____

_____

Social Development (page 81)

Socialization is the process of learning the rules of behavior in the culture where you live. To live with other people, children must learn what behavior is acceptable and unacceptable.

One part of socialization is learning when to apply the rules and when to bend them. A second part is gaining an identity. As children learn the society's values, they gain an identity as an individual member of a society, a member of different social categories, and a member of a family. A third part of socialization is learning to live with other people and with yourself. Children must learn that other people have rights and that they have limitations. For example, a child must learn that it is not acceptable to take another child's toy. Or, a child may discover that she cannot hit a baseball on the first try.

Sigmund Freud believed that all children are born with powerful sexual and aggressive urges. In learning to control these impulses, children gain a sense of right and wrong. Freud identified five stages of development. In the *oral stage*, infants associate erotic pleasure with the mouth, sucking at their mother's breast. In the *anal stage*, children associate erotic pleasure with the elimination process. The *phallic stage* occurs when children begin to associate

Copyright © by The McGraw-Hill Companies, Inc.

Reading Essentials and Study Guide

sexual pleasure with their genitals. During the phallic stage, children adopt the values and principles of the same-sex parent. This is called **identification**. At about age 5 or 6, children enter a *latency stage*. Sexual desires are pushed to the background, and children explore the world and learn new skills. This process of redirecting sexual impulses into learning tasks is called **sublimation**. Children reach the *genital stage* in adolescence. In this stage, they get as much satisfaction from giving pleasure as receiving it. Freud believed that personality development is complete as we enter adolescence.

Erik Erikson believed that a child's need for social approval is just as important as sexual urges. Unlike Freud, he saw development as a lifelong, interactive process among people. How we develop depends on how other people respond to our efforts. For example, a 1-year-old boy is delighted with his new ability to walk. Just learning this new skill gives him self-esteem. As he walks around exploring, however, he gets into things. If the adults around him praise his efforts, he will develop a sense of independence. If they punish him for being a nuisance, he may feel his desire for independence is bad.

Freud and Erikson stress the emotional part of social development. Other psychologists believe social development is simply a matter of conditioning and imitation. Children receive rewards for doing what others do. They begin to copy older children and adults to gain more rewards. These learning theories of development are discussed in Chapter 9.

Another theory is the cognitive-developmental approach. Cognitive means thinking. These psychologists believe that social development is the result of the child trying to make sense out of his experiences with the world around him. For example, when children play games, they make up rules. Much of their play involves **role taking**. They try on adult roles such as mother or teacher. This allows them to experience different points of view.

Lawrence Kohlberg identified six stages of moral development. In Stage 1, children are egocentric and consider no other points of view. In Stage 2, they evaluate acts in terms of consequences. They do not consider whether actions are right or wrong. In Stage 3, children want social approval so they apply other people's rules rigidly. In Stage 4, children see laws as moral rules to be obeyed. In Stage 5, people are concerned with whether a law is fair and just. Stage 6 involves accepting ethical principles as more important than any written law.

8. How does role taking help children experience different points of view?

_____

_____

_____

_____

_____

_____

Study Guide 4-1

Physical and Sexual Development

For use with textbook pages 93–99

Key Terms

initiation rites ceremonies or rituals in which an individual is admitted to new status or accepted into a new position (page 94)

puberty sexual maturation; the end of childhood and the point when reproduction is first possible (page 95)

menarche the first menstrual period (page 96)

spermarche period during which males achieve first ejaculation (page 96)

asynchrony the condition during adolescence in which the growth or maturation of bodily parts is uneven (page 96)

Drawing From Experience

When you were between 10 years old and 16 years old, did you notice changes in your body? Did you experience strong emotions as well? What was adolescence like for you?

This section discusses the physical and sexual changes people go through as they make the transition from childhood to adulthood. How people react emotionally to these changes affect what they will be like as adults.

Organizing Your Thoughts

Use the diagram below to help you take notes as you read the summaries that follow. Think about the physical changes that occur for males and females during adolescence. As you read, list some of the changes below.

Physical Changes

Females	Males
1.	6.
2.	7.
3.	8.
4.	9.
5.	10.

Read to Learn

Introduction (page 93)

Adolescence is the transition period between childhood and adulthood. It is a time when people begin to behave less like children and more like adults. They begin to prepare for adult responsibilities. Our society has many **initiation rites** that mark admission into adulthood. These are ceremonies or rituals, such as birthdays or graduations.

11. In what ways have you observed teenagers acting more like adults than children?

_____

Theories of Adolescence (page 94)

Psychologists disagree about the nature of adolescence. In 1904, G. Stanley Hall proposed that adolescence is a transition stage, full of "storm and stress." To Hall, adolescents were like a fully grown animal in a cage, trying to get free. Later researchers viewed adolescence as a period of growth that flows naturally out of childhood and into adulthood. One of these researchers, Margaret Mead, found that in some cultures, adolescence is a highly enjoyable time. She believed that adolescent storm and stress comes partly from our stressful society. She proposed that culture plays a role in development. Later studies support this view. They show that while adolescence is a difficult time, few adolescents have serious difficulties.

Great physical, mental, and emotional changes occur during adolescence. Robert Havighurst identified many of the challenges adolescents face. For example, they must accept their physical makeup, become emotionally independent of parents, prepare to make a living, and prepare for marriage and family.

12. What are some of the stresses adolescents feel?

_____

Physical Development (page 95)

Sexual maturation, or **puberty**, is the biological event that marks the end of childhood. Hormones set off a series of changes inside and outside the body. These hormones produce different growth patterns in boys and girls. Some girls start puberty as early as age 8. Some boys start at age 9 or 10.

Just before puberty, boys and girls have a growth spurt. The growth spurt is a rapid increase in weight and height. It reaches its peak at age 12 for girls and just after age 14 for most boys.

During this period, girls' breasts and hips fill out and they develop pubic hair. Between ages 10 and 17, they have their first menstrual period, or **menarche**.

At about 12, boys begin to develop pubic hair and larger genitals. Normally, between 12 and 13 they achieve their first ejaculation, or

spermarche. Boys' growth spurt begins 24 to 27 months later than that of girls, but it lasts about three years longer. Boys develop more muscle tissue and larger hearts and lungs than girls. Their voices deepen and they grow hair on their faces and chests.

During this growth period, parts of the body may grow at different rates in both boys and girls. This is called **asynchrony**. For example, hands and feet may be too large for the rest of the body. Later, the body parts assume their correct proportions.

These sudden changes in the body can make adolescents feel self-conscious. This is especially true if they are early or late to develop. They want to measure up to what is "right" or "ideal." Few can achieve the "ideal" body, because it is not realistic.

Individual differences in growth affect personality. Research shows that boys who mature early have an advantage. They often become sports heroes and leaders. Other boys often look up to them. Girls have crushes on them. As a result, they are often more self-confident and independent than other boys. Girls who mature early may feel embarrassed rather than proud of their height and figure at first. In their late teens, they may be more popular and have a more positive image of themselves than do girls who mature late.

The psychological reactions to physical growth may be the result of a self-fulfilling prophecy. For example, the boy who believes he does not meet his culture's physical ideal may think less of himself and not strongly pursue success. This may then bring about the failure he feared.

13. Why is it important for teenagers to feel good about their bodies?

_____

Sexual Development (page 98)

Adolescence is also a time when people develop attitudes about sex and the gender roles they will fill. The increase of sexual awareness and activity of today's teens has raised questions over the role of family, religion, and government in providing information about sex. About 1 million adolescent females get pregnant each year. There are about 3 million cases of sexually transmitted diseases each year. Studies show that children of teenage mothers are more likely to become teenage parents themselves, to do poorly in school, and to serve time in prison.

At first AIDS was associated only with homosexual sex and drug use so many Americans ignored it. Education has helped reverse this trend. Many teens are examining the risks and deciding that the only safe choice is abstinence from sexual intercourse. *Abstinence* is a choice to avoid harmful behaviors including sex before marriage and the use of drugs and alcohol. By choosing abstinence, some teens hope to avoid unwanted pregnancies, sexually transmitted diseases, and loss of self-respect.

14. What are some safe choices teenagers can make about sexual activity?

Study Guide 4-2

Personal Development

For use with textbook pages 101–108

Key Terms

rationalization a process whereby an individual seeks to explain an often unpleasant
emotion or behavior in a way that will preserve his or her self-esteem (page 102)

identity crisis a period of inner conflict during which adolescents worry intensely about who
they are (page 105)

social learning theory Albert Bandura's view of human development; emphasizes
interaction (page 107)

Drawing From Experience

Do you feel that you know who you are? What kinds of things make you
who you are? Have you ever worried about your future?

The last section discussed the physical and sexual changes that occur in
adolescence. This section focuses on the changes in thinking patterns that
occur during that period. You will also read about how adolescents gain a sense
of identity—a sense of who they are.

Organizing Your Thoughts

Use the diagram below to help you take notes as you read the summaries
that follow. Think about the key ideas in the theories of each researcher presented in this section. In the diagram below, record two key ideas for each theory of identity development.

IDENTITY DEVELOPMENT

Erikson's Theory

1. _____

2. _____

Marcia's Theory

3. _____

4. _____

Social Learning Theory

5. _____

6. _____

Read to Learn

Introduction (page 101)

Becoming an adult involves more than becoming physically mature. It also involves changes in reasoning patterns, moral thinking, personality, and sexual behavior.

7. Give an example of how a child thinks differently than an adult.

_____

_____

_____

_____

Cognitive Development (page 101)

From about age 11 or 12, most people's thinking becomes more abstract. For example, adolescents can think through hypothetical questions like "What would the world be like if people lived to be 200?" Young children cannot do this. This ability makes adolescents better able to solve problems. For example, a teenager who discovers that her car is making an unusual noise can consider the possible causes. Then she can try making different adjustments until she finds the root of the problem. This is the same ability scientists must have to conduct experiments.

When adolescents develop the ability to think about hypothetical questions, they can also understand abstract principles. This ability is important for studying higher-level science and math. It is also important for dealing with abstract ideas in their own lives, such as ethics and their own motivations.

These new thinking abilities also help adolescents deal with strong emotions by rationalizing. **Rationalization** is the process of trying to explain an unpleasant emotion in a way that will maintain self-esteem. For example, after failing a test, a person may rationalize that it happened "because I was worried about the date I might be going on next week."

Changes in personality and social interactions usually go along with these changes in thinking patterns. For example, adolescents tend to be very idealistic. This is because, for the first time, they can imagine how things might be. Also, adolescents usually become impatient with what they see as the failures of adults. For example, they do not understand why a person who dislikes his or her job does not just quit. Dr. David Elkind described some problems adolescents develop as a result of immaturity and abstract thought processes. For example, adolescents are self-conscious. They think mostly about themselves. They think that everyone else is thinking about them, too. Also, adolescents think they cannot be harmed. As a result, they may take many risks.

8. Suppose a scientist is conducting an experiment to find out if a new drug will cure a cold. What kind of thinking ability must the scientist have to do the experiment?

_____

_____

_____

_____

_____

Moral Development (page 103)

Some, but not all, adolescents go through changes in their moral thinking. You learned about Lawrence Kohlberg's stages of moral development in Chapter 3. Most people never progress beyond Stage 4. Their moral thinking remains rigid. Those who do progress usually do so in adolescence or young adulthood. In Stage 5, they are concerned with whether a law is fair or just. For example, people in Stage 5 might ignore a law to save a human life. Those who reach Stage 6 are concerned with making fair and just decisions. They believe that moral principles, like the Golden Rule, apply to everyone. They believe these principles cannot be broken and are more important than any law.

Reaching higher levels of moral thinking requires the abstract thinking gained in adolescence. People need to be able to see a situation from another's point of view. Abstract thinking, however, does not necessarily lead to higher levels of moral thinking. Only about 1 in 10 people progress to higher levels of moral thinking.

A person's moral development depends on many factors. The most important factor is the person's relationship with parents or other important people in his or her life. Moral development does not progress much in high school. It progresses more when the person is in college, away from home and experiencing different cultures and ideas.

9. Give an example of higher moral thinking. (It can be from Stage 5 or Stage 6 of Kohlberg's theory.)

_____

_____

_____

_____

_____

_____

Identity Development (page 104)

The changes adolescents go through influence their personality. According to psychologist Erik Erikson, building an identity is a task that is unique to adolescence. Children are aware of what other people think of them. They may dream of being this person or that person and act out these roles in their play. They do not worry, however, about who they are or where they are going in life. Children live in the present. Adolescents begin to think about the future.

To achieve a sense of themselves, most adolescents must go through what Erikson called an **identity crisis**. This is a time of inner conflict when they worry a great deal about who they are. Adolescents begin to see the future as real, not just a game. As they review their past and think about their future, adolescents begin to think about themselves. It is a painful process, full of inner conflict. They want to feel special but they also want to "fit in." Only by resolving this conflict do adolescents gain a sense of self.

Psychologist James Marcia supported Erikson's views. Marcia believed that the identity crisis arises because adolescents must make commitments on important issues like job, religion, and political beliefs. Marcia identified four attempts to achieve identity. (1) *Identity moratorium adolescents* are seriously considering the important issues but have made no commitments. (2) *Identity foreclosure adolescents* have made commitments about the issues but not based on their own choice. Rather, the commitments are based on the suggestions of others. (3) *Identity confused adolescents* have not yet seriously considered the issues. (4) *Identity achievement adolescents* have considered many identities and have freely committed to jobs and other important life matters.

A.C. Peterson had a different view. He argued that an identity crisis is not normal for adolescents. When a crisis does develop, it is caused by changes in the person's life rather than a biological cause. For example, divorce in the family may cause teenage rebellion and crisis.

Albert Bandura believed that human development is one continuous process. At all stages, individuals develop by interacting with others. This view is called **social learning theory**.

Margaret Mead also stressed the importance of the social environment to identity formation. She studied people in Samoa, a remote part of the world. There, adolescents did not experience an identity crisis.

All of these viewpoints contribute to an understanding of adolescent personality change and identity development. Erikson emphasized adolescents' need for their own identity. Studies by Bandura and Mead showed that society has an influence as well.

10. What are some of the "important issues" that adolescents face as they try to form a sense of identity?

_____

_____

_____

Study Guide 4-3

For use with textbook pages 109–115

Social Development

Key Terms

clique a small, exclusive group of people within a larger group (page 111)

conformity acting in accord with group norms and customs (page 111)

anorexia nervosa a serious eating disorder characterized by a fear of gaining weight that results in prolonged self-starvation and dramatic weight loss (page 114)

bulimia nervosa a serious eating disorder characterized by compulsive overeating usually followed by self-induced vomiting or laxative abuse (page 115)

Drawing From Experience

Do you have a group of friends? Do you dress and act like other people in the group? Have you ever felt pressure from your friends to do things that you normally would not do? Have you ever argued with your parents over some of the things you do?

In the last section, you read about how adolescents develop a sense of identity. This section discusses how parents and friends influence adolescent behavior and help shape them into the adults they will become. You will also learn about some difficulties adolescents may experience.

Organizing Your Thoughts

Use the diagram below to help you take notes as you read the summaries that follow. Think about the ways that parents and peers influence adolescents. Also think about the warning signs of adolescents in trouble.

Influences of Parents	Influences of Peers	Signs of Trouble
1.	5.	9.
2.	6.	10.
3.	7.	11.
4.	8.	12.

Read to Learn

Introduction (page 109)

During adolescence, people experience changes in their relationships with other people. No longer children and not yet adults, teenagers must find a new role in the family. They must also adjust to new, often stronger relationships with their peers. Peers are people their own age who are similar to them, such as classmates and friends.

13. Who are some of your peers?

_____

The Role of the Family (page 109)

One of the main tasks of adolescents is to become independent of their families. How to do this is not clear. Both parents and adolescents have mixed feelings about it. Parents may not want to let their children go. They may worry that their children are not ready to face the world as adults. Adolescents worry about this too. They worry about failing. This internal struggle often causes adolescents to act in unexpected ways. Parents may interpret this behavior as rebellion.

14. Why might parents have a hard time letting their children become independent?

_____

The Role of Peers (page 110)

Teenagers spend much of their time with friends. In high school, they divide into groups. Everyone knows who belongs to which group and what people in that group do with their time. Early in adolescence the groups are usually divided by gender. Later, the genders mix. Groups usually include people of the same social class. Middle-class and lower-class adolescents are seldom close friends.

Smaller groups also form within the larger group. A group within a group is called a **clique**. Belonging to a clique is very important to adolescents. The clique gives them a way to define themselves—an identity. The clique does this by helping them achieve self-confidence, feel more independent from family, clarify values, and experiment with new roles. For example, members of a clique may imitate each other's clothing, speech, and hairstyles.

Cliques also have drawbacks. One of the greatest drawbacks is the fear of being disliked. To avoid this, adolescents do what everyone else in the group is doing. This is called **conformity**. For example, teenagers are afraid to wear clothes that might set them apart from the rest of the clique. Conformity, however, can also lead to doing more serious things that do not reflect good judgment.

Cliques are not always the main influence on adolescents. Peers influence such things as taste in music and fashion. On basic matters like marriage, religion, and educational plans, however, adolescents tend to accept their parents' beliefs. Only on a few basic values might adolescents disagree with their parents. For example, some adolescents may view sex before marriage as more acceptable than their parents do. Adolescents tend to choose friends with values close to their parents' values. These friends help them make the transition from dependent child to independent adult.

15. What are some ways that students in your school conform to their cliques?

_____

_____

Difficulties During Adolescence (page 112)

With all the changes going on in their bodies and their lives, adolescents often experience *temporary* psychological difficulties. Most adjust quickly. Mental illness and suicide are rare among adolescents, although both are increasing.

Adolescents often have the false feeling that they cannot be caught or harmed. For example, they might think, "Others may get caught, but not me!" This false feeling can lead some teens to do things with peers that they would not do alone. Some examples are running away from home, abusing drugs, and doing poorly in school. Most adolescents outgrow these tendencies, although some do not. Without treatment, troubled teens may carry their problems into later life.

Teenage depression may be more common than many adults think. A major event, such as the loss of a loved one, can lead to depression. For example, if the family moves to another state, the adolescent may experience grief and anger over leaving a good friend behind. If the teen is not able to express these feelings in a safe atmosphere, depression may result. Another form of loss that may cause depression is the breakdown of the family unit through separation or divorce.

Depressed adults often look and feel sad. Depressed teenagers often appear angry. They may engage in rebellious behavior, such as skipping school or using drugs. Parents and teachers need to watch for warning signs of teenage depression and suicide. These include withdrawal from friends, doing dangerous things, talking about suicide, and being too hard on themselves. The best way to deal with teenage depression is to talk with the teens about their problems. A caring, listening parent or friend can help young people deal with their problems.

Some teenagers, especially females, develop eating disorders. **Anorexia nervosa** is a serious eating disorder in which fear of gaining weight results in long periods of self-starvation and weight loss. People with this problem see themselves as overweight and fat even though they are underweight and thin. Another serious eating disorder is **bulimia nervosa**. People with this problem constantly eat too much and then try to get rid of the calories they consumed by vomiting, taking laxatives, or eating nothing for a long time.

16. What warning signs can indicate that a teenager is in trouble?

_____

_____

Name _____ Date _____ Class _____

Study Guide 4-4

Gender Roles and Differences

For use with textbook pages 116–122

Key Terms

gender identity the sex group (masculine or feminine) to which an individual biologically belongs (page 117)

gender role the set of behaviors that society considers appropriate for each sex (page 117)

gender stereotype an oversimplified or distorted generalization about the characteristics of men and women (page 117)

androgynous combining or confusing traditionally male and female characteristics (page 117)

gender schema a set of behaviors organized around how either a male or female should think and behave (page 122)

Drawing From Experience

When you see a baby in a stroller, are there any clues that tell you that the baby is a boy or a girl? In what ways do boys act differently than girls? The last section discussed the influences of family and friends on adolescent behavior. In this section, you will learn how males and females differ from each other. You will learn which differences are real and which are stereotypes.

Organizing Your Thoughts

Use the diagram below to help you take notes as you read the summaries that follow. Think about the gender differences between males and females.

Gender Difference	Example of Male Behavior	Example of Female Behavior
Confidence	1.	2.
Aggression	3.	4.
Communication Style	5.	6.

Read to Learn

Introduction (page 116)

Your gender greatly influences how you dress, move, work, and play. It can influence your thoughts and what others think about you. Psychologists want to know if there are major differences between males and females.

7. What are some differences that you have noticed in the way male and female children play?

_____

Copyright © by The McGraw-Hill Companies, Inc.

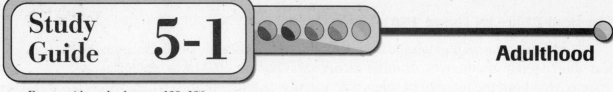

Study Guide 5-1

Adulthood

For use with textbook pages 129–136

Key Terms

menopause the biological event in which a woman's production of sex hormones is sharply reduced (page 131)

generativity the desire, in middle age, to use one's accumulated wisdom to guide future generations (page 135)

stagnation a discontinuation of development and a desire to recapture the past (page 135)

Drawing From Experience

Have you ever wondered what your life will be like when you are in your 30s or 40s, or even older? Do you worry about the changes to your body and mind as you age?

This section discusses the physical, mental, social, and personality changes that occur as adults age.

Organizing Your Thoughts

Use the chart below to help you take notes as you read the summaries that follow. Think about changes that occur as people age.

Changes in Adulthood	Men	Women
Physical	1.	4.
Cognitive	2.	5.
Social	3.	6.

Read to Learn

Introduction (page 129)

Adulthood is a time of opposites. There is success and failure, crisis and stability, joy and sadness. Adulthood is a time when you can mature fully into who you are, or allow life to get the better of you. How each of us reacts depends on circumstances and our general outlook on life.

7.   Why do you think it is important to have a positive outlook on life?

_____

_____

Physical Changes (page 130)

One theory claims that we age because, with time, our body's cells become less able to repair themselves. Another theory says that our cells have biological "clocks" that limit the number of times cells can divide and multiply. When they reach their limit, cells begin to die and aging occurs.

In general, adults are at their physical peak between ages 18 and 30. This is when we are strongest, healthiest, and have the quickest reflexes. Physical decline is usually slow and not easy to see. For example, a 20-year-old may carry four heavy bags of groceries. A 40-year-old may make two trips. Experience can also make up for some loss of physical ability. For example, a 60-year-old racquetball player may know the game's strategy so well that he can compete with a faster, less-experienced 30-year-old.

In middle age, hair starts to turn gray and thin. Skin becomes dry and wrinkles. In old age, muscles and fat break down, causing people to lose weight and become shorter. With time, the senses stop working as well as they did previously. Older people may not be able to see in the dark or hear as well as they used to. Reaction time slows.

Good health comes from a lifetime of making good choices. If you eat well, exercise, do not smoke, and avoid drugs and alcohol, you will look and feel younger than others who do not make healthy choices. The most common causes of death in later adulthood are heart disease, cancer, and cirrhosis of the liver. The fast-moving lifestyle of young adults can contribute to these diseases. Also, the tendencies of young adults to push physical limits can lead to accidental deaths.

Between the ages of 45 and 50, a woman's body begins to produce fewer sex hormones. This stage is called **menopause**. The woman stops producing eggs, stops having a menstrual period, and can no longer get pregnant. Menopause does not, however, reduce a woman's sexual drive or enjoyment of sex. Many women experience little or no discomfort during menopause. Men do not go through a biological change like menopause. The number of sperm a man's body produces declines over time, but men can father children even in old age.

About 90 percent of adults will marry. Between 40 and 60 percent of marriages end in divorce. Studies show that the success or failure of a marriage depends on two things. It depends on how couples handle conflict and how often couples share intimate and happy moments. Happy couples listen to each other and focus on solving problems. Unhealthy ways of dealing with conflict are ignoring the conflict, making the issues seem bigger than they are, and yelling at each other.

Sexual activity does not automatically decline with age. There is no physical reason to stop sexual activity with advancing age.

8. How might the experience gained with age help make up for the natural decline in physical abilities?

_____

Cognitive Changes (page 132)

People in their mid-20s are better at learning, solving problems, and shifting from one problem-solving method to another than they were in adolescence. People continue to learn new information and new words as they grow older. The ability to understand new material and to think improves with years and experience.

9. What kind of environment would help older adults remain mentally active?

_____

_____

Social and Personality Development (page 133)

An individual's basic character—his or her style of adapting to situations—remains about the same over the years. For example, confident young people tend to remain confident as adults. People do face many changes in their lifetimes, however. Like adolescents, adults must learn the skills needed to cope with problems.

Daniel Levinson identified transition periods for men at ages 30, 40, 50, and 60. At about age 30, men often look at the life choices they made in their 20s. They may question their choices of marriage partner, career, and life goals. They feel that if parts of their lives are not satisfying, they must make big changes now before it is too late. After resolving the age-thirty crisis, men settle down into a second life structure and focus on "making it" in the adult world.

At about age 40, men begin to ask themselves questions about their past and their future. For example, they may ask "What have I done with my life?" and "What do I still wish to accomplish?" At this time, men often become mentors to younger men. They have a desire to pass on their wisdom to the next generation. This desire is called **generativity**. The opposite, **stagnation**, can also occur. Men may choose to hang on to the past rather than continue to develop. Generativity or stagnation can occur for both men and women.

Far more studies have been done with men than with women. Some studies with women show, however, that for married women, midlife may be a time of opportunity rather than crisis, as it is for some men. As children become independent and leave home, mothers have more freedom to go back to work, to go to college, and focus on new interests.

Depression is common among middle-aged women. In early adulthood, women may feel a sense of personal worth in their roles as daughter, lover, wife, mother, and wage earner. These roles change as children grow, parents die, and marriages fail. Some women begin to feel useless. Many women welcome this time of life, however, when they no longer have to focus their attention on the needs of their children. Career women can draw a new sense of self-esteem from their work environment.

10. How do the transitions at midlife differ for men and women?

_____

_____

Study Guide 5-2

For use with textbook pages 137–143

Old Age

Key Terms

decremental model of aging misbelief that progressive physical and mental decline are inevitable with age (page 138)

ageism prejudice or discrimination against the elderly (page 138)

senile dementia decreases in mental abilities experienced by some people in old age (page 142)

Alzheimer's disease a condition that destroys a person's ability to think, remember, relate to others, and care for herself or himself (page 143)

Drawing From Experience

How would you describe what "being old" is like? What major life changes have older people in your life had to face? The last section discussed the changes we experience in adulthood. This section describes life changes and attitudes as we grow older.

Organizing Your Thoughts

Use the diagram below to help you take notes as you read the summaries that follow. Think about society's attitudes about older people. Give an example of what is real and what is a stereotype in each category below.

Category	Stereotype	Real
Health	1.	2.
Sexual Activity	3.	4.
Mental Ability	5.	6.

Read to Learn

Introduction (page 137)

Fear of growing old is very common in our society. Negative images of old age are all around us. Birthday cards make light of aging. Comedians joke about it. Companies encourage older workers to retire.

7. What negative images of aging have you seen on TV or in other media?

_____

Attitudes Toward Aging (page 138)

Many of our attitudes about aging are based on a **decremental model of aging.** This is the misbelief that people decline physically and mentally with age. In other words, their actual age is what makes them old. In fact, there are great differences in physical condition among the elderly. Some people who are 80 years old look 50, and vice versa. Negative views of the elderly are a form of prejudice known as **ageism**.

Young people tend to believe that the old suffer from poor health, live in poverty, and are often victims of crime. Studies show that the elderly seldom see themselves this way. Another common idea is that the aged withdraw from life and sit around doing nothing. This is false, too. Many musicians and actors are good examples of active older people.

Another false idea is that older people are inflexible or senile. Actually, a person who is flexible in early life will likely stay that way in old age. Also, only 10 percent of the aged are senile. This condition is usually caused by disease, not aging.

8. Give some examples of famous people who have made important contributions to society in their older years.

_____

Changes in Health (page 139)

Most people over 65 consider themselves to be in good health. If someone is healthy when they are young, they are likely to experience good health in old age. Healthy lifestyles today will lead to good health later.

All people, young and old, can get diseases. About 40 percent of the elderly have at least one illness that will last the rest of their lives. The four most common are heart disease, high blood pressure, diabetes, and arthritis. The major causes of death among the elderly are heart disease, cancer, and stroke.

The quality of health care for the elderly is usually not as good as for everyone else. Ageism among doctors may lead to incorrect treatment. Nursing homes are available for those unable to care for themselves. These homes, however, do not often have what they need to do a good job. Health care for the elderly needs to be improved.

9. What kinds of things lead to poor health care for the elderly?

_____

Changes in Life Situation (page 139)

Important changes in life for young people, like graduation and marriage, are usually positive. Important life changes for older people are likely to be negative, however. For example, retiring from a job can lead to fewer responsibilities and less contact with others. Often the saddest change is the loss of a husband or wife. Depression is common in older adults. Today, older people continue to learn and develop skills. Some skills do decline, but others remain normal or improve with age.

10. What are some major life changes that people face as they grow older?

_____

Changes in Sexual Activity (page 140)

Young people tend to think that sexual activity ends in old age. The majority of people over 65 with healthy partners, however, enjoy sex into their 70s and 80s. People usually behave about the same way in old age as they did when young. The reasons some do not engage in sexual activity are poor health or death of a husband or wife. Also, society's attitudes discourage sexual expression by older people. Families sometimes oppose an older person who wants to remarry after the death of a husband or wife. A change in such ideas will help older people enjoy a healthy sex life.

11. Why do you think a healthy sex life might be important for older people?

_____

Adjusting to Old Age (page 141)

Many of the changes older people face cause a loss of control over their environment. The loss of control is slow. It involves physical changes, such as illness. It also involves lifestyle changes, such as moving to a nursing home. Losing a husband is bad enough. It is made worse when the person must move to a nursing home and leave friends and home behind. Older people can improve their quality of life and self-image if they are helped to make the best of the options they have. To help older people adjust, society's attitudes need to change. Organizations like AARP (American Association of Retired Persons) speak out on issues important to older people.

12. How do you think an older person's life would change if he or she could no longer drive a car?

_____

Changes in Mental Functioning (page 141)

Mental ability does decline in old age, but less than most people think. John Horn proposed two types of intelligence. *Crystallized intelligence* is the ability to use knowledge in the right situations. This ability increases with age. *Fluid intelligence* is the ability to solve abstract problems and come up with new explanations. It increases as the nervous system matures. As people age, their nervous systems decline, and so does their fluid intelligence. Elderly people also have trouble calling up information from memory.

A small percentage of older people develop **senile dementia.** This is a decrease in mental abilities. It includes memory loss, forgetfulness, and a decline in the ability to think. The most common form of senile dementia is **Alzheimer's disease.** It is a condition that destroys people's ability to think, remember, relate to others, and care for themselves. Early signs are frequent forgetting, poor judgment, and withdrawal. Eventually, Alzheimer's disease patients lose their ability to understand simple questions or to recognize friends and family. There is no cure at present.

13. Give an example of something that might be a warning sign of Alzheimer's disease.

_____

Copyright © by The McGraw-Hill Companies, Inc.

Study Guide 5-3

Dying and Death

For use with textbook pages 144–147

Key Terms

thanatology the study of dying and death (page 144)

hospice a facility designed to care for the special needs of the dying (page 147)

Drawing From Experience

How would you react if a doctor told you that you were dying? How would you feel? What thoughts would go through your head? What would be important to you at that time?

The last section described the kinds of changes that old age brings. In this section, you will learn about the psychological stages that people often go through when they learn they are dying. You will also learn about new forms of care for the dying.

Organizing Your Thoughts

Use the diagram below to help you take notes as you read the summaries that follow. Think about the stages a dying person goes through on his or her way to accepting death. For each stage below, give an example of what happens in this stage.

Stage	Example of Behavior
Denial	1.
Anger	2.
Bargaining	3.
Depression	4.
Acceptance	5.

Read to Learn

Introduction (page 144)

Death is not just biological. When someone dies, there are legal, medical, psychological, and social aspects that need attention. Some customs involving death include care of the dying, place of death, and efforts to speed up or slow down the process. Other customs include disposing of the bodies, mourning, and the role of the family.

6. Give an example of something the family usually does when someone dies.

_____

_____

Adjusting to Death (page 144)

Thanatology is the study of dying and death. Elisabeth Kübler-Ross identified five stages of psychological adjustment people make when they know they are dying. The first stage is *denial*. When first told they are dying, people often do not believe that this is happening to them. They may even refuse treatment and pretend the problem does not exist.

The second stage is *anger*. They think, "Why me?" They may feel anger at fate and at every person who comes into their life.

The third stage is *bargaining*. People attempt to bargain with fate. For example, a woman may ask God for more time in return for good behavior.

After this short stage comes the fourth stage, *depression*. Dying people become aware of their losses, such as their loss of body tissue and their job, and the loss to come—losing everybody and everything. People should allow the dying to express their feelings rather than force them to act cheerfully.

In the final stage, patients *accept* death. The struggle is over. They feel a sense of calm.

Not all dying people go through these stages. Some go through them but in a different order, or may repeat some stages. For example, some people die in the denial stage because they are psychologically unable to go beyond it. Sometimes the illness does not give people time to get to the next stage. Patients at all stages hold on to hope.

Like all people, dying people need respect, dignity, and self-confidence. They need support and care. They need to know what is happening with their illness and with the legal and financial arrangements.

Many people have no direct experience with death, so they are afraid to talk about it. People used to die at home. Today Americans often die in nursing homes and hospitals. Machines can keep people alive long after they have stopped living a normal life.

A **hospice** is a facility designed to care for the special needs of the dying. It is part of a movement to bring dignity to the dying. The hospice gives patients pleasant, comfortable surroundings. Doctors at the hospice do not try to make life last longer. Instead, they try to improve the quality of life. Hospices provide drugs to relieve pain. Patients lead as normal a life as they are able. Family members provide care as much as possible. Another form of hospice service is home care provided by visiting nurses, aides, physical therapists, chaplains, and social workers. In-home care is becoming more common than care at a hospice.

7. Why might dying people prefer in-home care over care at a hospital or a hospice?

_____

_____

Reading Essentials and Study Guide

Study Guide **6-1**

**The Nervous System:
The Basic Structure**

For use with textbook pages 155–159

Key Terms

central nervous system (CNS) the brain and spinal cord (page 156)

spinal cord nerves that run up and down the length of the back and transmit most messages between the body and brain (page 156)

peripheral nervous system (PNS) nerves branching out from the spinal cord (page 156)

neurons the long, thin cells of nerve tissue along which messages travel to and from the brain (page 157)

synapse the gap that exists between individual nerve cells (page 157)

neurotransmitters the chemicals released by neurons, which determine the rate at which other neurons fire (page 158)

somatic nervous system (SNS) the part of the peripheral nervous system that controls voluntary movement of skeletal muscles (page 158)

autonomic nervous system (ANS) the part of the peripheral nervous system that controls internal biological functions (page 158)

Drawing From Experience

Have you ever wondered how your brain communicates with the rest of your body? What parts inside you cause your heart to beat and your lungs to take in air?

This section discusses the parts of the nervous system. You will learn how chemical messages travel throughout your body to control its activities.

Organizing Your Thoughts

Use the diagram on the next page to help you take notes as you read the summaries that follow. Think about how neurons transmit messages through the body. Label the parts of the neurons in the following diagram.

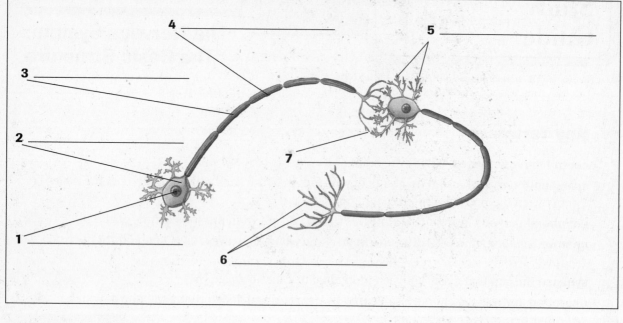

4 _____

5 _____

3 _____

2 _____

7 _____

1 _____

6 _____

Read to Learn

Introduction (page 155)

At some point during a long run, runners "push through the wall." They get a feeling of well-being called "runner's high." This feeling is caused by endorphins. These are substances the body produces in response to stress.

8. How does a physical activity like running actually change you?

_____

_____

_____

_____

_____

_____

How the Nervous System Works (page 156)

Your nervous system never rests, even when you are asleep. It controls your body functions, emotions, movements, thinking, and behavior. The nervous system has two parts. One part is the **central nervous system (CNS)**. This is the brain and spinal cord. The **spinal cord** consists of the nerves that run down the back and transmit most messages between the body and brain. The other part is the **peripheral nervous system (PNS)**. It includes the smaller nerves that branch out from the spinal cord. These nerves take information from the body's organs to the central nervous system and return information to the organs. All parts of the nervous system are protected. The skull protects the brain. The vertebrae protect the spinal cord. Sheathing protects the peripheral nerves.

The nerves are strings of long, thin cells called **neurons**. Messages travel along the neurons to and from the brain much as flame travels along a fire-cracker fuse. The neuron "fires" when it is stimulated past the minimum, or threshold level. Neurons have three parts: the cell body, dendrites, and the axon. The cell body contains the nucleus and produces the neuron's energy. The *dendrites* receive messages from other neurons and send them to the cell body. The *axon* carries messages from the cell body to the dendrites of another neuron. The *myelin sheath* protects the axon. The *axon terminals* branch out from the axon toward the dendrites of another neuron. The space between neurons is called the **synapse**. A neuron sends its message to another neuron across the synapse by releasing chemicals called **neurotransmitters**. The neurotransmitters can cause the next neuron to transmit a message, or they can stop it from transmitting.

There are three types of neurons. *Afferent neurons*, or sensory neurons, relay messages from sense organs (such as eyes and ears) to the brain. The *efferent neurons*, or motor neurons, send signals from the brain to the glands and muscles. The *interneurons* carry messages between neurons.

Some actions your body takes are voluntary. For example, you intentionally lift your hand to turn a page. Other actions are involuntary. For example, your heart beats without conscious effort by you. The **somatic nervous system (SNS)** is the part of the peripheral nervous system that controls voluntary activities. The **autonomic nervous system (ANS)** is the part of the nervous system that controls involuntary activities. The ANS has two parts: sympathetic and parasympathetic nervous systems. The sympathetic nervous system prepares the body for dealing with emergencies or strenuous activity. For example, it speeds up the heart to get oxygen and nutrients to the rest of the body quickly. The parasympathetic nervous system saves energy to help the body recover from strenuous activity. It reduces the heart rate and blood pressure. Both parts of the autonomic nervous system operate automatically.

9. What part of the system makes you breathe while you are asleep?

_____

_____

_____

_____

_____

_____

_____

Reading Essentials and Study Guide

Study Guide 6-2

Studying the Brain

For use with textbook pages 160–168

Key Terms

hindbrain a part of the brain located at the rear base of the skull that is involved in the basic processes of life (page 160)

midbrain a small part of the brain above the pons that integrates sensory information and relays it upward (page 161)

forebrain a part of the brain that covers the brain's central core (page 161)

lobes the different regions into which the cerebral cortex is divided (page 162)

electroencephalograph (EEG) a machine used to record the electrical activity of large portions of the brain (page 165)

computerized axial tomography (CAT) an imaging technique used to study the brain to pinpoint injuries and brain deterioration (page 167)

positron emission tomography (PET) an imaging technique used to see which brain areas are being activated while performing tasks (page 167)

magnetic resonance imaging (MRI) an imaging technique used to study brain structure and activity (page 167)

Drawing From Experience

What makes it possible for you to see objects, solve math problems, and create art? Why might a head injury cause different problems in one person than in another?

The last section discussed how the nervous system transmits messages from all parts of the body to the brain and back. In this section, you will learn how different parts of the brain control the body's functions. You will also learn how psychologists study the brain.

Organizing Your Thoughts

Use the diagram on the next page to help you take notes as you read the summaries that follow. Write the main function of each part of the brain in the diagram.

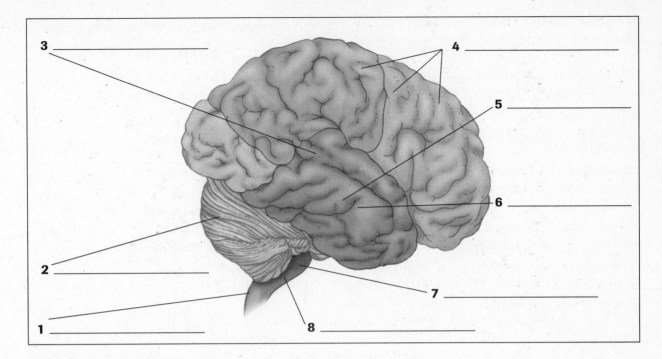

3 _____   4 _____

5 _____

6 _____

2 _____

7 _____

1 _____   8 _____

Read to Learn

Introduction (page 160)

In early times, people thought the heart, not the brain, was the source of thought and feeling. Then Greek physician Hippocrates observed the effect of head injuries on people's thoughts and actions. Since then, researchers have tried to explain how the mass of gray tissue known as the brain can think and create.

9. What might Hippocrates have observed that would lead him to believe that the brain was responsible for thought?

_____

The Three Brains (page 160)

The brain has three parts: the hindbrain, midbrain, and forebrain. The **hindbrain** is at the rear base of the skull. It is involved in the main processes of life. The parts of the hindbrain are the *cerebellum, medulla,* and the *pons*. The cerebellum is behind the spinal cord. It helps control posture and balance. The medulla controls breathing and many reflexes. The pons works as a bridge between the spinal cord and brain. It also produces chemicals needed for sleep.

The **midbrain** is a small part of the brain above the pons. It collects information from the senses and sends it upward. The medulla, pons, and midbrain make up the brain stem. The reticular activating system (RAS) goes across these parts. It alerts the rest of the brain to messages coming in and is involved in the sleep/wake cycle.

The **forebrain** covers the brain's central core. It includes the *thalamus,* which is the relay station for information traveling to and from the cortex. Just below the thalamus is the *hypothalamus*. It controls hunger, thirst, and sexual behavior. It also makes us sweat when we are hot and shiver when we are cold.

The forebrain is also where the higher thinking processes occur. The outside layer is the *cerebral cortex*. The inside layer is the *cerebrum*. The cerebral cortex and cerebrum go around the hindbrain and brain stem like a mushroom surrounds its stem. The cerebral cortex gives you the ability to learn and remember. It allows you to see, read, and understand this sentence.

The *limbic system* is at the core of the forebrain. It controls emotions and motivations. This system includes the hypothalamus, amygdala, thalamus, and hippocampus. Covering all these parts is the cerebrum.

The cerebrum has two sides called hemispheres. Fibers called the *corpus callosum* carry messages between the two sides. The cerebral cortex is divided into regions called **lobes**. The occipital lobe controls vision. The parietal lobe works with all of the senses. The temporal lobe controls hearing, memory, emotion, and speaking. The frontal lobe involves creative thinking and planning. Both hemispheres have these four lobes.

The hemispheres control movement on opposite sides of the body. The left hemisphere controls the right side of the body. The right hemisphere controls the left side of the body. The left hemisphere specializes in speech, math ability, and logic. The right hemisphere specializes in vision, creative ability, intuition, and relationships in space. For example, putting a puzzle together requires the ability to use space. Music and art would involve the right hemisphere's creative ability.

In a normal brain, the two hemispheres communicate through the corpus callosum. Some people have grand mal seizures, which are sudden attacks in the brain. To reduce the seizures, doctors cut the corpus callosum to split the hemispheres. Since the hemispheres can no longer communicate, these people then have two brains that work independently of each other. For example, if a person with a split brain held a ball in the right hand, he would say it is a ball. If the ball is placed in the left hand he would not be able to say what it was. The information went to the right hemisphere, but the speech center is in the left hemisphere. Research on split-brain patients has shown that the two hemispheres specialize in different functions and skills.

10. If a car accident injured someone's left hemisphere, where might the person lose feeling?

_____

_____

_____

How Psychologists Study the Brain (page 165)

Some methods psychologists use to explore the brain are recording, stimulating, lesioning (cutting or destroying), and imaging. Electrodes are wires that researchers put into the brain to record electrical activity. These wires can tell when neurons fire. An **electroencephalograph (EEG)** is a machine that

Reading Essentials and Study Guide

records the electrical activity of large parts of the brain. Psychologists have observed that overall electrical activity of the brain rises and falls in a rhythm. The patterns of these rhythms, or brain waves, are different when we sleep and when we are awake.

Researchers can also use electrodes to stimulate neurons to make them fire. Doctors can stimulate different parts of the brain to find the part that is not working well. Stimulation has also been used to relieve severe pain and control violent behavior.

Researchers sometimes create lesions by cutting or destroying part of an animal's brain. If the animal behaves differently after the operation, researchers assume that the destroyed part of the brain controls that behavior. For example, rhesus monkeys are normally fearful, aggressive, and vicious. After researchers removed a certain area of the brain, the monkeys became less fearful and less violent. The researchers could then conclude that the removed area controlled aggression.

Psychologists can also learn from accidents to the brain. For example, Phineas Gage was a respected railroad boss who showed good judgment and the ability to work well with other men. An explosion sent an iron bar through his head just below the left eye. He lived, but his personality changed. He became hard to get along with and said inappropriate things. After his death, psychologists examined his skull and found damage to parts of the frontal cortex. They concluded that these parts must give people the ability to control what they say. In another case, Dr. Paul Broca discovered where speech is located in the brain.

Today, modern machines can create images or pictures of the brain. **Computerized axial tomography (CAT)** scans can locate brain injuries. **Positron emission tomography (PET)** scans can capture a picture of the brain as different parts are being used. For example, PET scans show activity in different areas of the brain when a person is thinking, speaking, and looking at things. The pictures change as the activity changes. **Magnetic resonance imaging (MRI)** helps researchers study both activity and brain parts. It combines the features of both CAT and PET scans. Researchers use MRIs to study the structure of the brain as well as to find tumors and brain damage.

11. Give an example of one way a researcher might discover which part of the brain controls vision.

_____

_____

_____

_____

_____

_____

Study Guide 6-3

The Endocrine System

For use with textbook pages 170–173

Key Terms

endocrine system a chemical communication system, using hormones, by which messages are sent through the bloodstream (page 171)

hormones chemical substances that carry messages through the body in blood (page 171)

pituitary gland the center of control of the endocrine system that secretes a large number of hormones (page 171)

Drawing From Experience

Have you ever done something physically risky? Why did you do it? How did you feel when you were doing it?

In the last section, you learned about the parts of the brain and their functions. In this section, you will learn about another form of communication in the body, the endocrine system. You will learn how hormones affect different body functions.

Organizing Your Thoughts

Use the diagram below to help you take notes as you read the summaries that follow. Think about how hormones affect the body.

Hormone	Effect on the Body
Thyroxine	1.
Epinephrine or Adrenaline	2.
Cortical Steroids	3.
Testosterone	4.
Estrogen and Progesterone	5.

Read to Learn

Introduction (page 170)

Every year the people of Pamplona, Spain, release bulls to run through the town every morning during a nine-day holiday. Hundreds of people run with the bulls. They risk death by being speared by the bulls' horns. People do this for the "rush" they feel. The rush comes from a hormone produced by the endocrine system called adrenaline, or epinephrine.

6. Name another activity that people might do because of the "rush" it gives them.

_____

_____

The Endocrine Glands (page 171)

The nervous system is one of two communication systems for sending information to and from the brain. The other is the **endocrine system**. The endocrine system sends chemical messages, called **hormones**. Hormones are produced by the endocrine glands and put into the bloodstream. Hormones travel through the blood to the organ designed to receive them. Different hormones affect different body functions. Some encourage growth of muscles and bones. Others help the body turn food into energy. Still others prepare the body for action.

The **pituitary gland** acts as the "master gland." It produces a large number of hormones. Many of them control the amount of hormones other endocrine glands produce. The hypothalamus keeps track of the amount of hormones in the blood. It sends messages to the pituitary gland to correct imbalances.

The *thyroid gland* produces the hormone thyroxine. Too little thyroxine makes people feel lazy. Too much may cause people to be overactive and lose sleep.

The *adrenal glands* become active when a person is angry or afraid. They release epinephrine (adrenaline) and norepinephrine (noradrenaline) into the bloodstream. These hormones cause heartbeat and breathing to increase. They also heighten emotions and help generate energy to help a person handle a difficult situation.

There are two types of sex glands, *testes* in males and *ovaries* in females. Testes produce sperm and the sex hormone *testosterone*. Ovaries produce eggs and the sex hormones *estrogen* and *progesterone*. Females have small amounts of the male hormone, and males have small amounts of the female hormones.

7. How does the endocrine system send its messages?

_____

_____

Hormones vs. Neurotransmitters (page 172)

Both hormones and neurotransmitters affect the nervous system. In fact, the same chemical (such as norepinephrine) can work as both a hormone and a neurotransmitter. The difference is that a neurotransmitter is released right beside the cell it is supposed to affect. A hormone is released into the blood, which carries it to its receiver.

Early life-forms had just one communication system. As life-forms became more complex, however, the communication system split in two. One system, the nervous system, specialized in sending rapid, specific messages. The other system, using the bloodstream, specialized in sending slow and widespread messages. The chemical messengers of this second system developed into hormones.

8. When would norepinephrine be working as a hormone and when would it be working as a neurotransmitter?

Study Guide 6-4

Heredity and Environment

For use with textbook pages 174–176

Key Terms

heredity the genetic transmission of characteristics from parents to their offspring (page 174)

identical twins twins who come from one fertilized egg; twins having the same heredity (page 175)

genes the basic building blocks of heredity (page 175)

fraternal twins twins who come from two different eggs fertilized by two different sperm (page 176)

Drawing From Experience

Do you have a special ability? For example, are you good at drawing, dancing, or playing a musical instrument? Do you think you learned this ability, or were you born with it?

The last section described the role of hormones in your body. In this section, you will read about the argument over whether your behavior is learned or comes from the genes you received from your parents.

Organizing Your Thoughts

Use the diagram below to help you take notes as you read the summaries that follow. Think about the argument over whether behavior is inherited or learned. For each example below, decide whether it supports the "nature" or "nurture" side of the argument.

Example	"Nature" or "Nurture"?
1. In studies of many twins, identical twins were more likely to choose the same career than were fraternal twins.	1.
2. Identical twins separated at birth were raised in very different environments. Yet they both liked to bowl, sing in a choir, and wear the same designer clothes.	2.
3. A boy's parents were not very athletic, but they enjoyed watching sports. So they got him on a baseball team with a skilled coach. Later, the boy became a professional baseball player.	3.

Read to Learn

Introduction (page 174)

How much do genes determine our behavior? How much of our behavior do we learn from experiences in our environment? For example, do people learn to do well in school, or are they born good at it? This is the nature-nurture question. Some psychologists believe that genes are like a flower, and the environment is like rain, soil, or fertilizer. Genes say what we could be. Our environment shapes what we finally become.

4. Explain how genes are like a flower and the environment is like rain, soil, or fertilizer.

_____

_____

Heredity and Environment (page 174)

Parents pass on their genes to their children. Genes (or genetics) determine many of the children's traits. This passing of genes from parents to children is called **heredity**. The nature-nurture question is important because many people think that something learned can be changed. Something we are born with, however, will be difficult or impossible to change. Actually, genes (heredity or nature) and learning (environment or nurture) work together. Asking whether heredity or environment causes behavior is like asking, "What makes a cake rise, baking powder or heat?" Both work together to make the cake rise.

Nature refers to the characteristics people inherit, their biological makeup. Nurture refers to environmental factors, such as family, culture, education, and individual experiences. In 1869, Sir Francis Galton found that success ran in families and concluded that heredity was the cause. Other psychologists, such as John Watson, stress the importance of environment.

Genes are the basic building blocks of heredity. They affect behavior by building and changing the body's parts. For example, if your parents are musicians, you may have inherited a gene that influences your musical ability by developing the part of your brain that analyzes sounds well.

One way to find out if something is inherited is to study twins. **Identical twins** develop from a single fertilized egg and share the same genes. **Fraternal twins** come from two different eggs fertilized by two different sperm. Their genes are no more alike than those of any brother or sister. Psychologists have been studying identical twins who were separated at birth. Some research shows that even when raised in very different environments, the twins shared many common behaviors. For example, in one set of twins, both had done well in math and poorly in spelling. Both worked as deputy sheriffs and took vacations in Florida. They gave identical names to their children and pets, bit their fingernails, and liked building with wood. These shared behaviors suggest that heredity may play a major role in behaviors that appear to be learned.

5. In the nature-nurture argument, what is "nature" and what is "nurture"?

_____

Study Guide 7-1

Sleep and Dreams

For use with textbook pages 183–190

Key Terms

consciousness a state of awareness, including a person's feelings, sensations, ideas, and perceptions (page 183)

REM sleep a stage of sleep characterized by rapid eye movements, a high level of brain activity, a deep relaxation of the muscles, and dreaming (page 186)

circadian rhythm the rhythm of activity and inactivity lasting approximately one day (page 186)

insomnia the failure to get enough sleep at night in order to feel rested the next day (page 187)

sleep apnea a sleep disorder in which a person has trouble breathing while asleep (page 187)

narcolepsy a condition characterized by suddenly falling asleep or feeling very sleepy during the day (page 188)

nightmares unpleasant dreams (page 188)

night terrors sleep disruptions that occur during Stage IV of sleep, involving screaming, panic, or confusion (page 188)

sleepwalking walking or carrying out behaviors while asleep (page 188)

Drawing From Experience

Have you ever been awakened suddenly from a deep sleep? How did you feel? What kinds of dreams do you have? Did you ever try to figure out what they mean?

This section discusses the stages of sleep, sleep disorders, and some theories about dreams.

Organizing Your Thoughts

Use the diagram below to help you take notes as you read the summaries that follow. Think about the characteristics of sleep disorders.

Sleep Disorder	Characteristics
Insomnia	1.
Sleep Apnea	2.
Narcolepsy	3.
Nightmares	4.
Night Terrors	5.
Sleepwalking	6.

Read to Learn

Introduction (page 183)

Sleep is vital to mental health. Sleep is not unconsciousness. It is an altered state of consciousness in which certain patterns of brain activity occur. **Consciousness** is a state of awareness. People who are fully aware with their attention focused on something are conscious of that "something." Altered states of consciousness, like sleep, are different levels of awareness. Researchers study sleep with an electroencephalograph (EEG) that records the electrical activity of the brain.

7. How is an altered state of consciousness different from consciousness?

_____

_____

_____

_____

Why Do We Sleep? (page 184)

Some people believe that sleep is a time when the brain recovers from exhaustion and stress. Others believe we sleep to save energy, like hibernation. Some suggest that in earlier times, sleep was a way to keep humans out of harm's way at night. Still others believe we sleep to clear our minds of useless information.

8. How might sleeping at night have helped early humans survive?

_____

_____

_____

_____

Stages of Sleep (page 184)

In Stage I sleep, your pulse slows and your muscles relax. Your breathing becomes uneven and your brain produces theta waves. In Stage II, your eyes roll slowly from side to side. In Stage III, delta waves sweep your brain. Stage IV is the deepest sleep. Large, regular delta waves indicate deep sleep. Talking out loud, sleepwalking, and bed-wetting may occur in this stage.

Reading Essentials and Study Guide

People usually spend three quarters of their sleep time in Stages I through IV. Rapid eye movements mark your entrance into a more active type of sleep called **REM sleep**. Your pulse and breathing become uneven. Often your face and fingers twitch and your arms and legs are paralyzed. Your brain waves are like those of a person who is awake. For this reason, REM sleep is called active sleep. Stages I through IV are sometimes called NREM (non-REM) or quiet sleep. Almost all dreaming occurs during REM sleep.

9. Why is REM sleep called active sleep?

_____

_____

_____

_____

How Much Sleep? (page 186)

The amount of sleep you need is different at different ages. Newborns sleep about 16 hours a day. Sixteen-year-olds may sleep 10 or 11 hours. People 70 or older may need only 5 hours of sleep. Have you ever noticed that you are more alert at some times of the day than at others? A **circadian rhythm** is a pattern of activity and inactivity lasting approximately one day. Jet lag occurs when your internal circadian rhythms do not match the clock time. For example, when you travel from New York to Moscow, your body and your destination are on different time clocks. You may feel tired and confused.

10. Why do you think babies might need more sleep than 70-year-olds?

_____

_____

_____

_____

Sleep Disorders (page 187)

Everyone has a sleepless night sometimes. People with **insomnia**, however, never get enough sleep to feel rested. Anxiety, depression, or taking too much alcohol or drugs can cause insomnia.

Sleep apnea is a sleep disorder in which people have trouble breathing while asleep. Snoring is a common symptom. The snoring is actually caused by something blocking the air passage during sleep.

Narcolepsy is a condition in which people suddenly fall asleep or feel very sleepy during the day. People with narcolepsy may have sleep attacks throughout the day. Other symptoms are dreamlike hallucinations or a feeling of temporary paralysis.

Nightmares occur during the dream phase of REM sleep. The sleeper awakens with a sharp memory of the dream. On the other hand, **night terrors** occur during Stage IV sleep. They involve screaming, panic, or confusion. People usually have no memory of night terrors.

Sleepwalking is a disorder in which people walk or do other things while asleep with no memory of doing so. More children than adults sleepwalk, and most outgrow it. Sleep talking is also common and harmless. Most people do not remember talking in their sleep.

11. What kinds of social problems might a person with narcolepsy have?

_____

_____

_____

_____

Dreams (page 188)

Everyone dreams, but most people remember few of their dreams. As the night wears on, dreams become longer and more dramatic. Dreams often take place in ordinary settings. They include elements from everyday life mixed with fantasy. For example, the dreamer may wander through strange houses with endless doors. Sigmund Freud believed that dreams contain clues to thoughts the dreamer is afraid to express when awake. Another researcher proposes that dreams allow people to address problems they faced during the day. A third theory is that dreams are a way of removing unneeded memories. Some believe dreams serve no purpose at all.

12. Describe a dream you remember that included everyday activities mixed with fantasy.

_____

_____

_____

_____

_____

Study Guide 7-2

Hypnosis, Biofeedback, and Meditation

For use with textbook pages 191–195

Key Terms

hypnosis a state of consciousness resulting from a narrowed focus of attention and characterized by heightened suggestibility (page 191)

posthypnotic suggestion a suggestion made during hypnosis that influences the participant's behavior afterwards (page 193)

biofeedback the process of learning to control bodily states with the help of machines monitoring the states to be controlled (page 194)

meditation the focusing of attention on an image, thought, or external object to clear one's mind and produce relaxation (page 195)

Drawing From Experience

What do you do when you want to relax? Why do you think doing these things helps you relax? Do you think you could make your muscles relax if you tried?

In the last section, you learned about the altered states of consciousness called sleep and dreaming. This section discusses another altered state: hypnosis. You will also learn about how people can control their own body processes using biofeedback and meditation.

Organizing Your Thoughts

Use the diagram below to help you take notes as you read the summaries that follow. Give examples of how hypnosis, biofeedback, and meditation could be used to help you perform better in a sport, music recital, or other performance activity.

Method	Example of how it can help you perform better
Hypnosis	1.
Biofeedback	2.
Meditation	3.

Read to Learn

Introduction (page 191)

Surgery without pain-blocking drugs sounds like a trick but such operations have been done by hypnotizing the patient. Researchers are learning more about the connection between the mind and the body. Doctors and therapists use hypnosis to help people quit smoking, lose weight, manage stress, and reduce pain.

4. How is hypnosis a connection between the mind and body?

_____

_____

What is Hypnosis? (page 191)

Hypnosis is a form of altered consciousness in which people become highly suggestible. This means that the hypnotist can influence the person's behavior and thoughts by offering suggestions. The hypnotist can help people become aware of things they have forgotten, or become unaware of things they usually notice. For example, hypnotized people may recall in detail incidents they had forgotten. Or, they may feel no pain when pricked with a needle. People cannot be aware of everything they are thinking or feeling at a given time. For example, you are probably not aware of the position of your feet until this reading called attention to it. By mentioning your feet, this reading shifted your attention to your feet. Hypnosis shifts our awareness in the same way.

Hypnosis does not put the participant to sleep. A hypnotic trance is quite different from sleep. Hypnotized people are highly responsive. They can focus their attention on one small thing and ignore everything else. The hypnotist guides the participant into a trance by slowly persuading him or her to relax and lose interest in distractions.

The participant is not under the hypnotist's control, but can be convinced to do things he or she would not normally do. The participant is cooperating with the hypnotist. *Together* they try to solve a problem or learn more about how the participant's mind works. Anyone can resist hypnosis by simply refusing to open his or her mind to it.

Some psychologists, like Theodore Barber, argue that hypnosis is not a special state of consciousness. If given instructions and told to try their hardest, people who are not hypnotized can do anything a hypnotized person can do. Other psychologists, like Ernest Hilgard, believe that there is something special about the hypnotic state. Hilgard believes that consciousness includes many different aspects that may become separated, or dissociated, during hypnosis. This view is called the neodissociation theory. Other psychologists believe that hypnotized participants behave as they do because they have accepted the role. They know that hypnotized people are supposed to do as they are told, and they just play this role. Whether hypnosis is a special state or not, it does reveal that people have abilities that they do not use.

A **posthypnotic suggestion** is a suggestion made during hypnosis that influences the participant's behavior afterward. One thing hypnosis can do is block memory. For example, the hypnotist may suggest that, after awaking, the participant will be unable to hear the word "psychology." When the participant comes out of the trance, he or she may report that people around are speaking strangely. They seem to be leaving out words.

Hypnosis can also aid memory or help change unwanted behaviors, such as smoking or overeating. It can also reduce pain by reducing anxiety and encouraging relaxation. Therapists use hypnosis to help people become aware of their problems and look at their problems in new ways.

5. Give an example of a situation in which a person might want to be hypnotized to aid memory.

_____

Biofeedback (page 194)

Biofeedback is a way that people can learn how to control their body processes with the help of feedback from a machine. For example, you can be hooked up to a biofeedback machine so that a light will go on every time your heart rate goes over 80. You could then learn to keep your heart rate below 80 by trying to keep the light off. People have used biofeedback to learn to control many physical responses, including brain waves, blood pressure, and skin temperature. The basic principle of biofeedback is simple: feedback makes learning possible. Biofeedback machines tell people about very small changes in their bodies. These people can then experiment with different thoughts and feelings as they see how each affects their bodies. With time, they can learn to control their physical processes. In one study biofeedback helped people learn to control headaches by relaxing a certain muscle.

6. Give an example of feedback you received from someone that helped you learn a new skill.

_____

Meditation (page 195)

Meditation is focusing attention on an image, thought, or object to clear your mind and relax. Researchers have shown that people can change their physical states using meditation. There are three approaches to meditation. *Transcendental meditation* involves repeating in your mind a sound, called a mantra. *Mindfulness meditation* focuses on the present moment. For example, you would focus on each body part as you slowly move your focus through your body from the tips of your toes to the top of your head. You would pay special attention to areas that cause pain. *Breath meditation* is concentrating on your breathing, the process of breathing in and out.

Researchers generally agree that people can benefit from some sort of relaxation exercise like meditation. Meditation has helped people lower their blood pressure, heart rates, and breathing rates.

7. Why do you think meditation can help lower heart rates?

_____

Study Guide **7-3**

Drugs and Consciousness

For use with textbook pages 197–202

Key Terms

psychoactive drugs chemicals that affect the nervous system and result in altered consciousness (page 197)

marijuana the dried leaves and flowers of Indian hemp (*cannabis sativa*) that produce an altered state of consciousness when smoked or ingested (page 198)

hallucinations perceptions that have no direct external causes (page 199)

hallucinogens drugs that often produce hallucinations (page 200)

LSD a potent psychedelic drug that produces distortions of perception and thought (page 200)

Drawing From Experience

Have you observed anyone under the influence of alcohol or illegal drugs? How did he or she act? How do your friends feel about alcohol and drug use?

The last section discussed the uses of hypnosis, biofeedback, and meditation to help control physical problems, such as stress and pain. In this section, you will learn about mind-altering drugs. You will learn what they do and why many are dangerous.

Organizing Your Thoughts

Use the diagram below to help you take notes as you read the summaries that follow. Think about the harmful effects of each type of drug.

Drug	Harmful Effects
Marijuana	1.
LSD	2.
Opiates	3.
Alcohol	4.

Read to Learn

Introduction (page 197)

Marijuana is a serious threat to the health of young people. Parents must talk to their children about it. It is one of the **psychoactive drugs**. Psychoactive drugs are chemicals that affect the nervous system and result in altered consciousness. Psychoactive drugs include stimulants, like caffeine in coffee and colas, and depressants, like alcohol. They also include powerful drugs that cause hallucinations, like LSD.

5. Why do you think powerful psychoactive drugs are a threat to health?

_____

Marijuana (page 198)

Marijuana produces an altered state of consciousness when smoked or eaten. Hashish is a related drug that is also made from the Indian hemp plant. The sale and possession of marijuana and hashish are against the law in most states.

The drug affects people in different ways. The effects seem to depend on the setting in which the drug is taken and the user's past experience. In general, the drug heightens sensory experiences, both pleasant and unpleasant. If the user is psychologically unstable anyway, the drug can bring on mental illness.

Marijuana may not be physically addictive, although some researchers believe it is if used for a long time. It may also be psychologically addictive. Studies show that smoking marijuana may damage the lungs more than cigarettes do. Marijuana users hold the smoke in their lungs for 20 to 40 seconds, increasing the possibility of lung damage from tar and other chemicals. Marijuana users also have a harder time forming memories, making mental and physical tasks more difficult.

6. What might happen to a person who smoked marijuana when he was worried about an upcoming test in school?

_____

Hallucinations (page 199)

Hallucinations are perceptions of things that are not real. They are seeing, hearing, smelling, tasting, or feeling things that do not exist. Hallucinations can happen under normal conditions. People hallucinate when they are dreaming or have not slept for a long time. For example, truck drivers on long hauls have reported swerving suddenly to avoid stalled cars that do not exist.

Hallucinations are similar from person to person. Hallucinations may be similar in different people because the drug affects the same places in everyone's brain.

7. In what ways can hallucinations be dangerous?

_____

Hallucinogens (page 200)

Hallucinogens are drugs that produce hallucinations. These drugs are also called psychedelic because they create a loss of contact with reality. **LSD** is the strongest hallucinogen. Many hallucinogens come from plants, but LSD does not. It is synthetic (made rather than natural). An LSD trip can last 6 to 14 hours. During the trip, people can experience many perceptions. If they take the drug when they are in a bad mood, afraid, or depressed, the experience can be terrifying. Hallucinations are common with LSD use.

Users may think that LSD helps them think more clearly, but it actually hinders thinking. Panic is a common reaction. Users have described their experience as being trapped in the panic and afraid that they would never get out or would go mad. *Flashbacks* or reliving the experience can happen even months later.

8. LSD "trips" can be pleasant or terrifying. How might this fact influence someone's decision to use it?

_____

Opiates (page 201)

Opiates are usually called narcotics. They include opium, morphine, and heroin. They produce a pleasurable state users have described as somewhere between wake and sleep. Opiates are physically addictive. An overdose can cause loss of control of breathing, resulting in death.

9. What does it mean to be "physically addictive"?

_____

Alcohol (page 201)

Alcohol is the most used mind-altering substance in the United States. Alcohol may seem to stimulate the body, but it actually slows normal brain functions. Alcohol is a depressant. People who drink alcohol often act without the self-control they normally apply to their behavior. People experience slurred speech, blurred vision, and poor judgment and memory. Drinking heavily over a long period can cause permanent damage to the brain and liver.

10. Why do you think people drink alcohol in spite of the dangers?

_____

Drug Abuse and Treatment (page 202)

Drug abusers are people who regularly use illegal drugs or use legal drugs too much. Drug abuse has many dangers. It can cause injury or death from overdose or accident. It can damage a person's health. It can get people in trouble with the law. The greatest risk, though, is loss of control. Drug abuse can turn into addiction. Addiction is an overwhelming desire to get and use drugs. Treatment for drug abuse involves three steps. First, abusers must admit they have a problem. Then they must enter a treatment program. Finally, they must resist the temptation to go back to the drugs. Support groups can help abusers deal with temptation.

11. What kinds of things might drug addiction cause someone to do?

_____

Study Guide 8-1

Sensation

For use with textbook pages 207–213

Key Terms

sensation what occurs when a stimulus activates a receptor (page 208)

perception the organization of sensory information into meaningful experiences (page 208)

psychophysics the study of the relationships between sensory experiences and the physical stimuli that cause them (page 208)

absolute threshold the weakest amount of a stimulus that a person can detect half the time (page 209)

difference threshold the smallest change in a physical stimulus that can be detected between two stimuli (page 210)

Weber's law the principle that for any change in a stimulus to be detected, a constant proportion of that stimulus must be added or subtracted (page 211)

signal-detection theory the study of people's tendencies to make correct judgments in detecting the presence of stimuli (page 212)

Drawing From Experience

Have you ever noticed that you can ignore practically anything if you are around it long enough? Have you ever tried to study in a noisy room, and just when you were able to tune it all out, someone said something really loud, grabbing your attention?

This section discusses the ability of your senses to perceive and adapt to stimuli in your environment.

Organizing Your Thoughts

Use the diagram below to help you take notes as you read the summaries that follow. Design an experiment to determine the absolute threshold for sound. Make your experiment similar to the one researchers use to determine the absolute threshold for light given in the summary. Describe your experiment in four steps in the flowchart below.

■ 1. _____

　　■ 2. _____

　　　　■ 3. _____

　　　　　　■ 4. _____

Read to Learn

Introduction (page 207)

You gather information from your environment through your senses. But to understand the information, it must be organized in a way that you expect. For example, try to read the following sentences.

Yo umayn otrea lizeh owco mplexr eadi ngis. Afe wsim plech angesc anco nfus eyou!
You may not realize how complex reading is. A few simple changes can confuse you!

5.   What are some ways that we organize words into language that others can understand?

_____

_____

_____

_____

What is Sensation? (page 208)

A *stimulus* is any change in the environment that a living thing responds to. For example, an alarm, an electric light, and an aching muscle are all stimuli for humans. A **sensation** occurs any time a stimulus activates one of your senses. Your sense organs note physical changes in energy such as heat, light, sound, and physical pressure. Your skin notes changes in heat and pressure. Your eyes note changes in light.

A sensation combines with other sensations and your past experience to yield a perception. A **perception** is sensory information organized into something meaningful. For example, the jumbled sentences you tried to read in the introduction had no meaning until they were organized into words. Then, from your past experience with reading words, you could understand the meaning of the sentences.

Psychophysics is the study of the relationships between sensory experiences and the physical stimuli that cause them. For example, researchers want to know how the wavelengths of light affect the way we see color.

6.   When you are eating lunch in the school cafeteria, what stimuli do each of your five senses pick up?

_____

_____

_____

_____

Threshold (page 208)

Psychologists want to know how much of a stimulus is necessary for a person to sense it. For example, how much energy is required for someone to hear a sound or see a light? How much scent must be in a room before someone can smell it? To answer these questions, psychologists set up the following experiment. They put a person in a dark room and instruct him to watch the wall. The person is supposed to say "I see it" when he can see a light on the wall. The researchers shine a low-level light on the wall. They then increase the light until the person says "I see it." Then the researchers lower the light until the person states that he can no longer see it. Researchers do this kind of experiment with many people and average the results. From this, they determine the weakest amount of a stimulus that a person can detect. This is called the **absolute threshold.**

Researchers have determined an absolute threshold for each of the five senses. For example, on average, people can begin to hear a watch ticking when it is 20 feet away. They first detect sweetness when a teaspoon of sugar is dissolved in 2 gallons of water. These thresholds may seem impressive. But we miss a lot of the sensory world. We cannot see microwaves. Bloodhounds can smell more than we can. We can hear only about 20 percent of what a dolphin can hear. Human senses are rather limited.

7. What are some stimuli that your pet can sense before you can?

_____

_____

_____

_____

Sensory Differences and Ratios (page 210)

The **difference threshold** is the smallest amount of difference a person can detect between two stimuli. Going back to our light example, researchers would test for the difference threshold by gradually increasing the amount of light until the person says, "Yes, this light is brighter than the light I just saw." Using this kind of experiment, researchers can identify the *just noticeable difference (JND)*. This is the smallest increase or decrease in a stimulus that a person can detect.

Weber's law states that for any change in a stimulus to be detected, a constant proportion of that stimulus must be added or subtracted. For example, if you put a 3-pound package into an empty backpack, people will perceive that the weight of the backpack has greatly increased. But if you add the same amount to a backpack containing a 100-pound weight, people will perceive that the backpack's weight increased very little.

8. Say you turned up your car radio a certain amount. Then you went to a rock concert. During the concert, the musicians turned up the amplifiers the same amount as you did your radio. According to Weber's law, in which situation would you perceive a greater increase in sound?

_____

_____

_____

Sensory Adaptation (page 211)

Senses are tuned in to changes. They respond more to increases and decreases in new events rather than to unchanging stimuli. We can respond to changes in our environment because our senses have the ability to adapt, or adjust, to a constant level of stimulation. For example, after a short time in a darkened movie theater, your eyes adapt to the low level of light and you can then see things around you. Other senses adapt as well. When you first jump into a swimming pool, the water may feel cold. Soon, your skin adapts, and the water no longer feels cold. If your senses did not have the ability to adapt, you would feel the constant pressure of clothes on your body. Stimuli would seem to be bombarding all your senses at the same time.

9. Give an example of adaptation by your sense of hearing.

_____

_____

_____

Signal-Detection Theory (page 212)

Signal-detection theory is the study of people's tendencies to correctly detect the presence of stimuli. Detection thresholds involve recognizing some stimulus against a background of competing stimuli. A radar operator must be able to see airplanes on a radar screen, even when the blips on the screen are as faint as those caused by birds. In studying the difficulties faced by radar operators, psychologists have determined that there is not just one absolute threshold for detecting stimuli. Other factors affect detection, including motivation and competing stimuli.

10. When you are riding your bike with friends, what are some competing stimuli that might delay your detection of a dog running into your path?

_____

_____

_____

Study Guide 8-2

The Senses

For use with textbook pages 214–222

Key Terms

pupil the opening in the iris that regulates the amount of light entering the eye (page 215)

lens a flexible, elastic, transparent structure in the eye that changes its shape to focus light on the retina (page 215)

retina the innermost coating of the back of the eye, containing the light-sensitive receptor cells (page 215)

optic nerve the nerve that carries impulses from the retina to the brain (page 215)

binocular fusion the process of combining the images received from the two eyes into a single, fused image (page 216)

retinal disparity the differences between the images stimulating each eye (page 216)

auditory nerve the nerve that carries impulses from the inner ear to the brain, resulting in the sensation of sound (page 218)

vestibular system three semicircular canals that provide the sense of balance located in the inner ear and connected to the brain by a nerve (page 220)

olfactory nerve the nerve that carries smell impulses from the nose to the brain (page 220)

kinesthesis the sense of movement and body position (page 222)

Drawing From Experience

Have you ever tried to do something with one eye closed? Was the activity more difficult to do this way? Have you ever felt dizzy after riding on a roller coaster or a boat?

In the last section, you learned about the nature of sensations and their thresholds. This section discusses how your body receives and processes sensations from your environment.

Organizing Your Thoughts

Use the diagram below to help you take notes as you read the summaries that follow. Think about the path that light takes from the time it hits your eye until it becomes vision. Trace the steps in the process in the flowchart below.

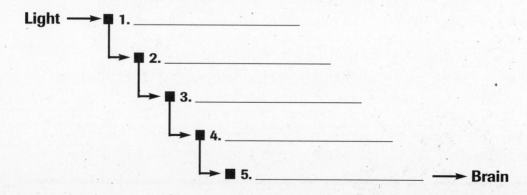

Copyright © by The McGraw-Hill Companies, Inc.

Read to Learn

Introduction (page 214)

You probably think that you have just five senses: vision, hearing, taste, smell, and touch. Actually, you have more. The skin has several senses. Plus, you have two "internal" senses: *vestibular* and *kinesthetic*. Each sense organ receives some sort of external stimulus, such as light, sound waves, or pressure. It then changes the sensation into a chemical-electrical message transmitted by the nervous system and interpreted by the brain.

6. What are the sense organs for the five familiar senses?

_____

_____

_____

_____

_____

Vision (page 215)

The vision process begins when light enters the eye through the **pupil** and reaches the **lens**. This is a flexible structure that changes its shape to focus light on the retina. The **retina** is a coating at the back of the eye. It contains two types of light-sensitive cells: *rods* and *cones*. These cells change light into impulses that the neurons carry over the **optic nerve** to the brain.

Cones require more light than rods before they begin to respond, so cones work best in daylight. Since rods can work in much lower light, they are the basis for night vision. There are many more rods than cones, but only cones are sensitive to color.

The colors we see are actually different wavelengths of light. We see color only after light waves hit objects and bounce back to us. For example, a pea looks green because green light bounces off of it and all other colors do not. We can sense differences in texture and solidity of objects by the speed at which the waves bounce back.

When the cones are not working well, the person can not see color very well. This condition is called color deficiency. For example, some people can not tell the difference between red and green. A few can't tell yellow from blue. A very few can't see any colors at all. They see the world in blacks, whites, and shades of gray.

Because we have two eyes, our visual system receives two images. But instead of seeing double, we see a combination of the two images. This is called **binocular fusion**. Each eye projects a slightly different image on the retina. This difference is called **retinal disparity**. For example, bring an object such as an eraser close to your eyes. Without moving it, look at the eraser first with one eye and then with the other. You will see a difference in the two images because of the different viewpoint each eye has. When you open both eyes, you will see no difference. You will see one eraser.

Retinal disparity is important to your sense of depth. Your brain knows that a large difference between the images each eye brings in (retinal disparity) means the object is near. A small difference means the object is far away.

7. Bring a small object very close to your face. Look at it with one eye and then the other. Notice the differences in the two images. Then do the same with a distant object. Which object creates the greatest difference in what each eye sees?

_____

_____

_____

_____

Hearing (page 218)

Hearing depends on sound waves. These are vibrations of the air. Sound waves from the air pass through several bones and fluids until they reach the inner ear. The inner ear contains tiny hairs that move back and forth, like a field of wheat in the wind. These hairs change the sound vibrations into signals that the neurons carry through the **auditory nerve** to the brain.

The amplitude, or height, of sound waves determines the loudness. The higher the amplitude, the louder the sound. Loudness is measured in *decibels*. The sound's *pitch* depends on the wave's frequency, or rate of vibration. Low frequencies produce deep bass sounds. High frequencies produce squeaks. You can hear more than one pitch at a time. For example, if you strike two piano keys at the same time, you can pick out two different pitches.

Your ears work together to tell you where the sound is coming from. For example, a noise on your right will reach your right ear first and then your left. It is also slightly louder in your right ear because it is closer to it. These differences tell you the direction of the sound.

Your outer ear directs sound waves down a short tube called the auditory canal. The vibration (sound wave) causes air in the auditory canal to vibrate, which in turn causes the eardrum to vibrate. The middle ear is filled with air and contains three bones: the hammer, anvil, and stirrup. These bones link to the eardrum on one end and the cochlea at the other. When the eardrum vibrates, the three bones in the middle ear vibrate and push against the cochlea.

The cochlea is the inner ear. It is a tube that contains fluids and neurons. The pressure against the cochlea makes the liquid in it move. Tiny hairs inside the cochlea pick up the motion. The hairs are attached to sensory cells. These cells turn the sound vibrations into impulses that the neurons in the auditory nerve carry to the brain.

8. When you hear sounds from a bass guitar, are you hearing waves with high frequency or low frequency?

_____

_____

_____

_____

Balance (page 220)

Your body's sense of balance comes from the **vestibular system** inside your inner ear. It has three *semicircular canals* filled with fluid. When you turn your head, this fluid moves, which bends hair cells in the fluid. The stimuli that your vestibular sense responds to are movements such as spinning, falling, and tilting your head. Too much stimulation of this sense can cause dizziness and "motion sickness." Without your sense of balance, you would be unable to walk without falling.

9. Give an example of an activity that might overstimulate your vestibular system.

_____

_____

_____

_____

Smell and Taste (page 220)

Smell and taste are chemical senses. Their sense organs respond to chemical molecules rather than to light energy or sound waves. To smell something, the right molecules must hit the smell receivers in your nose. These molecules enter your nose in vapors, which reach smell receivers in the nasal passages. These receivers send messages about smells through the **olfactory nerve** to the brain. To taste something, molecules must stimulate the taste buds on your tongue. The taste buds relay information about taste as well as texture and temperature of the substance to the brain.

Four sensory experiences make up taste: sour, salty, bitter, and sweet. The combination of taste, smell, and touch sensations create *flavor*. Much of what you taste is actually produced by your sense of smell. For example, when your nose is blocked by a cold, your food probably tastes bland.

Sensations of warmth, cold, and pressure also affect taste. Try drinking hot soda to see how temperature affects taste. Now think about the differences in texture between pudding and a crunchy chocolate bar. These textures influence taste as well.

10. Is the sense of smell better in dogs or humans? Give an example.

_____

_____

The Skin Senses (page 221)

Your skin provides at least four kinds of information to your brain: pressure, warmth, cold, and pain. Some spots on your skin are more sensitive to pressure than others because they contain more receivers. For example, your fingertips contain many receivers and are highly sensitive to pressure. Your calves have few receivers. Some skin receivers are sensitive to hot or cold. To create a hot or cold sensation, the temperature of the stimulus must be greater or less than the skin's temperature.

Stimuli such as scratches, punctures, and very high heat can produce pain. Pain is your body's emergency system. It warns you of possible damage to your body from such stimuli. Pain motivates you to stop the harmful activities and take care of injuries. There are two kinds of pain. Pain can be sharp and in a specific spot, or pain can be a dull ache over larger portions of your body.

According to the *gate control theory of pain*, we can reduce some pain by shifting our attention away from it, or we can send other signals to compete with the pain signals. Only so many impulses can get through the bottleneck, or gate. So by increasing nonpain impulses (like rubbing your stubbed toe), you decrease the pain impulses that get through.

11. Use the gate control theory of pain to explain why an injured athlete may be able to continue playing in the game.

_____

_____

The Body Senses (page 222)

Kinesthesis is the sense of movement and body position. It works with the vestibular system to control posture and balance. The receivers for kinesthesis are located near the muscles, tendons, and joints. These receivers send messages to the brain when movement occurs.

Without kinesthetic sensations, your movements would be uncoordinated. You would not know what your hand was doing if it went behind your back. You could not walk without looking at your feet. Complex activities like surgery would be impossible.

12. Give an example of a kinesthetic sensation needed to play tennis.

_____

_____

Study Guide 8-3

For use with textbook pages 223–231

Perception

Key Terms

Gestalt the experience that comes from organizing bits and pieces of information into meaningful wholes (page 224)

subliminal messages brief auditory or visual messages that are presented below the absolute threshold (page 226)

motion parallax the apparent movement of stationary objects relative to one another that occurs when the observer changes position (page 228)

constancy the tendency to perceive certain objects in the same way regardless of changing angle, distance, or lighting (page 229)

illusions perceptions that misrepresent physical stimuli (page 229)

extrasensory perception (ESP) an ability to gain information by some means other than the ordinary senses (page 230)

Drawing From Experience

Before you bite into a candy bar, how do you know it will taste good? If the first bite doesn't taste very good, are you likely to take one more bite before concluding that it isn't good?

The last section described how your senses gather sensations from the environment. In this section, you will learn how you organize sensations into meaningful perceptions.

Organizing Your Thoughts

Use the diagram below to help you take notes as you read the summaries that follow. Think about how your brain uses perceptual cues to make sense out of sensory information. Give an example of each type of perception below.

Type of Perception	Example
Figure-Ground Perception	1.
Perceptual Inference	2.
Monocular Depth Cue	3.
Binocular Depth Cue	4.
Constancy	5.

Read to Learn

Introduction (page 223)

Your brain receives information from the senses. It then organizes and interprets the information into something you can understand. This is the process of perception. For example, you do not just experience a mass of colors, noises, temperatures, and pressures. Rather, you see cars and buildings, hear voices and music, and feel pencils and desks. You do not have just sensory experiences; you perceive objects.

6. If you didn't have the ability to perceive, what would music sound like to you?

_____

_____

Principles of Perceptual Organization (page 224)

The brain makes sense of the world by creating "wholes" out of bits and pieces of information from the environment. This "whole" the brain constructs is a **Gestalt**. People tend to organize information from the senses into patterns. If elements of the pattern are close together or appear similar, we tend to perceive them as belonging to one another. For example, your hear melodies in music, not just single notes. Your brain grouped the notes that were close together. If a pattern your senses pick up is incomplete, your brain will fill in the gaps to make the whole. This is called *closure*. For example, if you write the letter "T" so that the top doesn't touch the stem, you will still perceive it as a "T." Your brain filled in the gap to complete the pattern that you recognize as a "T."

7. Give another example of a Gestalt.

_____

_____

Figure-Ground Perception (page 225)

Figure-ground perception is the ability to tell the difference between an object and its background. For example, when you see a tree against the sky, you can pick out the tree (*figure*) from its background, the sky (*ground*). Figure and ground are important in hearing as well as vision. When you follow one person's voice in a noisy room, the voice is the figure and the other sounds are the ground.

8. As you read this book, what is the figure and what is the ground?

_____

_____

Perceptual Inference (page 225)

Often we have perceptions that go beyond the sensory information. For example, when you take a seat in a dark theater, you assume it is solid, even though you can't see it. When you are driving up a steep hill, the road disappears from view at the top of the hill, but you assume that the road continues on the other side. It does not end suddenly at the top. These are examples of perceptual inference. Because you have experienced these stimuli before, you know what to expect from them.

9. When you hear barking as you approach your house, what does perceptual inference tell you it is?

_____

_____

Learning to Perceive (page 226)

Perceiving is something people *learn* to do. For example, infants under one month will smile at a nodding object the size of a human face, even if it does not have eyes, nose, and mouth. As the baby gets older, she learns to tell the difference between a human face and a blank oval. Later, the baby learns to identify her mother's face from other human faces.

Our needs, beliefs, and expectations influence what we perceive. When we want something, we are more likely to see it. For example, when researchers flash words quickly in front of hungry people, the people can identify food-related words faster than other words. Previous experience also influences what we see. For example, if you have always perceived all elderly women as honest, you might not even question an elderly woman at the next table when your wallet disappears in a restaurant. Your perception of elderly women as honest is your perceptual set. This set prepares you to see what you want to see.

Subliminal messages are brief sounds or visual messages presented below the absolute threshold. One advertiser claimed that the words "Eat Popcorn" were flashed on a movie screen so fast that none of the viewers noticed them. This was done over a period of weeks. The advertiser claimed that this "subliminal advertising" caused sales of popcorn to increase 58 percent. The idea of subliminal ads comes from questionable studies on *subliminal perception*. This is the ability to notice stimuli that affect only the unconscious mind. The studies had many flaws, so there is little support for this idea.

10. Say a child was bitten by a dog when young and is now afraid of dogs. If you show this child a picture of a dog, how might the child describe the dog in the picture?

_____

_____

Depth Perception (page 227)

Depth perception is the ability to recognize distances and three dimensions. To perceive distance and depth, people use many *monocular depth cues*. These are cues that can be used with a single eye. One cue is the size of an object. In the absence of other cues, bigger objects will seem nearer. We also use *relative height*. Objects that appear farther away from another object are higher in our view. *Interposition* is the overlapping of objects. For example, you see two people in the distance. You see the complete outline of the first person. The outline of the second person is interrupted by the first. From this you perceive that the first person is closer than the second. *Light* and *shadows* are also cues. Brightly lit objects appear closer. Objects in shadows appear farther away. *Texture-density gradient* means that the further away an object is, the less detail we can identify.

Motion parallax is the apparent movement of objects that occurs when the observer changes position. For example, look toward two objects in the same line of vision, one near you and the other at a distance. Then move your head back and forth. The near object will seem to move more than the far object. In this way, motion parallax gives you clues as to which objects are closer than others.

Binocular depth cues depend on the movement of both eyes. For example, your eyes turn inward to view objects closer to you. This is *convergence*. Another binocular cue is *retinal disparity*. You learned earlier that the brain interprets a large retinal disparity to mean a close object and a small disparity to mean a distant object.

11. Say you see a friend walking down the street toward you. How might the interposition cue tell you that your friend is closer than the next building?

_____

_____

Constancy (page 229)

Constancy is the tendency to perceive objects the same way, in spite of changing conditions. For example, you probably perceive the whiteness of this page to be fairly constant, even though you may have read the book under many lighting conditions. We perceive constancy in size, shape, brightness, and color. For example, a friend walking toward you does not seem to change into a giant even though the image your eye sees gets larger as she approaches. This is size constancy. Information you receive about distance helps you perceive the friend as being the same size, in spite of the enlarging eye image.

As an example of brightness and color constancy, look out a window at night and see that the trees, grass, or parked cars do not appear to be the same color or brightness as they are during the day. You already know, though, that the grass is green. You perceive this quality even under different lighting conditions.

12. If you didn't have size constancy, which person would appear taller: a 6-foot person standing 50 yards away or a 5-foot person standing 3 feet away?

_____

_____

Illusions (page 229)

Illusions are incorrect perceptions. They occur when perceptual cues are distorted so that our brains cannot correctly interpret space, size, and depth cues. For example, look at Figure 8.18 in your textbook. Which lines are longer? Measure the lengths of the two pairs of lines with a ruler. Then look again. Do the lines *look* as long now that you *know* they are the same? Most people say no.

Figure 8.19 shows two individuals in a room. Their sizes look very different because you perceive the room as rectangular. In fact, the ceiling and walls are slanted so that the back wall is shorter and closer on the right than on the left. Yet even when you know how this illusion was achieved, you still accept the odd difference in the sizes of the two people because the windows, walls, and ceiling appear rectangular. Your experience with rectangular rooms overcomes your knowledge of how this trick is done.

13. Give an example of an illusion you have seen, either performed by a magician or in a "fun house" at an amusement park or fair.

_____

_____

Extrasensory Perception (page 230)

Extrasensory perception (ESP) is the ability to receive information by some means other than the ordinary senses. There are four types of ESP—(1) Clairvoyance is perceiving objects or information without input from the senses. (2) Telepathy is reading someone else's mind or transferring thoughts. (3) Psychokinesis means using mental effort to move objects. (4) Precognition is the ability to foretell events.

14. How do you think fortune-tellers can predict your future in a believable way?

_____

_____

_____

Study Guide 9-1

Classical Conditioning

For use with textbook pages 241–248

Key Terms

classical conditioning a learning procedure in which associations are made between a natural stimulus and a learned, neutral stimulus (page 241)

neutral stimulus a stimulus that does not initially elicit any part of the unconditioned response (page 242)

unconditioned stimulus (UCS) a stimulus that elicits a certain predictable response typically without previous training (page 242)

unconditioned response (UCR) an organism's automatic reaction to a stimulus (page 242)

conditioned stimulus (CS) a once-neutral event that has come to elicit a given response after a period of training in which it has been paired with an unconditioned stimulus (page 242)

conditioned response (CR) the learned reaction to a conditioned stimulus (page 242)

generalization responding similarly to a range of similar stimuli (page 244)

discrimination the ability to respond differently to similar but distinct stimuli (page 244)

extinction the gradual disappearance of a conditioned response when the conditioned stimulus is repeatedly presented without the unconditioned stimulus (page 245)

Drawing From Experience

Have you ever reached for your phone after hearing a ring on the television? Do you have a pet that runs to its food dish the minute you walk in the house? This section discusses how classical conditioning affects human and animal behavior.

Organizing Your Thoughts

Use the diagram below to help you take notes as you read the summaries that follow. Think about how a neutral stimulus becomes a conditioned stimulus.

Before Conditioning	During Conditioning	After Conditioning
1. A neutral stimulus results in _____.	3. A conditioned stimulus is paired with the _____.	5. A conditioned stimulus results in a(n) _____.
2. An unconditioned stimulus results in a(n) _____.	4. The result is a(n) _____.	6. The conditioning will last unless _____ occurs.

Read to Learn

Introduction (page 241)

What is learning? Learning takes place when a person or an animal has an experience that changes his or her behavior, more or less permanently. **Classical conditioning** is a type of learning. When something makes you react in a certain way, it is called a stimulus. During classical conditioning, people and animals learn to respond to a new stimulus the same way that they respond to one they already know.

7. Who was the first person to explain how classical conditioning worked?

_____

_____

_____

_____

_____

Classical Conditioning (page 242)

A stimulus that you respond to without training is called an **unconditioned stimulus (UCS).** Your response is called an **unconditioned response (UCR).** A **neutral stimulus** is one that has nothing to do with your response. Ivan Pavlov gave an unconditioned stimulus and a neutral stimulus to a dog at the same time. He discovered that the dog would eventually learn to respond to the neutral stimulus in the same way as it did to the unconditioned stimulus.

If you watch an action movie, you will feel tense at certain times during the movie when the main characters are in danger. If the movie plays the same song every time the characters are in danger, you will eventually feel tense when you hear the music, even if you are not watching the movie. The song is a neutral stimulus. It did not make you feel tense before you saw the movie. After conditioning, the neutral stimulus (the song) is called a **conditioned stimulus (CS).** Your response is called a **conditioned response (CR).**

Classical conditioning works gradually. Sometimes you will respond to a neutral stimulus that is similar to the conditioned stimulus. This is called **generalization.** For example, if you are conditioned to feel tense when you hear a certain song, you might feel tense when you hear other songs with a similar beat. If you did, that would be generalization. Eventually, you will learn to tell the difference between a conditioned stimulus and a similar neutral stimulus. This is called **discrimination.** If you learn to feel tense only when you hear the song from the movie, and not when you hear other songs with a similar beat, you have learned discrimination.

Classical conditioning is not always permanent. If the conditioned stimulus and the unconditioned stimulus are not given together for a long time, the conditioned stimulus stops working. The conditioned response stops. This is called **extinction.** If you were conditioned to feel tense when you heard a song during a movie, but then never watched the movie again, you would eventually stop feeling tense when you heard the song. If the unconditioned stimulus and the conditioned stimulus are again put together, the conditioned response comes back quickly. This is called spontaneous recovery.

8. If you strongly dislike broccoli, green beans, and spinach, what is your reaction likely to be if you are served green peas? Which process of classical conditioning would you be using?

_____

_____

_____

_____

Classical Conditioning and Human Behavior (page 246)

A person can be conditioned on purpose or by accident. To stop children from wetting the bed, parents can use a device called a bell and pad. The pad is put on the bed and wired to a bell. When the child starts to wet the bed, the pad gets wet causing the bell to ring. The child wakes up and uses the bathroom. The bell is an unconditioned stimulus. A child will always respond to it. By ringing the bell when the child's bladder is full, the child learns to wake up when he or she needs to go to the bathroom. The full bladder becomes a conditioned stimulus.

A taste aversion is an example of accidental classical conditioning. Suppose you eat snails for the first time. Later in the evening, you feel sick. You will probably think the snails made you sick and you will not like the smell or thought of them the next time someone serves them.

9. If you develop a taste aversion, what can you do to overcome it?

_____

_____

_____

_____

Study Guide 9-2

Operant Conditioning

For use with textbook pages 250–258

Key Terms

operant conditioning a form of learning in which a certain action is reinforced or punished, resulting in corresponding increases or decreases in the likelihood that similar actions will occur again (page 250)

reinforcement a stimulus or event which follows a response and increases the likelihood that the response will be repeated (page 251)

primary reinforcer a stimulus that is naturally rewarding, such as food or water (page 252)

secondary reinforcer a stimulus such as money that becomes reinforcing through its link with a primary reinforcer (page 252)

fixed-ratio schedule a schedule of reinforcement in which a specific number of correct responses is required before reinforcement can be obtained (page 253)

variable-ratio schedule a schedule of reinforcement in which an unpredictable number of responses are required before reinforcement can be obtained each time (page 254)

fixed-interval schedule a schedule of reinforcement in which a specific amount of time must elapse before a response will elicit reinforcement (page 254)

variable-interval schedule a schedule of reinforcement in which changing amounts of time must elapse before a response will obtain reinforcement each time (page 255)

shaping the technique of operant conditioning in which the desired behavior is "molded" by first rewarding any act similar to that behavior and then requiring closer and closer approximations to the desired behavior before giving the reward (page 255)

response chain learned reactions that follow one another in sequence, each reaction producing the signal for the next (page 256)

aversive control the process of influencing behavior by means of unpleasant stimuli (page 256)

negative reinforcement increasing the strength of a given response by removing or preventing a painful stimulus when the response occurs (page 256)

escape conditioning the training of an organism to remove or terminate an unpleasant stimulus (page 257)

avoidance conditioning the training of an organism to remove or withdraw from an unpleasant stimulus before it starts (page 257)

Drawing From Experience

Have you ever touched a hot iron and immediately pulled your hand away? Would you touch the iron again without testing it? We learn not to repeat behaviors that are harmful to us.

In the last section, you read about classical conditioning. Classical conditioning is one type of learning. In this section you will read about another type of learning called **operant conditioning.** This type of learning occurs when we receive rewards or punishments for our behavior.

Organizing Your Thoughts

Use the diagram below to help you take notes as you read the summaries that follow. Think about the various kinds of reinforcement that affect behavior and fill in examples of reinforcers.

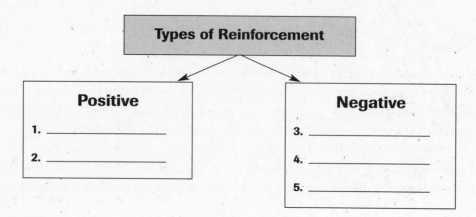

Types of Reinforcement

Positive
1. _____
2. _____

Negative
3. _____
4. _____
5. _____

Read to Learn

Introduction (page 250)

Every day we do many things. How things turn out affects what we do in the future. We learn from our actions. We tend to repeat actions that result in rewards and avoid actions that result in punishment. This is operant conditioning.

6. Name something you did in the past 24 hours that resulted in some kind of reward.

_____

_____

Reinforcement (page 251)

B.F. Skinner believed that people do things based on whether or not they will receive a reward or a punishment. If a reward makes you more likely to do something, it is called a **reinforcement.** There are two kinds of reinforcement. You can give people something as a reward for their behavior. This is called positive reinforcement. You can also reward people by taking away something unpleasant or painful. This is called negative reinforcement.

The strongest reinforcers are the ones that satisfy the basic needs of our body. These are called **primary reinforcers.** For example, food is a basic need. We need food to live. Food is a primary reinforcer. Reinforcers that are not directly connected to the needs of our body are called **secondary reinforcers.** Secondary reinforcers only work when we are conditioned to associate them with a primary reinforcer. If someone gives us money as a reward, it will strongly affect our behavior. Money is just a piece of paper or a round piece of metal. We cannot eat it or drink it. We have been conditioned, however, to associate money with our basic needs. We know we can buy food and other basic needs with money. Money is a secondary reinforcer.

7. Would you use a primary or secondary reinforcer to train a dog to shake hands? Why?

_____

_____

Schedules of Reinforcement (page 253)

Rewards can be given in various ways. The plan for giving rewards is called a reinforcement schedule. You can reward people based on how often they do something. This is called a ratio schedule. If you reward people after they do something a specific number of times, you are using a **fixed-ratio schedule.** For example, if you pay a typist every time he or she types 10 pages for you, the typist is on a fixed-ratio schedule.

If people know they will be rewarded for their behavior, but do not know how often they have to do the behavior to get the reward, they are on a **variable-ratio schedule.** A slot machine uses a variable-ratio schedule. If you pull the handle enough times, eventually the machine will pay out money. The problem is that you do not know when you will be rewarded for pulling the handle.

Reinforcement schedules can also be based on time. This is called an interval schedule. You can reward people at specific times regardless of how often they have done something. If you reward people at the exact same time, you are using a **fixed-interval schedule.** Many teachers use a fixed-interval schedule for tests. The students know that the test will take place whether they study a lot or very little.

If you reward at random times, you are using a **variable-interval schedule.** A surprise quiz is an example of a teacher using a variable-interval schedule. Students know that a quiz could come at any time. In order to be ready, students need to study regularly since they cannot predict when they will be tested.

8. Which types of schedules have a long-lasting effect on behavior? Why?

_____

_____

Shaping and Chaining (page 255)

Operant conditioning can be used to teach new skills. One type of operant conditioning that is good for teaching skills is called **shaping.** Shaping teaches a new behavior step by step. At first, you are given a reward for behavior similar to the skill you are learning. To keep getting the rewards, however, you must get better at the skill. The rewards shape your behavior.

If you want to learn a complex skill, you need to learn several different behaviors. You also have to learn how to put the behaviors together in the right order. For example, if you want to learn how to swim, you have to learn several behaviors. You have to learn how to kick your feet. You have to learn how to stroke with your arms. You have to learn how to breathe. Then you have to link these behaviors together. Linking behaviors together is called a **response chain.** Many complex activities require you to learn several response chains. You then have to put the chains together. Once you master the response chains, you will no longer have to think about each chain. Your actions become natural. You have learned a new skill.

9. You have to teach a friend a cheerleading routine. Would you be more likely to use shaping or chaining to teach the skill? Defend your choice.

_____

_____

Aversive Control (page 256)

Another way to condition someone is to use an unpleasant or painful stimulus. This is called **aversive control.** There are two kinds of aversive control. You can reward someone by taking away something that is unpleasant or painful. This is called **negative reinforcement.** You can also inflict something unpleasant or painful on someone to make them do something. This is called punishment.

Negative reinforcement works in two different ways. People can learn to behave a certain way to stop something unpleasant or painful. This is called **escape conditioning.** For example, a child who dislikes liver whines and gags when liver is placed in front of her. When her father removes the liver, the gagging and whining stop. The liver is a negative reinforcement. The child has learned that gagging and whining make liver go away. She has been conditioned to whine in order to escape from the liver.

People can also learn to behave a certain way to prevent something unpleasant or painful from starting. This is called **avoidance conditioning.** If the child's father dislikes hearing his daughter whine, he may stop serving liver. In his case, the whining is a negative reinforcement. The father has been conditioned to avoid the whining by not serving liver.

The other type of aversive control is punishment. Most people are familiar with how punishment works. If you do not change your behavior, something painful or unpleasant happens to you. Punishment is the opposite of negative reinforcement. Negative reinforcement makes people repeat their behavior. Punishment makes people stop their behavior.

Punishment can change behavior, but it can also cause fear, aggression, or rage. It can also teach someone that the way to avoid punishment is to stay away from the punisher. Punishment can teach you what not to do, but it cannot teach you the right behavior. Children need to be taught acceptable behavior as well as be punished for wrong behavior.

10. How might a child use avoidance conditioning to escape punishment for her action?

_____

Study Guide 9-3

Social Learning

For use with textbook pages 259–266

Key Terms

social learning a form of learning in which the organism observes and imitates the behavior of others (page 259)

cognitive learning a form of learning that involves mental processes and may result from observation or imitation (page 260)

cognitive map a mental picture of spatial relationships or relationships between events (page 260)

latent learning alteration of a behavioral tendency that is not demonstrated by an immediate, observable change in behavior (page 260)

learned helplessness a condition in which repeated attempts to control or influence a situation fail, resulting in the belief that the situation is uncontrollable and that any effort to cope will fail (page 261)

modeling learning by imitating others, copying behavior (page 262)

behavior modification a systematic application of learning principles to change people's actions and feelings (page 263)

token economy a form of conditioning in which desirable behavior is reinforced with value-less objects or points, which can be accumulated and exchanged for various rewards (page 264)

Drawing From Experience

Everyone has habits. Do you have any habits you would like to change? In the last section, you learned how positive and negative reinforcement help people learn. Many psychologists think that people can choose to learn things. They do not have to be conditioned or given reinforcement. This type of learning is called **social learning.** Social learning refers to the way people make decisions and use information.

Organizing Your Thoughts

Use the diagram below to help you take notes as you read the summaries that follow. Think about the decisions you make that affect your actions.

Type of Social Learning	Examples
Cognitive learning	1.
Modeling	2.
Behavior modification	3.

Read to Learn

Cognitive Learning (page 260)

One type of social learning is called **cognitive learning.** Every day we receive a lot of information. Psychologists who study cognitive learning are trying to understand our mental processes. They look at how we get information, how we organize it, and how we use it.

Sometimes, people do not immediately show what they have learned. For example, you need to get to a store that you have been to only once before. You are not sure how to get there. As you drive, you see signs and landmarks that you remember from the first trip. This is an example of one type of cognitive learning. It is called **latent learning.** You did not try to learn the signs and landmarks on your first trip, but you were still able to remember what they looked like when you needed them.

Latent learning is possible because we create **cognitive maps** to help us remember and learn. Cognitive maps are mental pictures. We create them naturally as we explore our surroundings. A cognitive map helps us to remember how things are related to one another. For example, a rat in a maze will explore the maze to find the shortest route to the food. If the shortest route is blocked, the rat will switch to the next shortest route. He does not need to explore the maze again because he has created a mental map of the maze.

Another type of social learning is called **learned helplessness.** When people repeatedly try to change a situation and fail each time, they may decide that they cannot change things. They will no longer even try. They become convinced that they are helpless.

Learned helplessness has three elements. The three elements are stability, globality, and internality. Stability means you believe you can never change a situation. Globality means you believe that because you cannot change one situation, you cannot change anything. Learned helplessness also includes internality because you blame yourself for your failures. People can either blame themselves or their circumstances. People who blame themselves internalize the failure. As a result of these elements, learned helplessness can lead to depression, guilt, and self-blame.

4.   What types of cognitive maps do humans develop?

_____

_____

Modeling (page 262)

The second type of social learning is called **modeling.** When you watch other people and copy their behavior, you are using modeling. There are three kinds of modeling: simple modeling, observational modeling, and disinhibition.

Simple modeling involves copying the exact behavior of others. If other people look up, you look up. Simple modeling does not involve learning. You already know the skill. You simply copy the behavior of people around you.

The second type of modeling is observational learning. You use observational learning when you copy another person to learn a new skill. You may watch someone perform a dance step. By watching, you are able to learn the step and then do it yourself.

The third type of modeling is disinhibition. This type of modeling helps people do things that they are afraid of doing. When you watch someone do something you fear, and not get hurt, you are more willing to try it for yourself. This type of modeling may be used to treat phobias. For example, imagine you are afraid of snakes. If you watch someone else hold a snake without anything bad happening, it may help reduce your fear of snakes.

5. How do simple modeling and observational learning differ?

_____

_____

Behavior Modification (page 263)

It is possible to use classical conditioning, operant conditioning, and social learning to deliberately change someone's behavior. This is called **behavior modification.** It begins by clearly defining a problem. A plan is then developed using the different learning techniques.

Computer-aided instruction uses operant conditioning to teach new information. The information is broken down into very small pieces. Students learn the easiest information first. Then, step by step, they progress to the more difficult information. Each question builds on the ones that came before. Learning occurs in a planned, systematic manner.

A **token economy** is another kind of behavior modification. It has many uses. For example, it can be used to change the behavior of troubled students. Students earn tokens for good behavior. The tokens are secondary reinforcers. They can be exchanged for rewards. Studies show that students will change their behavior in order to earn tokens.

Behavior modification can teach people self-control. People using self-control create their own rewards and punishments. They do this to control their own behavior. Self-control begins by figuring out what behavior you want to control. You then make a contract with yourself. You promise yourself a reward if you change your behavior. For example, you know that you need to study more. You also know that you like soda. You might make a deal with yourself. After you study for an extra 30 minutes, you get a soda to drink. Using systems similar to this, students have been able to greatly improve their study habits.

6. What rewards would you use to improve your study habits?

_____

_____

Study Guide 10-1

For use with textbook pages 273–280

Taking in and Storing Information

Key Terms

memory the storage and retrieval of what has been learned or experienced (page 274)

encoding the transforming of information so that the nervous system can process it (page 274)

storage the process by which information is maintained over a period of time (page 274)

retrieval the process of obtaining information that has been stored in memory (page 274)

sensory memory very brief memory storage immediately following initial reception of a stimulus (page 274)

short-term memory memory that is limited in capacity to about seven items and in duration by the subject's active rehearsal (page 276)

maintenance rehearsal system for remembering that involves repeating information to oneself without attempting to find meaning in it (page 276)

chunking process of grouping items to make them easier to remember (page 277)

semantic memory knowledge of language, including its rules, words, and meanings (page 279)

episodic memory memory of one's life, including time of occurrence (page 279)

declarative memory memory of knowledge that can be called forth consciously as needed (page 279)

procedural memory memory of learned skills that does not require conscious recollection (page 279)

Drawing From Experience

Have you ever remembered something from long ago and wondered why you still know it? Have you ever wondered how you can learn everything expected of you in school? This section discusses how you create and store memories.

Organizing Your Thoughts

Use the diagram below to help you take notes as you read the summaries that follow. Think about how people learn, and the different types of memories. Give an example of each concept below.

Memory Concept	Example
Maintenance Rehearsal	1.
Chunking	2.
Primacy-Recency Effect	3.
Semantic Memory	4.
Episodic Memory	5.

Read to Learn

Introduction (page 273)

What would life without memory be like? Think of all the material you have stored in your memory: your best friend's phone number, the capital of South Dakota, the names of your favorite musicians. What kind of wonderful filing system allows you to quickly recall a line from your favorite movie? How does all that information fit in your head?

6. Give an example of something you remembered recently that you thought you had forgotten long ago.

_____

The Processes of Memory (page 274)

Memory is the storage and retrieval of what you learned and experienced. There are three memory processes. The first, **encoding**, is transforming information so that the nervous system can process it. You use your senses to encode and create a memory. When you are trying to remember something by repeating it out loud or to yourself, you are using *acoustic codes*. For example, when you learned the alphabet, you may have repeated "A," "B," "C," and so on. Or, you may have tried to remember the letters by keeping a mental picture of them. If so, you were using *visual codes*. Another way you might have tried to remember the letters is by making sense of them. Then you would be using *semantic codes*. For example, "A is for Apple," "B is for Boy," and so on.

After you encode the information, it goes through a second memory process, **storage**. This is the process of keeping the information for a period of time. You can store information for a few seconds or much longer, depending on how much effort you put into encoding it. The third memory process is **retrieval**. This means bringing information back to mind from storage.

7. Describe something you learned recently. What method of encoding did you use to try to remember it?

_____

Three Stages of Memory (page 274)

Once you learn something, your brain must store it for future reference. There are three types of memory: sensory, short-term, and long-term. In **sensory memory**, the senses of sight and hearing hold a bit of information for less than a second before it disappears. For example, researchers flashed letters in front of people for a twentieth of a second. Later, the people could name four or five of the letters. Sensory memory that holds visual information is called *iconic memory*. Sensory memory that holds sound is called *echoic memory*.

The things you have in your conscious mind at any one moment are in **short-term memory**. Short-term memory has limited storage space. Usually people can hold only about seven items in short-term memory at a time. To keep something in short-term memory for more than a few seconds, you have to repeat it to yourself. This is called **maintenance rehearsal**. For example, when you look up a phone number, you can remember the seven numbers long enough to dial them if you repeat them several times. If you make a mistake in dialing, you will probably have to look up the number again.

The maximum of seven items we can hold in short-term memory can be any kind of items. They can be unrelated words or numbers. But an "item" can also be a set of information grouped together in a "chunk." For example, the call letters of your favorite radio station would be one "chunk." You could hold in short-term memory seven "chunks" of call letters or initials, like "ESP." Grouping items to make them easier to remember is called **chunking**. For example, you probably remember phone numbers in two or three chunks (555-6794 or 555-67-94) rather than as a string of seven numbers (5-5-5-6-7-9-4).

The *primacy-recency* effect refers to the fact that we are better able to recall information at the beginning or end of a list. For example, if you read through your shopping list quickly, you will likely remember only the first and last few items on the list.

Short-term memory is also called *working memory*. It includes both events that just occurred as well as information recalled from long-term memory for use now. Long-term memory is the storage of information over a long time. Your long-term storage space seems to be unlimited. Suppose you go to a movie. As the actors say their lines, the sounds flow through your sensory storage. The words gather in short-term memory and form meaningful phrases and sentences that form chunks in your memory. An hour or two later, you will have forgotten all but the most striking lines, but you have stored the meaning of the lines and actions in long-term memory. Months later, the details of the movie are more difficult to recall, but they are still in long-term memory.

One theory suggests that we have two types of long-term memory. **Semantic memory** is our knowledge of language, including its rules, words, and meanings. **Episodic memory** is our memory of our own life. Another theory suggests that the two types of memory are declarative and procedural. **Declarative memory** is memory of information that we can call up consciously as needed. This includes both episodic and semantic memory. **Procedural memory** is memory of learned skills that does not require conscious recall of past learning to affect our performance. This would include memory of how to ride a bicycle.

8. Give an example of semantic memory.

_____

Memory and the Brain (page 279)

Changes occur in the brain when people store something in long-term memory. During learning, a complex chemical process takes place. Then new connections form between neurons. How and where memories are stored remains unclear.

9. How might knowledge about how learning occurs benefit people?

_____

Study Guide 10-2

Retrieving Information

For use with textbook pages 282–288

Key Terms

recognition memory retrieval in which a person identifies an object, idea, or situation as one he or she has or has not experienced before (page 283)

recall memory retrieval in which a person reconstructs previously learned material (page 283)

reconstructive processes the alteration of a recalled memory that may be simplified, enriched, or distorted, depending on a person's experiences and attitudes (page 284)

confabulation the act of filling in memory gaps (page 284)

schemas conceptual frameworks a person uses to make sense of the world (page 284)

eidetic memory the ability to remember with great accuracy visual information on the basis of short-term exposure (page 284)

decay fading away of memory over time (page 285)

interference blockage of a memory by previous or subsequent memories (page 286)

elaborative rehearsal the linking of new information to material that is already known (page 287)

mnemonic devices techniques for using associations to memorize information (page 288)

Drawing From Experience

Have you ever had something "on the tip of your tongue" and just couldn't bring it to mind? Have you ever "remembered" an event, and someone else "remembered" it completely differently? This section discusses how you bring memories back from storage.

Organizing Your Thoughts

Use the diagram below to help you take notes as you read the summaries that follow. Think about some things that get in the way of accurate recall. For each problem below, describe how it affects recall.

Problem	Effect on Recall
Confabulation	1.
Schemas	2.
Interference	3.
Repression	4.
Amnesia	5.

Read to Learn

Introduction (page 282)

Stored information is useless if you can not retrieve it from memory. The problem of memory is to store thousands of items in such a way that you can find the one you need when you need it. The solution is good organization.

6. You must remember many things in your daily life—birthdays, dates with friends, due dates for schoolwork. How do you organize these things so you can retrieve the information when you need it?

_____

_____

_____

_____

Recognition (page 283)

Recognition is the process of identifying an object, idea, or situation as one you have or have not experienced before. Memory is organized in a way that makes recognition easy. For example, you might not remember the name of your first-grade teacher, but would probably recognize the name if you heard it. The ability to recognize is also the reason that multiple choice tests can bring out knowledge that a student might not be able to show on an essay test.

The process of recognition gives clues to how we store information in memory. We recognize the sound of a particular musical instrument, no matter what tune it is playing. We can also recognize a tune no matter which instrument is playing it. This pattern of recognition suggests that a single item of information may be "indexed" under several "headings," so we can retrieve it in a number of ways. The more categories an item is filed in, the more easily we can retrieve it.

7. How is the organization of information in memory like a card catalog or indexing system in a library?

_____

_____

_____

_____

Recall (page 283)

Recall is the reconstruction of information from memory. Recall involves more than searching for bits of information. The brain is not like a video recorder that plays things back without change. Remembering is an active process. We reconstruct memories, not just call them up. In the process, we may simplify, enrich, or distort them. The processes involved in changing memories are called **reconstructive processes**. **Confabulation** is a mistake in which someone seemingly remembers information that was never stored in memory. Sometimes we reconstruct memories to match our **schemas**. These are the frameworks we use to make sense of the world. We may remember things the way we expect them to be rather than how they actually were.

About 5 percent of children do not reconstruct memories. They have a form of photographic memory called **eidetic memory**. They can form sharp visual images of something and later recall the entire image.

People can more easily recall information when they are in the same set- ting or emotional state as they were when they first learned it. This is called *state-dependent learning*. For this reason, it helps to study in the same room where you will take the test. Being in the same setting while taking the test will help you recall stored information.

8. Suppose a police officer asks a witness to describe the gun used in a robbery. The witness recalls a gun, even though the robber did not have one. What does this show about the way we recall memories?

_____

_____

_____

_____

Relearning (page 285)

Relearning is evidence of procedural memory. Suppose you learned a poem as a child but have not recited it in years. If you can relearn it with less practice than someone learning it for the first time, you have benefited from your childhood learning.

9. Give an example of something you relearned. Was relearning easier than learning it for the first time?

_____

_____

_____

Forgetting (page 285)

When information that was once in long-term memory cannot be retrieved, it is said to be forgotten. Some memories may fade away, or **decay**, over time. Items in sensory and short-term memory do decay, but long-term memories may not. Instead, interference or repression causes people to lose track of them. **Interference** refers to a memory being blocked by an earlier or later memory. Suppose you move to a new home. At first you may have trouble remembering your new phone number. The memory of your old one gets in the way. According to Sigmund Freud, sometimes blocking is no accident. A person may subconsciously block memories of embarrassing or frightening experiences. This kind of forgetting is called *repression*. The information is in memory, but the person's brain is blocking recall.

Amnesia is a loss of memory that may result from a blow to the head or brain damage.

10. Why might someone be unable to recall the details of a bad car accident that her or she had been involved in?

_____

_____

_____

_____

Improving Memory (page 287)

You learned that maintenance rehearsal, or repeating things, helps you remember them. A more efficient way is to use **elaborative rehearsal**. In this method, you relate the new information to something you already know. For example, you would be more likely to remember the six letters DFIRNE if you arranged them to form the word FRIEND.

A good way to protect memory from interference is to overlearn it. Keep rehearsing it even after you think you know it well. Another way is to avoid studying similar material together. Instead of studying history right after social studies, study biology in between.

Mnemonic devices are methods for using associations to memorize. For example, the rhyme we use to recall the number of days in each month ("Thirty days has September. . .") is a mnemonic device.

11. Suppose you want to memorize your friend's phone number. You note that the number is the same as yours, except the last digit is a 6 instead of an 8. What memory improvement method would you be using?

_____

_____

_____

Study Guide 11-1

Thinking and Problem Solving

For use with textbook pages 295–302

Key Terms

thinking changing and reorganizing the information stored in memory to create new information (page 296)

image a visual, mental representation of an event or object (page 296)

symbol an abstract unit of thought that represents an object or quality (page 296)

concept a label for a class of objects or events that share at least one common attribute (page 296)

prototype a representative example of a concept (page 296)

rule a statement of relation between concepts (page 297)

metacognition the awareness of one's own cognitive processes (page 297)

algorithm a step-by-step procedure for solving a problem (page 299)

heuristic a rule-of-thumb problem-solving strategy (page 299)

mental set a habitual strategy or pattern of problem solving (page 299)

functional fixedness the inability to imagine new uses for familiar objects (page 300)

creativity the capacity to use information and/or abilities in a new and original way (page 300)

flexibility the ability to overcome rigidity (page 301)

recombination rearranging the elements of a problem to arrive at an original solution (page 301)

insight the apparent sudden realization of the solution to a problem (page 301)

Drawing From Experience

Have you ever tried to solve a problem the same way you always solve such problems, only this time it didn't work? Have you ever quit working on a problem in frustration, only to have the solution suddenly pop into your head?

In this section, you will learn about different kinds of thinking. You will also learn about problem-solving strategies and the nature of creativity.

Organizing Your Thoughts

Use the diagram on the next page to help you take notes as you read the summaries that follow. List the five units of thought and give an example of each.

Units of Thought	Example
1.	6.
2.	7.
3.	8.
4.	9.
5.	10.

Read to Learn

Introduction (page 295)

The human mind can do more than just store and retrieve information. We can use information to think and solve problems. With these abilities, we can create new ideas.

11. Give an example from history of a new idea that someone invented to solve a problem.

_____

_____

Thinking (page 296)

Thinking is changing and reorganizing information stored in memory to create new information. For example, you can put together any combination of words from memory to create new sentences.

Images, symbols, concepts, prototypes, and rules are the building blocks of mental activity. An **image** is a visual, mental representation of something. A representation is not an exact copy. Rather, it contains only the highlights of the original. For example, if an adult tried to visualize an image of a grandmother who died when he was seven years old, he would probably remember only a few details, such as hair color or a piece of jewelry she wore.

A **symbol** is an abstract representation of something. The most common symbols in thinking are words. Words are symbols that stand for something. For example, the word "cat" is a symbol for the animal. Symbols make it possible to think about things that are not present and imagine things that never were or will be.

A **concept** is a label for a class of objects or events that have at least one thing in common. Animals, music, and liquid are examples of concepts. They represent groups of things that are alike. So the concept animal separates a group of things from other things such as cars and carrots. Concepts allow us to chunk large amounts of information. We don't have to treat each new piece of information as unique.

When we think of a concept, we often think of an example, or **prototype**, of it. For example, when you think of a vehicle, you might picture a truck. A more complex unit of thought is a **rule**. This is a statement of a relation between concepts. For example, one rule is that a person cannot be in two places at once. Images, symbols, concepts, prototypes, and rules give us the ability to think, reorganize, and create.

People think in different ways. *Directed thinking* is step-by-step thinking aimed at a goal such as solving a problem. *Nondirected thinking* is a free flow of thoughts with no particular plan. It often uses images and feelings such as daydreams and fantasies. This kind of thinking can produce creative ideas. A third type of thinking is **metacognition**. This is thinking about thinking. For example, when you have trouble solving a math problem, thinking about your approach to the problem can help you change to a new strategy that works better.

12. You are trying to put together a new desk from written instructions. What kind of thinking would this involve?

_____

_____

_____

_____

Problem Solving (page 297)

Problem solving is trying to bridge the gap between a present situation and a desired goal. The gap may be between hunger (the present situation) and food (the goal); or the gap may be between a column of numbers and a total. Getting from a problem to a solution requires directed thinking.

Problem solving requires you to use strategies, or methods for approaching problems. One strategy is to break down complex problems into smaller subgoals that are easier to solve. For example, you have a number of assignments to finish in the next few days. You solve the problem by breaking it into subgoals. First, you study for the exam. Next, you finish the paper. Then you do the project. Another problem might require you to examine different ways of reaching the goal. For example, suppose you want to get to the mall. You could walk, ride your bike, or ask your parents for a ride. Since you want to get there fast, you decide to ask for a ride.

To decide which strategy to use, we analyze the problem to see if it is like one we experienced in the past. A strategy that worked before will likely work again. An **algorithm** is a step-by-step procedure that will lead to a solution. Math formulas are algorithms. If you follow the rules of multiplication, 3 x 2 will yield the correct solution, 6. To play checkers, you follow algorithms, a set of rules.

People often take shortcuts to solving problems. We use **heuristics**, which are rules-of-thumb that simplify problems. For example, if a friend comes to you for advice, you may offer something that worked for you before. But short-cuts may lead to poor decisions. You may not have considered important facts about your friend's situation.

When a problem-solving strategy becomes a habit, it is called a **mental set**. You might try to solve problems the same way every time, even when the strategy doesn't work very well. This is called rigidity. **Functional fixedness** is a form of mental set that can interfere with problem solving. It is the inability to imagine new ways of using familiar objects. You can overcome rigidity by looking for new approaches to problems.

13. To start a car, you put the key in the ignition, then you turn the key, and then you let it go. What kind of problem-solving strategy is this?

_____

_____

_____

_____

Creativity (page 300)

Creativity is the ability to use information in new and meaningful ways. All problem solving requires some creativity, but some approaches are more creative than others. Creative thinking requires **flexibility**. This is the ability to overcome rigidity. For example, think of all the ways you can use a paper clip. The more you can think of, the more creative you are. Creativity also requires **recombination**. This is the ability to rearrange elements of a problem to arrive at an original solution. For example, creative people can discover new truths by looking at current knowledge in a field in new ways.

Insight occurs when a solution suddenly emerges in the process of recombining elements. For example, as you are trying to look at a frustrating problem in new ways or even when you are doing something else, the solution may suddenly pop into your head. This sudden insight is sometimes called the "aha" experience.

14. Why do you need to be able to think creatively to be a good problem solver?

_____

_____

_____

_____

Study Guide 11-2

Language

For use with textbook pages 304–308

Key Terms

language the expression of ideas through symbols and sounds that are arranged according to rules (page 304)

phoneme an individual sound that is a basic structural element of language (page 305)

morpheme the smallest unit of meaning in a given language (page 305)

syntax language rules that govern how words can be combined to form meaningful phrases and sentences (page 305)

semantics the study of meaning in language (page 305)

Drawing From Experience

Have you observed an infant's language develop from simple sounds, to words, and finally to sentences? How do you think the infant learned to do this? Have you watched two pets communicate with each other? Do you think they were using language?

The last section described the nature of thinking, problem solving, and creativity. In this section, you will learn what language is and how it develops.

Organizing Your Thoughts

Use the diagram below to help you take notes as you read the summaries that follow. Think about the four rules or parts in the structure of language. List them next to the appropriate example below.

Example	Language Rule
th in *there*	**1.**
A sentence must have a subject and a verb.	**2.**
The word *can* has different meanings, depending on the context.	**3.**
ed in *talked*	**4.**

Read to Learn

Introduction (page 304)

Understanding and speaking language is one of the most complex and important things we do. We must learn thousands of words and grammar rules to communicate.

5. If there were no grammatical rules for how to combine words into sentences, what would communication be like?

_____

_____

The Structure of Language (page 304)

Language is a communication system that combines symbols and sounds into words and sentences by arranging them according to rules. Language has four rules, or parts: phonemes, morphemes, syntax, and semantics. A **phoneme** is the smallest unit of sound in a language. Phonemes can be a single letter, such as *t*, or a combination of letters that form a single sound, such as *sh*. We can produce about 100 different sounds, but not every language uses every sound.

A **morpheme** is the smallest unit of meaning in a language. It is made up of one or more phonemes. Morphemes can be a word, a letter, a prefix (*un* in *uncertain*), or a suffix (*ly* in *slowly*). For example, the word *love* has a single morpheme. *Loves* has two morphemes (*love* and *s*).

Syntax is a set of rules for combining words to form meaningful phrases and sentences. For example, this sentence does not make sense: *Boy small bike small rode.* In English we follow grammatical rules, such as placing adjectives in front of nouns. If you apply grammatical rules, the sentence makes sense: *The small boy rode a small bike.*

Semantics is the understanding of the meaning in language. Words can mean different things in different contexts. The word "mind" has different meanings in these two sentences. *A mind is a terrible thing to waste. Do you mind if I sit next to you?* From your knowledge of semantics, you knew that "mind" is a noun in the first sentence and a verb in the second.

6. List the phonemes in the word *fearlessness*.

_____

_____

Language Development (page 306)

B.F. Skinner believed that children learn language through conditioning. When children say something similar to adult speech, adults reward them with smiles and attention. Eventually, children learn speech. But there is evidence that children understand language before they speak and before they receive rewards. Social learning theories propose that children learn language by observing, exploring, and imitating. Children use language to get attention or ask for help. Noam Chomsky theorized that the ability to learn grammar is innate.

7. How might an infant learn to say "mama"?

_____

_____

How Language Develops (page 307)

Infants go through four stages of language development.

Stage 1: At around 4 months, infants progress from making sounds and cooing noises to babbling. Babbling, such as *dadada*, includes sounds found in all languages. When babbling, infants learn to control their vocal cords and imitate sounds their parents make. At around 9 months, their babbling begins to sound more like their native language.

Stage 2: At around 12 months, infants begin to say single words to describe familiar things, such as *doggie*, or to express longer thoughts. For example, *da* may mean "Where is my father?"

Stage 3: Near the end of their second year, children can put two words together to express an idea. They may say "Me play" to mean "I want to play." The child is beginning to learn the rules of grammar.

Stage 4: At around age 4, children begin to form sentences. The first sentences are *telegraphic speech*. This is a pattern of leaving out articles (the), prepositions (with), and parts of verbs. For example, "I go to park."

8. If a child says "Cat go" to mean the cat left the room, what stage of language development is she in?

_____

Do Animals Learn Language? (page 308)

Animals communicate with one another. But do animals learn language? Language is more than just communicating. It involves combining words or phrases into meaningful sentences, using grammatical rules. Animals do not have the ability to use grammatical rules.

9. Give an example of animal communication that you observed. What makes you think that the animals understood each other?

_____

Gender and Cultural Differences (page 308)

Do people who speak different languages actually think differently from one another? Benjamin Whorf argued that language affects our basic perceptions of the world. He used the term *linguistic relativity* to refer to the idea that a person's language influences his or her thoughts. For example, the Inuit people who live in the far north have many words for *snow*. Whorf believed that they need these words because their survival depends on traveling and living in snow. The different terms help Inuits see the different types of snow as different. Others argue that Americans, too, have different words for *snow* (flurry, blizzard, powder).

Certain words in language may create gender stereotypes. For example, the word *chairman* can mean a man or a woman. But the use of "man" at the end of the word suggests that the chairman is a man. Pronouns also affect our thinking. Secretaries and teachers are often referred to as *she*. Doctors and engineers are often referred to as *he*. Many organizations now have guidelines for using nonsexist language.

10. Suppose that everything a girl read or heard while growing up used the pronoun *he* with doctor and *she* with nurse. How might this affect the girl's view of what she can be when she grows up?

_____

Study Guide 12-1

Theories of Motivation

Key Terms

motivation an internal state that activates behavior and directs it toward a goal (page 314)

instincts innate tendencies that determine behavior (page 314)

need a biological or psychological requirement of an organism (page 314)

drive a state of tension produced by a need that motivates an organism toward a goal (page 315)

homeostasis the tendency of all organisms to correct imbalances and deviations from their normal state (page 315)

incentive an external stimulus, reinforcer, or reward that motivates behavior (page 316)

extrinsic motivation engaging in activities that either reduce biological needs or help us obtain external incentives (page 316)

intrinsic motivation engaging in activities because they are personally rewarding or because they fulfill our beliefs and expectations (page 316)

Drawing From Experience

Have you ever done something and then wondered why you did it? If you have a job, why do you work? Have you ever done something just for the fun of it? This section describes different theories about why we do what we do. You will learn about needs, drives, and rewards both inside and outside of you that prompt you to act.

Organizing Your Thoughts

Use the diagram below to help you take notes as you read the summaries that follow. Think about the four theories of motivation presented in the chapter. For each theory listed below, give an example that supports it.

Theory	Supporting Example
Instinct Theory	1.
Drive-Reduction Theory	2.
Incentive Theory	3.
Cognitive Theory	4.

Read to Learn

Introduction (page 313)

Research on motivation and emotion focuses on why we behave the way we do. **Motivation** is an internal state that prompts us to act toward achieving a goal. We can not see motivation directly, so we assume it from the behavior we observe. For example, we see Mikko working after school at a job he doesn't like. We know he wants to buy a car, so we assume he is "motivated" to earn money for the car. Motivations can come from outside or inside of us.

5. You have been working so hard that you forgot to eat lunch. Now your stomach is growling in protest. What might this internal state motivate you to do?

_____

Instinct Theory (page 314)

In the 1900s, William McDougall proposed that instincts motivate human behavior. **Instincts** are inborn tendencies that determine how an animal will behave in certain situations. Instincts do not involve reason. Instinctive behavior will be about the same for all members of a species. For example, salmon have instinctive urges to swim up rivers to reproduce in the exact spot where they were spawned. Instincts do not explain human behavior, however. Psychologists have since focused on other theories.

6. Deer have a mating season, a time every year when males and females get together to reproduce. Do you think this is instinctive behavior? Explain.

_____

Drive-Reduction Theory (page 314)

Something that motivates us moves us to action. That "something" starts with a need and leads to a drive. A **need** is a physical or psychological requirement. We need oxygen and food to survive (physical needs). We may also need love and the approval of our friends (psychological needs).

A need produces a drive. A **drive** is a feeling of tension caused by an unmet need. This tension motivates us to do something to meet the need. We have different drives with different goals. For example, hunger drives us to eat. Curiosity drives us to find out something.

Drive-reduction theory came from the work of Clark Hull. According to Hull, when an organism (living thing) is missing something it needs, it becomes tense and restless. This state of tension throws the organism out of its normal, balanced state. When an organism finds itself out of balance, it tries to correct the imbalances to return to **homeostasis**, its normal state. So to relieve the tension and return to homeostasis, the organism takes random actions. If a behavior reduces the drive, the behavior becomes a habit. That is, when the organism feels the drive again, it will first try the behavior that worked before. In short, drive-reduction theory states that physical needs drive an organism to act randomly or according to habit until it satisfies its needs.

Later research showed some flaws in this theory. According to drive-reduction theory, infants become attached to their mothers because their mothers relieve drives such as hunger and thirst. In an experiment, Harry Harlow took baby monkeys away from their mothers and put them in cages with two substitute mothers made of wire. One wire mother had a bottle attached. The other had no bottle but was covered with soft cloth. If drive-reduction theory was correct, the babies would become attached to the wire mother with the bottle, because this was their only source of food. But in test after test, the babies preferred to cling to the cloth mother, especially when frightened.

Another argument against drive-reduction theory is that people sometimes intentionally do things that increase tension rather than try to relieve it. For example, you may enjoy riding roller coasters or watching scary movies.

7. According to drive-reduction theory, how would an elephant act if it were thirsty and needed to find water?

_____

_____

Incentive Theory (page 316)

Incentive theory stresses the role of the environment in motivating behavior. A drive is something inside us that causes us to act, but our actions are directed toward a goal, or incentive. An **incentive** is the result we are trying to achieve by our actions. Drives push us to reduce needs, but the results we are after pull us toward obtaining the incentives. For example, hunger may cause you to walk to the cafeteria, but the incentive is the sandwich you intend to eat. If your drive (hunger) is very strong, you may eat the sandwich even if you know it won't be very tasty. But if your drive (hunger) is weak, the incentive must be strong to motivate you to action. So, if you aren't very hungry but you really like peanut butter sandwiches, you may eat one anyway.

8. When you ask your teacher for help in solving a math problem, what is the drive and what is the incentive?

_____

_____

Cognitive Theory (page 316)

Cognitive theory proposes that we act because of extrinsic and intrinsic motivations. *Extrinsic* means "outside ourselves." So **extrinsic motivation** means that we do things to reduce physical needs or to obtain incentives or rewards from our environment (that is, from outside ourselves). *Intrinsic* means "inside ourselves." So **intrinsic motivation** means that we do things because the activities are personally rewarding or because they meet our own internal goals. For example, if you spend hours playing basketball because you want to excel at the sport, you are following intrinsic motivation. If you spend hours playing basketball because your parents want you to excel at the sport, you are following extrinsic motivation. But if you play basketball just for the fun of it, you are following intrinsic motivation.

You are often motivated by both intrinsic and extrinsic rewards at the same time. For example, you may go out to dinner with friends because you need to satisfy your hunger (an extrinsic motivation), but you also do it because you like to socialize with them (an intrinsic motivation).

9. What extrinsic and intrinsic rewards are motivating you to take this course?

_____

_____

Study Guide 12-2

Biological and Social Motives

For use with textbook pages 319–327

Key Terms

lateral hypothalamus (LH) the part of the hypothalamus that produces hunger signals (page 320)

ventromedial hypothalamus (VMH) the part of the hypothalamus that can cause one to stop eating (page 321)

fundamental needs biological drives that must be satisfied to maintain life (page 326)

psychological needs the urge to belong and to give and receive love, and the urge to acquire esteem (page 326)

self-actualization needs the pursuit of knowledge and beauty or whatever else is required for the realization of one's unique potential (page 326)

Drawing From Experience

When someone invites you to eat, have you ever looked at your watch to see if it is "time" to be hungry? When you face a difficult task, do you tackle it with all you've got, or do you avoid it because you think you can't do it?

The last section discussed different theories of human motivation. In this section, you will learn about motivations that come from inside your body and those that come from your experiences with other people.

Organizing Your Thoughts

Use the diagram below to help you take notes as you read the summaries that follow. Think about the motivations that we learn from our environment. Complete each statement below.

1. A person with high need for achievement _____.

2. A person who fears failure might _____.

3. A person who fears success might _____.

4. A person trying to satisfy psychological needs might _____.

Read to Learn

Introduction (page 319)

Eating satisfies a physical need for food, but it also satisfies psychological or social needs. We may eat when we feel stressed (psychological). Eating is also a form of entertainment, such as eating lunch with friends (social). Social needs, such as achievement, also influence our behavior.

5. What have you done because you wanted to achieve something?

_____

_____

_____

_____

Biological Motives (page 320)

Like other animals, humans must satisfy some physical needs to survive. The nervous system requires a balance of elements such as water, oxygen, salt, and vitamins to stay healthy. When your body senses an imbalance, it will motivate actions aimed at returning itself to balance. For example, when your body temperature falls below a certain level, you shiver, some blood vessels make themselves smaller, and you put on more clothes. These activities reduce heat loss and bring your body back to its correct temperature. When your body temperature gets too high, you sweat, some blood vessels expand, and you remove some clothes. These activities cool you. The body's tendency to correct imbalances and return to its normal state is *homeostasis*.

You eat for many reasons. The smell of a pizza may lure you into a restaurant. You may eat out of habit. For example, you may always eat lunch at 12:30. But if you go without food for a long time, your body will demand food. You will feel an ache in your stomach. A part of the hypothalamus called the **lateral hypothalamus (LH)** produces this hungry feeling. It provides the "go" signal that tells you to eat. Another part of the hypothalamus called the **ventromedial hypothalamus (VMH)** produces the feeling of being full. It provides the "off" signal that tells you to stop eating.

The *glucostatic theory* suggests that the hypothalamus watches the amount of glucose, a kind of sugar, in the blood. Glucose provides energy to the body. When the glucose level in the blood gets too low, the LH prompts you to eat. At the same time, the pancreas releases *insulin* to change incoming calories into energy. You will use some of this energy right away. Some will be stored as fat for later use. After your meal, as your glucose level drops, the pancreas releases *glucagon*, which converts stored energy back into useful energy.

Your body tends to keep a stable weight over a long time. This weight is your *set-point*. The hypothalamus considers your set-point, glucose level, and body temperature in determining whether or not to motivate you to eat.

We also eat for social reasons, called *psychosocial hunger factors*. When others are eating, we tend to eat more. You may eat popcorn at a movie because you always do. You may also choose not to eat because you want to look like a model. Psychosocial factors can lead to eating disorders, such as binge eating or self-starvation.

Growing evidence suggests that genes play a big role in a person's weight. The genes you inherit may give you a tendency to be overweight. People are overweight if they are 20 percent above their ideal weight. They are obese if they are 30 percent over their ideal weight. Studies show that obese people eat because of external cues (signals from their environment), not because they are hungry. For example, they may eat because a food looks good or because their watches tell them it is time to eat. Normal-weight people tend to respond more to internal signals, such as a feeling of hunger. Anxiety and depression are not causes of overeating. These conditions occur just as often among people of normal weight as among those who are overweight.

6. What would happen if you didn't have a ventromedial hypothalamus?

_____

_____

_____

Social Motives (page 323)

Social motives are learned from our experiences with other people. The achievement motive is the desire to set challenging goals and keep trying to reach them, in spite of the roadblocks along the way. David McClelland used a Thematic Apperception Test (TAT) to try to measure achievement. In this test, researchers showed people a series of pictures. They told the people to describe what is happening in each picture. There were no right or wrong answers. It was not clear what was actually happening in the pictures. So, people's stories had to come from their own beliefs and attitudes. The researchers "coded" the stories for certain themes that related to needs, such as achievement, setting goals, and competing. For example, a story would be scored as high in achievement if the main character was concerned with excellence, high performance, or special accomplishments.

People who score high in achievement in the test tend to set difficult but realistic goals and pursue them strongly, compete to win, and choose challenging careers. McClelland followed the careers of people who scored high in achievement on the test as students. He found that 11 years after graduation, 83 percent of the people who scored high on achievement had chosen challenging careers.

Some people are motivated by a fear of failure. A person may not try out for the baseball team because she thinks she can't make it. People display fear of failure when they choose easy tasks in which failure is unlikely. The fear of failure may motivate a student to study only enough to pass an exam but not enough to get a good grade.

Fear of success can also motivate people. Matina Horner found that the thought of succeeding in a traditionally male profession made many women anxious. The women seemed to think that success in traditionally "male" careers such as medicine or law must mean failure as a woman. Horner discovered that bright women who had a very good chance of high achievement showed a stronger fear of success than did average women. Fear of success is found in both men and women.

Expectancy-value theory states that how motivated we are depends on how likely we are to be successful in the task (*expectancy*) and how much the reward for success is worth to us (*value*). *Competency* theory suggests that we tend to choose tasks that are reasonably difficult, so we can find out how competent (skilled) we are. Tasks that are too easy or too hard will not tell us anything about our skill.

Abraham Maslow believed all people have certain needs. He arranged the needs in a hierarchy or triangle, ordered from the most basic needs to the highest needs. Maslow proposed that after we satisfy the needs at the bottom of the triangle, we advance to the next level and try to satisfy those needs. **Fundamental needs** are the physical drives that must be satisfied to live, such as hunger. These needs are at the bottom of the triangle. If we are hungry, our main motivation will be to find food. Until we relieve our hunger, we will not be interested in other needs.

The second level of the triangle are the **psychological needs**. These are the needs to belong, to give and receive love, and to feel good about ourselves through achievement. Once these needs are met, we start trying to satisfy the highest level of needs: **self-actualization needs**. These include the pursuit of knowledge, beauty, and anything else that will help us reach our full potential. Other research suggests that while we may all have these needs, we may not have to satisfy them in a certain order.

7. Horner did her studies in the 1970s. Do you think women may not fear success as much now as they did then? Explain.

_____

_____

_____

_____

_____

_____

_____

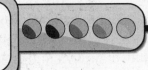

Study Guide 12-3

Emotions

For use with textbook pages 328–336

Key Term

emotion a set of complex reactions to stimuli involving subjective feelings, physiological arousal, and observable behavior (page 329)

Drawing From Experience

When you have to speak in front of a group, what kinds of reactions do you feel in your body? Have you ever tried to "read" someone's face or body language to try to figure out what the person is feeling?

In the last section, you learned about motivations, both physical and social. In this section, you will learn what emotions are and some theories about how they occur.

Organizing Your Thoughts

Use the diagram below to help you take notes as you read the summaries that follow. Think about the four things that happen when you experience an emotion.

1. _____

2. _____.

3. _____.

4. _____.

Read to Learn

Introduction (page 328)

When a person is frightened, physical changes occur. The heart races, breathing quickens, the senses become more aware, and blood rushes toward the brain, heart, and other muscles. So with all these physical changes, why do we call fear an "emotion" instead of a physical drive? It depends on whether we want to describe the source of our behavior or the feelings that go with it. Physical drives and emotions go together. Sometimes emotions work like physical drives. Our feelings might push us to pursue a goal. Other times we do things we think will make us feel good. The good feelings we expect to receive are the rewards of the behavior. Finally, emotions help us make decisions and communicate what is going on inside us.

Emotional intelligence is the ability to understand emotions and use that information to make decisions. For example, you want to tell your friends a joke. First you must judge whether they will like the joke or think it is in bad taste. Judging the emotions involved in this situation is a sign of your emotional intelligence.

5. Give an example of a decision you have made based on emotions.

_____

_____

Expressing Emotions (page 329)

An **emotion** is a feeling brought on by a real or imagined object or event that is important to you. Four things happen when you experience an emotion. (1) You are faced with a stimulus that causes you to react. (2) You have a feeling, such as fear or happiness. (3) You experience physical responses, such as an increased heart rate. (4) You display a visible behavior, such as smiling or crying.

All emotions have three parts: physical, behavioral, and cognitive. The physical part has to do with the changes inside the body caused by the emotion. The behavioral part is the outward expression of the emotion, such as body language and tone of voice. The cognitive part concerns the meaning we attach to the situation (stimulus) causing the emotion. For example, if someone says hello, we may think that the person is being friendly, hostile, or mocking. The meaning we apply affects our emotional response.

Charles Darwin argued that all people express basic feelings the same way. Without knowing a person's language, you can tell whether the person is pleased or angry just by looking at the person's face. Later research supported this view. It suggested that basic facial expressions are *innate*, that is, inherited as part of our physical makeup. For example, children born without sight and hearing cannot learn expressions from other people. Yet they laugh, frown, and pout like other children.

Carroll Izard identified 10 different emotional states from studying changes in parts of the face, such as eyebrows, eyes, and mouth. For example, when people are angry, their eyebrows go down and draw together and their eyes narrow.

James Averill believes that we learn our emotional reactions from social expectations and consequences. We learn to experience and express emotions in the company of other people. How others react to our emotional expressions help shape them. For example, parents shape their children's emotions by getting angry at some outbursts, giving sympathy with others, and occasionally ignoring them. In this way children learn which emotions are considered appropriate in different situations.

Learning explains the differences among cultures once we go beyond such basic expressions as laughing or crying. Children imitate the expressions of the parents or caregivers. So, all of us are born with emotions and with some basic forms of expression, but when, where, and how we express different feelings are mostly learned.

Some psychologists believe emotions come from physical changes. Others believe they come from mental processes. William James was one psychologist who stressed the physical causes of emotions. He believed that emotions are the perception of certain changes within the body. While some psychologists thought that emotions trigger changes in the body, James saw it the other way around. He argued that the body's physical reactions occur first, and we feel emotions when we recognize these changes. Because Carl Lange came to the same conclusion at about the same time, the theory became known as the *James-Lange theory*.

Carroll Izard's theory is similar. He believed that the way we experience emotion results from what we feel the muscles in our faces doing. To check this out, smile for two minutes and notice how you feel. Then frown for two minutes and notice the difference.

One argument against the James-Lange theory is that some emotions, such as anger and fear, cause the same physical changes. Another argument is that complex emotions such as jealousy and love require thought.

William B. Cannon and Philip Bard opposed the James-Lange theory. According to the Cannon-Bard theory, the brain sends two reactions—one waking the body's processes and the other an experience of emotion. One does not cause the other. They occur together.

Psychologists who believe that emotions result from mental processes are cognitive theorists. They believe that the body's changes and thinking work together to produce emotions. Physical changes are only half the story. What you feel depends on the meaning or interpretation you apply to these changes. The Schachter-Singer experiment supported this view. It demonstrated that the internal parts of emotion affect a person differently, depending on the person's perception of the social situation. When people cannot explain their physical reactions, they take cues from their environment. Therefore, perception and physical changes work together to create emotions. Opponents of this theory say that sometimes you feel an emotion first, and then your body reacts.

The body has sympathetic and parasympathetic systems. The sympathetic system prepares the body for action. The parasympathetic system calms the body. The opponent-process theory states that these two systems act together to control our emotions. This process is similar to other ways that the body corrects imbalances to return to homeostasis. According to the opponent-process theory, proposed by Richard Solomon and John Corbit, when the stimulus for one emotion is removed, you feel the opposite emotion.

6. If someone pointed a gun at you, what physical, behavioral, and cognitive reactions might you have?

_____

_____

Reading Essentials and Study Guide

Study Guide 13-1

Characteristics of Psychological Tests

For use with textbook pages 343–347

Key Terms

reliability the ability of a test to give the same results under similar conditions (page 344)

validity the ability of a test to measure what it is intended to measure (page 345)

percentile system ranking of test scores that indicates the ratio of scores lower and higher than a given score (page 346)

norms standard of comparison for test results developed by giving the test to large, well-defined groups of people (page 346)

Drawing From Experience

Have you ever taken a test given to everyone in your class? Did you know what your score meant? Did you think the test was fair?

In this section, you will learn about what makes a good test. You will also learn how to tell what your score means on some types of tests.

Organizing Your Thoughts

Use the diagram below to help you take notes as you read the summaries that follow. Think about the three requirements for a test to be fair and useful as a measurement tool.

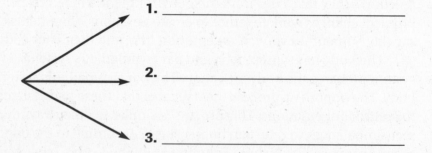

For a test to be fair and useful, it must be . . .

1. _____

2. _____

3. _____

Read to Learn

Introduction (page 343)

All tests make it possible to find out a lot about someone in a short time. Some tests forecast how well a person might do in a certain career. Others help people see what types of tasks they like and have the ability to do. Still others reveal psychological problems. Tests can show how one individual compares to many others, measure behavior, and predict in general how people will perform. They do not determine how any individual will behave. People should consider other things, not just test scores, when making decisions about their future.

4. How might a test that shows your interests and abilities help you make decisions about your future?

_____

_____

Test Reliability (page 344)

For a test to be fair and useful, it must be reliable. **Reliability** is a test's consistency. It is the test's ability to give the same results in similar situations. For example, you take a test today and then take it again a week later. If the test is reliable, your scores should be about the same. If your scores are very different, then the test is not reliable. This method for judging reliability is called *test-retest* reliability.

Another way to judge a test's reliability is to have more than one person grade it. For example, both your teacher and another teacher grade your essay. One gives you a B and the other, a D. In this case, the test is not reliable. The score depends more on who grades the test than on you. This is called *interscorer* reliability. Suppose the same teacher scores the same essay differently at different times. If so, the test is not reliable. This method of judging reliability is called *scorer* reliability. On a reliable test, your score would be the same no matter who graded it or when it was graded.

Another way to judge reliability is to randomly divide the test items in half and score each half separately. The two scores should be about the same. This is called *split-half* reliability. For example, if the test is supposed to measure reading ability, you should not score high on one section and low on the other.

5. Say you took a test that showed you are better at math than 60 percent of everyone else who took the test. You took the test again a month later, and it said you are better at math than 61 percent of others who took the test. Is this test reliable?

_____

_____

Test Validity (page 345)

For a test to be fair and useful, it must be valid as well as reliable. **Validity** is the test's ability to measure what it is supposed to measure. For example, a vocabulary test would not be a valid test of your math skills. A history test that asks questions not covered in class is not a valid test of what you learned in class. One way to judge a test's validity is to find out how well it predicts performance. This is *predictive* validity. For example, people take a test designed to measure management ability. If the test is valid, then most people who score high on the test should turn out to be good managers. If they do not, then the test is not valid. It does not measure what it is supposed to measure. If the test does do well at predicting who will make good managers, then the company might use it to help decide whom to hire as managers.

6. The people who score high on the management ability test turn out to be good at getting their employees to produce more. Many of these managers, however, make poor decisions. Is the test valid? Explain.

_____

Standardization (page 345)

For a test to be fair and useful, it has a third requirement. It must be *standardized* as well as reliable and valid. Standardization refers to two things. First, the people who give the test must give the same instructions and score the test the same way every time. Second, a standardized test must have norms, or average scores, determined from the scores of many people.

Suppose a child answers 32 of 50 questions correctly on a fifth grade vocabulary test. What does this score mean? If the test is reliable and valid, then the score means that the child will probably understand a certain percentage of the words in a book written at the fifth grade level. In other words, the score predicts how the child will perform at the fifth grade reading level. Yet this "raw" score does not tell us where the child stands in relation to other fifth graders. If most fifth graders answered 45 or more questions correctly, then 32 is a low score. If most answered 20 questions correctly, then 32 is a high score.

People who make standardized tests use norms to set up a scale for comparing. They do this by turning raw test scores into a **percentile system**. This is like "grading on a curve." First, they order the test scores actually achieved on the test from lowest to highest. Then they compare each score with this list and assign a percentile according to the percentage of scores that fall above or below this score. For example, if half the fifth graders in the above example scored 32 or below, then the score of 32 would be at the 50th percentile. If 32 were the top score, then it would be the 100th percentile. If one-fourth (25%) of all fifth graders taking the test scored higher than 32, then the score of 32 would put the child in the 75th percentile. This means that the child scored higher than three-fourths and lower than one-fourth of the others taking the test.

The test makers give the test to a large number of people in the group to be measured. For example, if they designed the test for fifth graders, they give it to many fifth graders. If the test is designed for engineers, then they give it to a large group of engineers. They determine percentiles from the scores achieved by this sample group. These percentiles then become the standards of comparison, or the test's **norms**. Test takers can then compare their scores to these norms to see how they stack up to others who took the test. For example, your percentile on the Scholastic Assessment Test (SAT) shows your standing among people your own age and grade. Remember that norms are averages. They are not some exact standard that you "should" meet.

7. If you scored at the 60th percentile on a standardized test, what does this mean?

_____

Study Guide 13-2

Intelligence Testing

For use with textbook pages 348–357

Key Terms

intelligence the ability to acquire new ideas and new behavior and to adapt to new situations (page 348)

two-factor theory proposes that two factors contribute to an individual's intelligence (page 349)

triarchic theory proposes that intelligence can be divided into three ways of processing information (page 350)

emotional intelligence includes four major aspects of interpersonal and intrapersonal intelligence (page 351)

intelligence quotient (IQ) standardized measure of intelligence based on a scale in which 100 is average (page 352)

heritability the degree to which a characteristic is related to inherited genetic factors (page 355)

cultural bias an aspect of an intelligence test in which the wording used in questions may be more familiar to people of one social group than to another group (page 356)

Drawing From Experience

Think about someone you think is really smart. What makes you think this person is smart? Based on what you have observed about this person, what are some characteristics of an intelligent person?

In the last section, you learned what makes a test reliable, valid, and standard. This section discusses different theories of intelligence and the tests that try to measure it.

Organizing Your Thoughts

Use the diagram below to help you take notes as you read the summaries that follow. Think about the theories that define intelligence in different ways. For each theory listed, name two types of intelligence the theory identifies.

Theory	One Type of Intelligence	Another Type of Intelligence
Two-Factor Theory	1.	2.
Thurstone's Theory	3.	4.
Gardner's Theory	5.	6.
Triarchic Theory	7.	8.
Emotional Intelligence	9.	10.

Read to Learn

Introduction (page 348)

Psychologists do not agree on the meaning of the word *intelligence*. Most believe that **intelligence** is the ability to learn new ideas and new behavior and to adapt to new situations. Others think intelligence allows you to do well in school and on tests.

11. Do you think someone could be intelligent but do poorly in school? Explain.

_____

_____

_____

Views of Intelligence (page 348)

According to Charles Spearman's **two-factor theory**, intelligence is the combination of a person's general intelligence and specific mental skills. General intelligence is the person's ability to perform difficult mental work, such as problem solving. Specific mental skills are things like verbal (language) or math skills.

L.L. Thurstone did not support the idea of general intelligence. Instead, he believed that intelligence is made up of seven mental abilities. These are the ability to (1) understand words and ideas (verbal comprehension), (2) use numbers to solve problems (numerical ability), (3) see patterns in things in space (spatial relations), (4) perceive things quickly (perceptual speed), (5) use words easily (word fluency), (6) recall information (memory), and (7) understand general rules based on information (inductive reasoning).

Howard Gardner identified eight types of intelligence. They are (1) ability with words; (2) math reasoning; (3) spatial ability, the ability to find your way around in an environment and mentally picture it; (4) musical ability; (5) physical skills, the ability to do small movements like thread a needle; (6) interpersonal skills, the ability to understand the feelings of others; (7) intrapersonal skills, knowledge of oneself; and (8) naturalist intelligence, the ability to identify patterns in nature.

Robert Sternberg's **triarchic theory** proposes that intelligence is made up of three ways of processing information. The first way is *analytical* thinking, or the ability to solve problems. The second way is *creative* thinking, which is the ability to find new ways to solve problems and deal with new situations. The third way is *practical* thinking, which helps you adjust to your environment.

Another proposed type, **emotional intelligence**, is similar to Gardner's interpersonal and intrapersonal intelligence. It includes the ability to (1) perceive and express emotions, (2) use emotions while thinking, (3) understand emotions and use this understanding, and (4) direct one's emotions toward personal growth.

12. The theories of Spearman, Thurstone, Gardner, and Sternberg are similar in some ways. Name two types of ability that are included in at least two of these theories.

_____

_____

_____

_____

The Development of Intelligence Tests (page 352)

In 1904, schools in France asked Alfred Binet and Theodore Simon to prepare a test that would pick out "slow learners." Then the schools could place these slow learners in special classes. Binet was not able to define intelligence. However, he believed that whatever it is, it increases with age. That is, older children have more intelligence than younger children. Therefore, in selecting items for his test, he included only items on which older children did better than younger children. By asking the same questions of many children, Binet determined the average age at which a certain question could be answered. For example, he discovered that some questions could be answered by most 12-year-olds but not 11-year-olds. If a child of 11, or even 9, could answer these questions, that child was said to have a mental age of 12. If a 12-year-old could answer questions no higher than those for 9-year-olds, then that child was said to have a mental age of 9. Slow learners were those with mental ages below their actual ages.

The Stanford-Binet Intelligence Scale currently in use still groups test items by age level. The **intelligence quotient (IQ)** score is based on a scale in which 100 is average for the person's age group. For example, if you have an IQ of 100, this means that half the test takers your age did better than you and half did worse than you.

The Stanford-Binet test has been largely replaced by the Otis-Lennon Ability Test. This test tries to measure mental abilities that relate to a student's ability to succeed in school. It measures a student's verbal (language) and non-verbal skills.

The Wechsler-Adult Intelligence Scale (WAIS) uses a different version for different age groups. These tests give percentile ratings for several areas, including vocabulary, arithmetic, picture arrangement, and others. Graders use these ratings to compute separate IQ scores for verbal and performance areas.

13. If someone had an IQ of 96 on the Stanford-Binet test, what would this mean?

_____

_____

_____

The Uses and Meaning of IQ Scores (page 353)

Most intelligence tests set norms in such a way that most people score near 100. About 95 percent of people score between 70 and 130. Only a little more than 2 percent score at or above 130. These people are in at least the 97th percentile. Those who score below 70 have been classified as mentally handicapped. Mental handicaps are classified more specifically from mildly handicapped (55–69) to profoundly handicapped (below 25).

IQ scores do accurately predict which people will do well in school. Yet does success in school or the ability to take a test really indicate intelligence? This question is at the heart of the argument over IQ tests.

14. Look at Figure 13.9 in the text. If your IQ is 104, how would your intelligence be classified?

_____

_____

_____

_____

Controversy Over IQ Testing (page 355)

Differences in IQ scores may be due to genetics (the intelligence people inherit) or to the environment they come from. This is the familiar nature versus nurture debate. **Heritability** is a measure of how much of a characteristic is genetic. Studies show that between 52 percent and 70 percent of differences in IQ scores is related to heredity. Studies also show that environmental factors such as richness of the home environment, quality of food, and the number of brothers and sisters in the family also affect IQ.

Intelligence tests also have a **cultural bias**. That is, the wording of the questions may be more familiar to people of one social group than another. For example, on one intelligence test the correct response to the question "What would you do if you were sent to buy bread and the grocer said he did not have any more?" was "try another store." However, many minority students responded "go home." When questioned, they said that their neighborhood has only one store.

15. How might an IQ test be culturally biased against a Hispanic student?

_____

_____

_____

_____

Study Guide 13-3

Measuring Achievement, Abilities, and Interests

For use with textbook pages 359–362

Key Terms

aptitude test estimates the probability that a person will be successful in learning a specific new skill (page 360)

achievement test measures how much a person has learned in a given subject or area (page 360)

interest inventory measures a person's preferences and attitudes in a wide variety of activities to identify likely areas of success (page 361)

Drawing From Experience

Have you ever wondered what career would be right for you? What kinds of activities do you like? If a test could help you narrow your choices, would you take it?

In the last section, you learned about the nature of intelligence and intelligence testing. This section describes tests designed to measure your ability to learn new skills, your current knowledge in certain subjects, and what career choices might interest you.

Organizing Your Thoughts

Use the diagram below to help you take notes as you read the summaries that follow. Think about the three types of tests discussed in this chapter. For each example below, name the test that is designed to reveal this kind of result.

Test Result	Type of Test
You scored higher than others in your grade level in your knowledge of algebra.	1.
You show a strong talent for art and mechanical drawing.	2.
You would prefer a job in which you work with your hands over one that requires you to sit at a desk all day.	3.

Read to Learn

Introduction (page 359)

Intelligence tests are just one type of test. Psychologists have developed other tests to reveal special abilities and experiences. These include aptitude tests, achievement tests, and interest tests.

4. How might a test help you decide which careers to consider?

_____

_____

_____

Aptitude Tests (page 360)

Aptitude tests try to discover a person's talents and to predict how well he or she will be able to learn a new skill. Two such tests are the Differential Aptitude Test (DATE) and the General Aptitude Test Battery (GATB). Test results show a person's promise for a large number of occupations (job fields). The SAT and American College Test (ACT) are general aptitude tests. They are designed to predict a student's success in college. The best predictor of how well students will do in college is their performance in high school. Colleges use both high school grades and the results of tests like the ACT to predict college success.

5. Why might you want to pursue a career that matches your talents?

_____

_____

_____

Achievement Tests (page 360)

Achievement tests measure how much a person has already learned in a subject area. Achievement tests and aptitude tests overlap in what they measure. Aptitude is defined as inborn ability. Tests that measure aptitude also measure some learning. Achievement tests often predict job talents as well as measure how much a student already knows. Because of the overlap, the two types of tests are classified by purpose more than content. Thus, a test used to predict future ability is considered an aptitude test. A test used to determine what someone already knows is an achievement test.

Adaptive testing is a type of achievement test given by a computer. The computer changes the difficulty of the questions to adapt to the test taker's performance. For example, if you answer several problems correctly, the computer will challenge you with harder problems. The purpose is to measure your ability by finding the right difficulty level for you.

6. How do achievement tests overlap with aptitude tests in what they measure?

_____

_____

_____

_____

_____

_____

Interest Inventories (page 361)

Tests that measure abilities have right and wrong answers. Interest inventories do not. The purpose of an **interest inventory** is to measure your interests in some activities over others. Interest inventories try to find out what you like, not what you know. They compare the individual's responses to those of people in particular job fields. If your answers are like those of people in a certain job, then you would probably enjoy and succeed in that field. Suppose that the responses of most engineers on the inventory showed that they would rather be astronomers than coaches. If you responded like the engineers on many such questions, the inventory would rate your interests as high in engineering. The purpose of inventories like the Kuder Preference Record is to help people find the right career.

7. Why don't interest inventories have right and wrong answers?

_____

_____

_____

_____

_____

_____

Study Guide 13-4

For use with textbook pages 363–368

Personality Testing

Key Terms

personality test assesses an individual's characteristics and identifies problems (page 363)

objective test forced-choice test (in which a person must select one of several answers) designed to study personal characteristics (page 364)

projective test unstructured test in which a person is asked to respond freely, giving his or her own interpretation of various ambiguous stimuli (page 366)

Drawing From Experience

Do some people you know like to go to parties with lots of people, while others prefer to be with just one or two close friends? Do you relate to some people differently than others because you know how each is likely to respond?

The last section discussed aptitude, achievement, and interests. In this section, you will learn about different types of personality tests.

Organizing Your Thoughts

Use the diagram below to help you take notes as you read the summaries that follow. Think about the differences among the personality tests. For each test listed below, give a major characteristic that makes it different from the other tests.

Test	Major Difference
MMPI-2	1.
CPI	2.
Myers-Briggs test	3.
Rorschach test	4.
TAT	5.

Read to Learn

Introduction (page 363)

Psychologists use **personality tests** to identify personality characteristics and problems. These tests can also help predict how a person might behave in the future.

6. Think about someone who has a personality very different from yours. When faced with a crisis, how would you expect this person to act compared to how you would act?

_____

_____

_____

Objective Personality Tests (page 364)

Objective tests are usually limited- or forced-choice tests. That is, each question gives a few choices, and you must select one of them. One objective test, the Minnesota Multiphasic Personality Inventory (MMPI), consists of statements to which a person can respond *true, false,* or *cannot say*. The items on the MMPI reveal habits, fears, and symptoms of psychological disorders. Statements related to a certain characteristic, such as depression, are scattered throughout the test. When psychologists score the test, they group these answers together into a single depression scale. The MMPI has 10 such scales. Psychologists look for patterns of responses, not scores on individual items. The MMPI-2, a revision, was published in 1990.

The questions were selected for the test because studies showed that these questions can help separate people into different personality categories. For example, if you answer *false* to "I attend religious services frequently," you will score one point on the depression scale. This and other items like it were included because more depressed than nondepressed people answer *false* to this item.

The California Psychological Inventory (CPI) is similar to the MMPI, but was developed for more general use. It does not contain questions that reveal mental illnesses. It measures traits such as responsibility, self-control, and tolerance. The CPI is used to predict things like adjustment to stress, leadership, and job success.

The Myers-Briggs test focuses on how a person takes in information, makes decisions, and approaches day-to-day tasks. The test groups personality on four scales: extraversion vs. introversion, intuition vs. sensing, feeling vs. thinking, and judging vs. perceiving. For example, an extravert prefers activities with other people, while an introvert enjoys being alone. The idea behind the test is that each person's personality is a combination of these characteristics. The characteristics that are stronger in your personality will influence your communication style, how you conduct relationships, your work style, and your lifestyle choices. The purpose of the test is to help you understand your own personality, so that you can better understand how you relate to others and others relate to you. Hopefully, this knowledge will help you live a more rewarding life. Businesses use the test to make better hiring and promotion decisions.

7. How might the Myers-Briggs test help businesses decide whom to hire as a salesperson?

_____

_____

_____

_____

Projective Personality Tests (page 366)

Projective tests encourage test takers to respond freely, giving their own thoughts about each test item. These tests invite people to tell stories about pictures, diagrams, or objects. Because the test items have no set meaning, the story a person tells must say something about the person's needs, wishes, fears, and other aspects of personality. The test taker "projects" his or her unconscious feelings onto the test items.

The Rorschach inkblot test has 10 cards containing inkblot designs. The psychologist hands the ink blots one by one to the test taker and asks the person to say what he or she sees. There are no right or wrong answers. The theory is that what the person says reveals personality.

The Thematic Apperception Test (TAT) is a series of 20 cards with pictures of vague situations. Test takers are asked to tell a story about the situation. The interpreter focuses on the themes in the stories and the needs of the main characters. The responses are used to identify motivation and personality characteristics and problems.

8. Have you ever looked up at the clouds and seen patterns, such as a dog or person? How is this activity similar to a Rorschach test?

_____

_____

_____

_____

Study Guide 14-1

Purposes of Personality Theories

For use with textbook pages 375–377

Key Term

personality the consistent, enduring, and unique characteristics of a person (page 375)

Drawing From Experience

What are you "like"? What kinds of things make you different from every other person? What characteristics do you like best about your best friend?

This section discusses the purposes of personality theories. It also introduces you to the major schools of thought in personality theory that you will read about in the rest of this chapter.

Organizing Your Thoughts

Use the diagram below to help you take notes as you read the summaries that follow. Think about the major theories of personality that you will read about in this chapter. In the diagram below, list each major school of thought and what each one emphasizes.

School of Thought	Emphasis	
1.	7.	
2.	8.	
3.	9.	
4.	10.	
5.	11.	
6.	12.	

Read to Learn

Introduction (page 375)

People have something inside them that makes them think, feel, and act differently from each other. That "something inside" is personality. **Personality** is the consistent and long-lasting characteristics of a person that make the person unique. That is, a person's personality makes him or her an individual, different from every other person.

Reading Essentials and Study Guide

13. Give an example of a characteristic of your personality.

_____

_____

Purpose of Theories (page 375)

Personality theories provide ways to organize the characteristics of people. People may be outgoing or shy, quick-tempered or calm, fun-loving or gloomy. These words describe behaviors that characterize an individual. Researchers develop theories about what characteristics go together, why a person has some characteristics and not others, and why someone might show different characteristics in different situations. Theories vary, but all try to discover patterns in the ways people behave.

A second purpose of personality theories is to explain differences between individuals. Some say that differences in motives explain differences in people. Others try to find out how motives developed. Still others look for explanations in childhood conflicts.

A third purpose of personality theory is to look at how people conduct their lives. Researchers try to explain why problems arise in people's lives and why some people can deal with the problems better than others.

A fourth purpose of personality theories is to determine how people can improve their lives. People need to grow and change. Yet what are the goals of growth and change? How can we cope with the conflicts that will come up?

Personality theories are used to guide research. They are precise statements of possible explanations for human behavior. Researchers then test how well the theories explain behavior.

14. In your own words, describe how theories guide research.

_____

_____

Major Schools of Personality Theory (page 376)

There are several conflicting theories, or schools of thought, about personality. Sigmund Freud's psychoanalytic theories stress the importance of motives hidden in the unconscious mind. B.F. Skinner and the behaviorists study how rewards and punishments shape our actions. Social learning theories look at how parts of personality may be learned by observing others. Cognitive theories focus on how our thoughts, perceptions, and feelings shape our personalities. Humanistic theories stress one's human potential for growth. Finally, trait theories try to understand basic personality characteristics such as friendliness and aggression.

You will learn about each of these theories in this chapter. Each has a different image of human nature. What they have in common is that they all try to understand differences among people.

15. Give an example of a way you often behave that you think you learned from someone else.

_____

Study Guide 14-2

Psychoanalytic Theories

For use with textbook pages 378–386

Key Terms

unconscious the part of the mind that contains material we are unaware of, but that strongly influences conscious processes and behaviors (page 379)

id the part of the unconscious personality that contains our needs, drives, and instincts, as well as repressed material (page 379)

ego the part of the personality that is in touch with reality and strives to meet the demands of the id and the superego in socially acceptable ways (page 380)

superego the part of the personality that inhibits the socially undesirable impulses of the id (page 380)

defense mechanisms certain specific means by which the ego unconsciously protects itself against unpleasant impulses or circumstances (page 380)

collective unconscious the part of the mind that contains inherited instincts, urges, and memories common to all people (page 384)

archetype an inherited idea, based on the experiences of one's ancestors, which shapes one's perception of the world (page 384)

inferiority complex a pattern of avoiding feelings of inadequacy rather than trying to overcome their source (page 385)

Drawing From Experience

Have you ever made excuses for doing something wrong? Have you ever been angry with someone, but took it out on someone else? Why do you think you did these things? The last section introduced the major schools of thought in personality theory. In this section, you will learn more about one of them: the psychoanalytical theories.

Organizing Your Thoughts

Use the diagram on the next page to help you take notes as you read the summaries that follow. Think about the defense mechanisms the people unconsciously use to protect their egos. Give an example of each one listed.

Defense Mechanism	Example
Rationalization	1.
Repression	2.
Denial	3.
Projection	4.
Reaction Formation	5.
Regression	6.
Displacement	7.
Sublimation	8.

Read to Learn

Introduction (page 378)

Sometimes people slip when speaking and say something they did not mean to say. Have you ever said something that hurt a friend and later wondered why you said it? If you think about it, you might discover that you were really angry with your friend. According to Sigmund Freud, slips like this are not accidental. They are intentional ways of expressing unconscious desires.

9. Think about a time when someone said something he or she did not mean to say. How did you react? Did you think the slip had meaning?

_____

_____

Sigmund Freud and the Unconscious (page 378)

Sigmund Freud was a doctor in Vienna, Austria, in the late 1800s and early 1900s. He specialized in nervous disorders. His patients told him about their personal lives, conflicts, fears, and desires. He concluded that the most powerful influences on human personality are things we are not conscious of. He suggested that every personality has an **unconscious**—the part of the mind that contains material we are unaware of. Freud believed that many of our experiences, especially painful events of childhood, are not forgotten. Instead, we store them in our unconscious. Although we may not consciously recall these experiences, they continue to influence our behavior. For example, a child who never pleases her demanding parent may feel unhappy and will doubt her abilities to succeed. As an adult, she may feel unworthy and lack confidence in her abilities in spite of how able she really is. Freud believed that unconscious feelings people experience as children have a huge impact on adult personality and behavior. Freud also believed that between the conscious and the unconscious is the preconscious—thoughts that can be recalled with little effort.

10. Suppose a child's parents gave him lots of praise whenever he tried new things, even when he failed. According to Freud's beliefs, how might this child behave as an adult?

_____

_____

The Id, Ego, and Superego (page 379)

Freud explained personality as an energy system, like a steam engine. The energy comes from two instincts: the life instinct and the death instinct. The life instinct is the most important. It appears as pleasure-seeking urges. The death instinct shows up as destructive behavior and aggression. Freud introduced a model of how the brain works. The parts of his model are the id, ego, and superego. He did not believe that these parts really exist. Rather, he used them as a way to describe his view.

The **id** is the part of the unconscious that holds our needs, drives, and instincts. The id is the lustful, impulsive, fun part of the unconscious. It operates on the *pleasure principle*. It seeks immediate satisfaction of desires, regardless of the consequences. Hurting someone's feelings, lying, and having fun are examples of the id's influence.

The part of personality that is mostly conscious is the **ego**. It is the reasonable, thoughtful part. It operates on the *reality principle*. If you were hungry, your id would drive you to eat everything available. Your ego would recognize that your body will need food in the future and would cause you to save some for later.

Suppose that you thought of stealing the desired food from someone else. The part of the personality that would stop you is the **superego**. It is the moral part of personality, your conscience. It operates on the *moral principle*. It is also the source of guilty feelings if you do something that your conscience tells you is wrong.

The id is concerned with what the person *wants* to do. The ego is concerned with what she *can* do. The superego is concerned with what she *should* do. The id and superego often conflict. Neither is concerned with reality. The ego tries to satisfy the demands of the id without offending the superego.

11. Suppose you found a wallet containing $100. You chose to find the owner and give the money back. What part of your personality would be behind this behavior?

_____

_____

Defense Mechanisms (page 380)

The ego's job is so difficult that all people unconsciously resort to psychological defenses. Rather than face intense conflict, people deceive themselves into believing nothing is wrong. These **defense mechanisms** unconsciously defend the ego from the stress of failing in its tasks. To some degree, defense mechanisms are necessary for psychological well-being. They help people through emotional crises. If a person uses them too much, however, they will avoid facing and solving their problems realistically.

Rationalization is a defense mechanism that involves making up excuses. If you failed a test and blamed the failure on "bad test questions" rather than admit that you did not study, you would be rationalizing.

If you are very angry at someone and the anger causes your ego too much stress, you may push these feelings down into your unconscious. This defense mechanism is called *repression*. However, the feelings remain in the unconscious and may show themselves as cutting remarks, slips of the tongue, or in dreams.

You are in *denial* if you refuse to accept the reality of something that stresses you out. A feeling like "it won't happen to me" is an example of denial.

Another way the ego avoids stress is to believe that feelings coming from within are really coming from other people. For example, a person who dislikes himself may feel that others dislike him. This defense mechanism is called *projection*. The person is throwing or "projecting" his inner feelings onto others. We all do this from time to time.

Reaction formation involves replacing an unacceptable feeling with an opposite one. For example, you might put up a front and act confident when you are really scared.

Regression means going back to an earlier, less mature pattern of behavior. When under severe pressure, a person may throw a temper tantrum or sleep a lot like he did as a child. If you were ever tempted to pout when you could not have your own way, then you have experienced regression.

Displacement occurs when you cannot take out your anger on the source of your frustrations. Instead, you "displace" it. You take it out on someone else. For example, if you wanted to hit your father but were afraid to, you might hit your little brother instead.

Sublimation means directing a forbidden desire into a socially acceptable desire. For example, suppose that you are very angry at your friend. Instead of acting on that anger, you work extra hard at soccer practice. You have channeled your aggressive feelings into physical activities.

12. Suppose that your parents warn you that if you do not wear a helmet when you skateboard, you could be seriously injured. Yet, you refuse to wear one anyway.

What defense mechanism would you be using?

_____

_____

Evaluating Freud's Contribution (page 383)

Freud's greatest contribution was the idea that strong forces exist in the human personality and that these forces are difficult to control. Freud thought that conflict was the result of the savage part of people coming to terms with the rules of society. The id is the savage part. The superego represents society's rules. In a healthy person, the ego is strong enough to handle the struggle.

Freud claimed that personality develops mostly in the first 5 years of life. Freud identified five stages of development in children. Conflicts develop at each stage. How children deal with these conflicts determines how their personalities develop.

13. What might happen if someone had no superego?

_____

_____

In Freud's Footsteps (page 384)

Carl Jung disagreed with Freud on two major points. First, he took a more positive view of human nature. He believed that people try to develop their potential as well as handle their urges. Second, he proposed a second type of unconscious, a **collective unconscious**. This is a storehouse of instincts, urges, and memories of the entire human species throughout history. He called these inherited ideas **archetypes**. Every person has the same archetypes. They reflect common experiences of humanity. Jung found that the same themes (archetypes) appear again and again in stories, myths, and religions. For example, the story of Jack and the Beanstalk is nearly the same as the story of David and Goliath. Both tell how a small, weak, good person triumphs over a big, strong, bad person. Jung believed such stories are common because the situations they describe have occurred throughout history. They have been stored as archetypes in the collective unconscious in every person.

Alfred Adler believed that the driving force in people's lives is a desire to overcome feelings of inferiority. According to Adler, everyone struggles with inferiority, feeling that they are not good enough. A person who constantly avoids feelings of inferiority rather than tries to overcome them has an **inferiority complex**. Children first feel inferior because they are so little and dependent on adults. They slowly overcome this feeling as they learn to do things adults can do. The patterns people use to overcome inadequacies throughout life is called their *lifestyle*. Adler believed that the way parents treat their children influences the lifestyles they choose. An overly pampered child becomes a self-centered adult who expects everyone else to do what he wants.

Erich Fromm's theory centered on the need to belong and the loneliness that freedom brings. Karen Horney stressed the basic anxiety children feel because of their helplessness and resentment toward their parents that accompanies the anxiety. Erik Erikson outlined eight stages that every person goes through from birth to old age.

14. Give an example of something a child might do that would help the child develop self-confidence and reduce the feeling of inferiority.

_____

_____

Study Guide 14-3

For use with textbook pages 387–390

Learning Theories

Key Terms

behaviorism school that holds that the proper subject matter of psychology is objectively observable behavior—and nothing else (page 387)

contingencies of reinforcement the occurrence of rewards or punishments following particular behaviors (page 388)

Drawing From Experience

When you do something really well, such as make a goal in soccer, snag some tickets to a hot concert, or buy just the right outfit, how do your friends react? Does this reaction make you want to do the same thing again? The last section discussed psychoanalytical theories of personality. This section describes two types of learning theories, behaviorism and social cognitive theory.

Organizing Your Thoughts

Use the diagram below to help you take notes as you read the summaries that follow. Think about behaviorism and social cognitive theory. Describe the core idea behind the key words below.

Key Word	Core Idea
Reinforcement	1.
Observational Learning	2.
Reciprocal Determinism	3.

Read to Learn

Introduction (page 387)

John Watson believed that psychologists should study behavior that can be observed. He believed that you cannot study what you cannot see. His beliefs led to the school of thought called **behaviorism**. Behaviorists believe that our personalities develop from what we learn from our environment. People have different learning experiences. They learn different behaviors, so their personalities are different.

4. Why do you think this school of thought is called behaviorism?

_____

_____

_____

_____

_____

B.F. Skinner: Behaviorism (page 388)

B.F. Skinner focused on what causes a person to act a certain way. He was less concerned with understanding behavior than in predicting and controlling it. For example, Ruben has been depressed lately. Freud would seek the roots of Ruben's childhood unhappiness. Skinner would take a more direct approach. He would want to know exactly how Ruben behaves. The answer may be that Ruben spends most of the day in his room, cuts his classes, and rarely smiles or talks to anyone.

Skinner would then try to understand the **contingencies of reinforcement**. These are the rewards and punishments that follow particular behaviors. What reward does Ruben receive for not leaving his room? One hypothesis (possible answer) is that Ruben's girlfriend, Brandi, has unintentionally reinforced this behavior by spending a lot of time with him trying to cheer him up. Note that Skinner's approach immediately suggests a hypothesis that can be proved true or false. If paying attention to Ruben encourages him to stay in his room, then ignoring him should decrease this behavior. If Brandi ignores him and he starts leaving his room, then she has discovered the reinforcement for his behavior. If he does not leave his room, then that hypothesis was wrong, and she should try something else. The behaviorist approach may seem to suggest that Ruben is faking his depression. Skinner would not make this assumption. Ruben could be unaware of the rewards that are shaping his behavior. To behaviorists, Ruben's feelings do not matter. What matters is his behavior. The point is to identify the behavior and find out what causes it. To change behavior, we must change the reinforcer.

5. Give an example of something you like to do. What is reinforcing that behavior?

_____

_____

_____

_____

_____

Albert Bandura: Social Cognitive Theory (page 389)

Skinner stresses reinforcement in his view of how personalities develop. Albert Bandura agreed with this but added another way personalities develop—by observing and imitating. In *observational learning*, a person learns a new behavior by watching the actions of someone else. For example, to teach a child how to hit a baseball, you could demonstrate the correct way to hold the bat and swing at the ball.

Bandura believed that a young child's behavior and personality develop by exposure to everyday models. In his view, people can direct their own behavior by their choice of models. When your parents object to your choice of friends, they are trying to change the models you use.

According to Bandura's social cognitive theory, your personality is shaped by an interaction among three things. The first is you—your beliefs, expectations, emotional makeup, and genes. The second is your behavior. The third is your environment—social and cultural influences and your personal learning experiences. The interaction of these three things is called *reciprocal determinism*.

One strong influence on behavior is your view of your chances to succeed. Bandura called this *self-efficacy*. For example, you are thinking about going on a date. You consider your environment—your potential date's recent behavior and your parents' state of mind. You also consider what happened the last time you tried to date this person. From these considerations, you assess your chances of success. If you believe you have a good chance of getting the date, you will likely try.

Psychoanalytical theories stress childhood experiences and unconscious forces. In contrast, learning theories focus on behavior, something that can be tested and measured.

6. Give an example of something you learned to do mostly by watching someone else do it.

_____

_____

_____

_____

_____

_____

_____

Reading Essentials and Study Guide

Study Guide 14-4

Humanistic and Cognitive Theories

For use with textbook pages 391–397

Key Terms

humanistic psychology a school of psychology that emphasizes personal growth and the achievement of maximum potential of each unique individual (page 392)

self-actualization the humanist term for realizing one's unique potential (page 392)

self one's experience or image of oneself, developed through interaction with others (page 395)

positive regard viewing oneself in a positive light because of positive feedback received from interaction with others (page 395)

conditions of worth the conditions a person must meet in order to regard himself or herself positively (page 395)

unconditional positive regard the perception that individuals' significant others value them for what they are, which leads the individuals to grant themselves the same regard (page 396)

fully functioning an individual whose person and self coincide (page 396)

Drawing From Experience

Do you know anyone who seems to really enjoy life? How do they behave toward other people? How do they cope with the problems of life?

The last section discussed the behaviorist and social cognitive theories on personality. In this section, you will learn about the approaches of humanism and cognitive theory.

Organizing Your Thoughts

Use the diagram below to help you take notes as you read the summaries that follow. Think about the characteristics of self-actualized people. Describe five of these characteristics in the diagram below.

Characteristics of Self-Actualized People

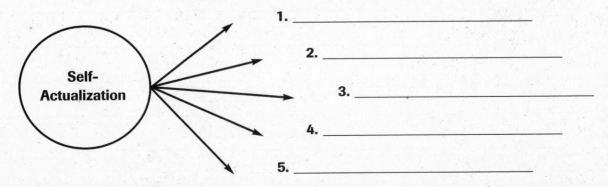

1. _____

2. _____

3. _____

4. _____

5. _____

Self-Actualization

Read to Learn

Introduction (page 391)

When Jackie Robinson broke the color barrier in professional baseball, he had everything going against him. His teammates did not want him. Pitchers threw at him. Fans mocked him. However, through it all he held onto a strong belief in his own abilities, which helped him succeed. The idea that people's perception of themselves can become their reality is part of the humanistic and cognitive theories of personality.

6. Give another example of a famous person who believed in himself or herself and succeeded against the odds.

_____

_____

_____

_____

_____

_____

Humanistic Psychology (page 392)

Humanistic psychology may be viewed as a rebellion against the negative view of human nature in personality theory of the early 1900s. Psychoanalysts saw human nature as a struggle to control the demands of the id and superego. Behaviorists saw human behavior in mechanical terms. Humanistic psychology stresses instead our ability to create and live by personal standards and perceptions. It is founded on the belief that all human beings strive for **self-actualization**. That is, we all try to reach our full potential.

7. In what way is the humanistic view of human nature positive?

_____

_____

_____

_____

_____

_____

Abraham Maslow: Growth and Self-Actualization (page 392)

Abraham Maslow was one of the pioneers of humanistic psychology. He based his theory of personality on studies of healthy, creative, self-actualizing people. Psychoanalysts based their theories on studies of disturbed people. Maslow wanted to learn more about people who led exceptional lives. He found that self-actualized people share a number of traits. First, they perceive reality accurately. They also accept themselves, other people, and their environment better than other people do. Most of us deny our shortcomings and try to change things around us. Self-actualized people accept themselves as they are.

Because self-actualized people feel better about themselves, they can focus more on tasks than on themselves. They are more likely to base decisions on ethical principles than on the possible costs or benefits to themselves. They have a good sense of humor and laugh with people, not at them. Maslow also found that self-actualized people do not try to be anything other than themselves. They can keep their integrity in the face of unpopularity and rejection. They value privacy and focus on deep, loving relationships with a few close friends.

The people Maslow studied appreciated even the simplest things. They approached their lives with a sense of discovery that made each day new. They were rarely bored and had moments of intense joy or "peak experiences." They enjoyed life.

Maslow believed that to become self-actualized, a person must first satisfy basic needs, such as food, shelter, safety, love, and self-esteem.

8. Think of someone you know who you think is self-actualized. What qualities of self-actualization does this person have?

_____

_____

_____

_____

_____

_____

Carl Rogers: Self Theory (page 395)

Carl Rogers believed that many people suffer from a conflict between what they value in themselves and what they believe other people value in them. Rogers believed that people are constantly trying to become more complete. Anything that helps them toward this goal is good. Each person also has what Rogers called a **self**. The self is your image of who you are and what you value in yourself, in others, and in life. You gain your sense of self gradually over the years by seeing how other people react to you. You want approval or **positive**

regard. This means viewing yourself in a positive light because of positive feed-back you get from others. For example, you may ask yourself, "How does she see me?" If the answer is "She likes me," then you begin to develop positive regard. Often the other person puts conditions on positive regard. She may like you *if* you do what she wants. Then you develop **conditions of worth**. These are conditions you must meet in order to regard yourself positively.

Rogers believed that people cope with conditions of worth by denying parts of themselves that do not fit their self-concept. For example, if your mother grew distant whenever you became angry, you learned to deny yourself the right to express anger. The gap between your image of yourself and who you really are limits you. Rogers believed the cure for this situation is **unconditional positive regard**. If people important to you let you know that they value you as you are, you will learn to grant yourself unconditional positive regard. You will be able to accept yourself and become **fully functioning**. This means that you and your self image are the same. You are free to develop to your full potential.

9. According to Rogers, why is it important to have unconditional positive regard?

_____

_____

_____

_____

Cognitive Theory (page 396)

Cognitive theory is based on analysis of our own perceptions, thoughts, and feelings. George Kelly believed that our personality is made up of our thoughts about ourselves. His *personal construct theory* focused on psychological processes within each of us. We channel these processes according to what we think will happen in our world. The emphasis is on the individual and his or her plans, including biases, errors, and false conclusions. His view took an optimistic view of humans. In his view, we are masters rather than victims of our destiny.

10. Why is it important to see yourself as a master rather than a victim of your destiny?

_____

_____

_____

_____

Study Guide 14-5

Trait Theories

For use with textbook pages 398–403

Key Terms

trait a tendency to react to a situation in a way that remains stable over time (page 398)

cardinal trait a characteristic that is so pervasive that the person is almost identified with the trait (page 400)

factor analysis a complex statistical technique used to identify the underlying reasons variables are correlated (page 401)

surface trait a stable characteristic that can be observed in certain situations (page 401)

source trait a stable characteristic that can be considered to be at the core of personality (page 401)

extravert an outgoing, active person who directs his or her energies and interests toward other people and things (page 401)

introvert a reserved, withdrawn person who is preoccupied with his or her inner thoughts and feelings (page 401)

Drawing From Experience

Do certain words, such as friendly, outgoing, or shy, seem to describe people you know? Do these people seem to act this way no matter what the situation? In this section, you will learn about trait approaches.

Organizing Your Thoughts

Use the diagram below to help you take notes as you read the summaries that follow. Think about the "robust five" personality traits. On the scales below, write each of the five traits on one end and their opposite trait on the other.

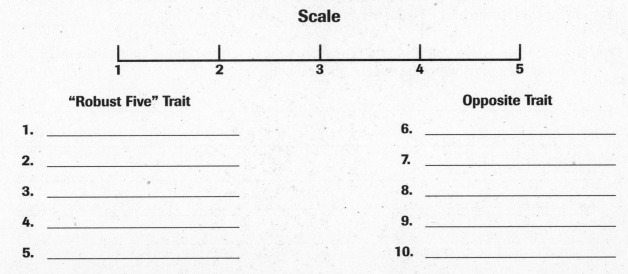

Scale

1 2 3 4 5

"Robust Five" Trait   **Opposite Trait**

1. _____   6. _____

2. _____   7. _____

3. _____   8. _____

4. _____   9. _____

5. _____   10. _____

Read to Learn

Introduction (page 398)

Terms such as *nice*, *smart*, and *friendly* refer to personality traits. A **trait** is a tendency to respond the same way in different situations. It is a way that one individual differs from another.

11. What traits do you think your friends would say are part of your personality?

_____

_____

_____

_____

What Is the Trait Theory of Personality? (page 399)

People who study traits assume two things. First, every trait applies to all people. For example, everyone has some amount of friendliness. Second, we can measure the amount of a trait someone has. For example, we can create a scale on which a very friendly person scores a 10 and a very unfriendly person scores a 1. Most people fall somewhere between these two extremes. We can understand people by identifying their traits. We can predict their future behavior from this understanding.

Trait researchers also try to discover why people tend to act the same way most of the time. They might ask the following: What is the best way to describe someone's behavior? What trait best explains this behavior?

If Freud noticed that some people are stingy, he would try to explain this behavior in terms of instincts. Trait researchers would not start by trying to understand stinginess. Rather, they would try to determine whether stinginess is a trait. That is, they would try to find out if people who were stingy in one type of situation were also stingy in others. Then they might try to determine whether stinginess is a sign of a more basic trait like possessiveness. The main question for trait researchers is: What behaviors go together?

12. Suppose a person rated a "2" on the "friendly" scale described above. How might this person act at a party where he did not know anyone?

_____

_____

_____

_____

Copyright © by The McGraw-Hill Companies, Inc.

Gordon Allport: Identifying Traits (page 400)

Gordon Allport believed that a person's traits will be consistent in different situations. By studying words that describe personality in a dictionary, Allport created a list of traits. He defined common traits as those that apply to everyone. Individual traits are those that apply more to a particular person. Allport described three kinds of individual traits. A **cardinal trait** is a trait that is so strong in someone that the person seems almost identified with it. For example, Scrooge in *A Christmas Carol* almost defines stingy. *Secondary traits* are traits that tend to change, such as food and music preferences. These are less important. A *central trait* is one that best describes a person, such as shy, loyal, or generous.

13. Think of two people you know. What do you think is the central trait for each person?

_____

_____

_____

_____

Raymond Cattell: Sixteen Trait Theory (page 401)

More recent trait researchers studied what Allport called *common traits*. They tried to measure how strongly different traits relate to each other. To do this, they used a complicated mathematical method called **factor analysis**. Using factor analysis, Raymond Cattell identified 46 **surface traits**. These are traits that someone can observe. He then found that some surface traits occur in clusters. He identified 16 **source traits**. These are traits at the core of personality. He believed that by measuring source traits, psychologists could predict people's behavior in certain situations.

14. How are source traits different from surface traits?

_____

_____

_____

_____

Hans Eysenck: Dimensions of Personality (page 401)

Hans Eysenck concluded that there are two basic parts of personality. The first part is *stability versus instability*. This refers to how much control people have over their feelings. At the emotionally-stable end of this scale are people who are easygoing, relaxed, and well-adjusted. At the instability end of the scale are people who are moody, stressed, and restless. The second part of personality is *extraversion versus introversion*. **Extraverts** are outgoing, active, lively people. **Introverts** are thoughtful, reserved, quiet, and not very social.

Years later Eysenck added a third part of personality, *psychoticism*. At one end of this scale are self-centered, aggressive people who act without much thought. People at the other end have what Freud labeled superego. They are sensitive, caring, and easy to work with.

15. If a scale rated extreme extraverts as a 1 and extreme introverts as a 10, how would you rate yourself? Why?

_____

_____

_____

_____

_____

The Robust Five (page 401)

Over years, psychologists have shown that five traits appear again and again in different studies. These traits are called the "five robust factors." (1) *Extraversion* is identified with warmth and being talkative and energetic. (2) *Agreeableness* means being sympathetic to others, kind, and trusting. (3) *Conscientiousness* identifies people who are responsible, organized, and dedicated to completing tasks. (4) *Openness to experience* describes people who are open-minded and willing to try new experiences and ideas. (5) *Emotional stability* identifies people who experience things easily without getting upset.

Think of each big five trait as a scale. Each trait has an opposite that is on the other end of the scale. For example, conscientiousness at one end includes responsible and dependable people. At the other end would be people who are careless and not dependable.

16. Describe a person who would be at the opposite end of the emotional stability scale.

_____

_____

_____

_____

Study Guide 15-1

For use with textbook pages 413–419

Sources of Stress

Key Terms

stress a person's reaction to his or her inability to cope with a certain tense event or situation (page 413)

stressor a stress-producing event or situation (page 414)

stress reaction the body's response to a stressor (page 414)

distress stress that stems from acute anxiety or pressure (page 414)

eustress positive stress, which results from motivating strivings and challenges (page 414)

conflict situation when a person must choose between two or more options that tend to result from opposing motives (page 414)

Drawing From Experience

Have you ever had to decide between two options, when both options were bad? How did this situation make you feel? Have you ever stressed out over something that didn't seem to bother a friend at all?

In this section, you will learn about the nature of stress. You will also learn about some of the sources of stress in your life.

Organizing Your Thoughts

Use the diagram below to help you take notes as you read the summaries that follow. Think about the components or parts that make up stress. List each component in the diagram.

Components of Stress

1. _____   3. _____

STRESS

2. _____   4. _____

5. _____

Read to Learn

Introduction (page 413)

Stress has several definitions. To some psychologists, stress is an event that produces tension. Others describe it as a physical or psychological *response* to such an event. Still others believe it to be a person's *perception* of the event. This chapter defines **stress** as the feeling of tension that comes from our reaction to our inability to cope with a situation.

6. Have you ever felt stress? What does it feel like?

_____

_____

_____

_____

Components of Stress (page 414)

A **stressor** is an event or situation that causes stress. An event that is a stressor for one person may not be for another. For example, traveling in an airplane may be a stressor for someone who has never flown, but not for a flight attendant. Stress is a person's reaction to a stressor. A **stress reaction** is the body's physical response to a stressor.

Stress may seem like a bad thing. However, there are two types of stress. Negative stress, or **distress**, comes from extreme tension or pressure. It can harm mind and body. Positive stress, or **eustress**, comes from striving to meet life's challenges. Stress is a normal part of life. It goes hand in hand with working toward a goal or facing any challenge. In fact, stress can spur us on to greater achievements. For example, the stress of playing in the big game can motivate athletes to high performance. We cannot escape stress. We can learn to cope with it, though, so that it makes life interesting rather than overwhelming.

Another part of stress is how a person perceives and evaluates a situation. This is called the cognitive model of stress. We size up a situation and decide if it is stressful. For example, if we perceive a situation as dangerous, we react with stress.

7. Give an example of a time when someone might experience eustress.

_____

_____

_____

Conflict Situations (page 414)

In our daily lives, we often have to decide between two or more options. For example, should you go to a movie with friends or study for the test? These choices result from opposing motives: the desire to be with your friends versus the desire to do well in school. Such choices are **conflict situations**. There are four types.

In an *approach-approach conflict*, a person must choose between two attractive options. Suppose two excellent colleges accept you. You must decide which to attend. This type of conflict does not produce much stress and is usually easy to resolve.

An *avoidance-avoidance conflict* requires a choice between two unattractive options. For example, suppose you have been looking for a job for a long time. You find one that does not pay well. Should you accept it or continue looking? Both options are frustrating, so this kind of conflict produces a great deal of stress.

Say you really want to do something, but are afraid to. This is an *approach-avoidance conflict*. For example, you may want to ask for a raise, but are afraid you will be fired if you ask. The amount of stress in this type of conflict depends on how strong your desire is and how fearful the threat is.

In the *double approach-avoidance conflict*, you must choose between options that each have attractive and unattractive aspects. For example, you are unable to decide whether to go to the beach or visit your grandmother. The beach would be exciting but expensive. Visiting your grandmother would be inexpensive but not very exciting.

The amount of stress you feel depends on how you size up the situation. *Primary appraisal* is your first evaluation of the situation. Suppose your teacher announces a pop quiz. You may feel neutral about it. You think you know the material and the teacher doesn't give hard quizzes. You may feel positive about it. You know the material so well that you look forward to a good grade. Or, you may see the situation as negative. You have not studied in a long time. This appraisal will cause you stress. A *secondary appraisal* involves deciding how to deal with the situation. You would size up the situation and choose a coping strategy. You will learn more about this later.

8. Give an example of an approach-avoidance conflict you have faced.

_____

_____

_____

_____

_____

Environmental Stressors (page 416)

Some things in your environment cause stress. For example, constant noise around you can be stressful. Also, crowding can be stressful. Most people feel tense when others get too close. Yet crowding can make people feel better if the situation is pleasant to them. For example, being in a crowd at a baseball game can increase the excitement if you enjoy baseball games.

Major changes in your life, such as a new job or moving, can cause stress. The stress may come from the separation from family and friends that such events cause. Even positive changes, such as marriage, can be stressful. Thomas Holmes and Richard Rahe tried to determine how much stress different life changes cause. From their research, they developed the Social Readjustment Rating Scale. This scale ranks 43 life events in terms of the stress they cause. The top stressor is the death of a spouse. Getting fired ranks eighth. Moving to a new home ranks 32nd. People who have many of these stressors score high on the rating scale. Some studies have related a high score on this scale to illness. A major life change can also lead to other stressors. For example, marriage may mean a change in financial status and moving to a new home.

In addition to major life changes, you also have small, day-to-day stressors called *hassles*. Hassles may be losing your car keys, being late for school, or getting stuck in traffic. Research has found a connection between hassles and health problems. Perhaps hassles slowly weaken the body's defenses, making it harder to fight off illness. Small, positive events, called *uplifts*, may protect against stress. Uplifts are things that make you feel good.

9. What are some hassles you have experienced in the last week?

_____

_____

_____

_____

_____

_____

_____

_____

_____

_____

_____

Study Guide 15-2

Reactions to Stress

For use with textbook pages 420–429

Key Terms

anxiety a vague, generalized apprehension or feeling that one is in danger (page 422)

anger the irate reaction likely to result from frustration (page 422)

fear the usual reaction when a stressor involves real or imagined danger (page 422)

social support information that leads someone to believe that he or she is cared for, loved, respected, and part of a network of communication and mutual obligation (page 428)

Drawing From Experience

Have you ever felt so stressed that you just couldn't think? Have you ever been under a lot of pressure over some major event in your life, but then blew up over something really small?

The last section discussed the nature and sources of stress. In this section, you will learn about physical, psychological, and behavioral reactions to stress.

Organizing Your Thoughts

Use the diagram below to help you take notes as you read the summaries that follow. Think about the variety of reactions we have to stress. List three examples of each type of stress reaction.

Physical Reactions	Psychological Reactions	Behavioral Reactions
1.	4.	7.
2.	5.	8.
3.	6.	9.

Read to Learn

Introduction (page 420)

A person who faces a stressor that is strong or long-lasting will react to it. Some reactions to stress are harmful. Others are helpful. Many are automatic. Just as the body reacts to a cut by producing new tissue, it has ways to heal the wounds of stress—crying, for example. People react differently to stress. Reactions can be physical (our body's reaction), psychological (how we feel emotionally), or behavioral (how we act). Yet these reactions are not separate from each other. The human body is *holistic*. Everything works together to make up the whole person. Our physical well-being affects how we think and behave. For example, poor mental health can lead to physical illness.

10. When you are very nervous, do you ever laugh? How does the laughter affect how you feel physically?

_____

_____

_____

_____

Fight-or-Flight Response (page 421)

No matter what is causing the stress, the body quickly becomes alert. The adrenal glands produce (a) hormones that speed up energy production and (b) adrenaline, which speeds up heartbeat and breathing to help the body use energy quickly. These responses prepare you for self-defense. This is called the *flight-or-fight response*. In wild animals, this response is needed for survival. It prepares them to either run from danger (flight) or stand and fight. This response prepares humans in the same way to deal with dangerous or stressful situations.

11. Describe how your body feels during times of great stress.

_____

_____

_____

_____

General Adaptation Syndrome (page 421)

Hans Selye identified three stages of the body's stress reaction: alarm, resistance, and exhaustion. He called this the *general adaptation syndrome*. In the *alarm* stage, the body starts its fight-or-flight defenses. The person becomes very alert to things going on around him or her. For example, a hiker comes upon a rattlesnake. He freezes in his tracks and suddenly becomes aware of every sound around him. He tries not to panic.

In the *resistance* stage, the person finds a way to cope with the stressor and ward off strong emotions. For example, after recovering from the initial shock of seeing the snake, the hiker may tell himself to stay calm and wait for the snake to move off.

If the stressful situation continues, the person reaches the stage of *exhaustion*. At this point, the adrenal and other glands involved in the fight-or-flight response have reached their limit. They can no longer supply hormones. The person reaches the breaking point. He or she becomes exhausted and confused.

12. Why is the resistance stage important to dealing with a stressful situation?

_____

_____

_____

Emotional and Cognitive Responses (page 422)

Stress reactions may be emotional or cognitive (involving thought processes). A common emotional response is **anxiety**. This is a feeling that some unclear threat is about to happen. If your boss passes you in the hall without saying hello, you might develop anxiety about the possibility of being fired. **Anger** is the likely response to frustration. **Fear** is the usual response if the stressor involves real danger, such as a fire. Fear directs you to run away, but in severe cases you may panic and be unable to act. Common examples of emotional stress reactions are reacting too strongly to minor hassles, feeling no joy in daily pleasures, and doubting your abilities.

Cognitive reactions include difficulty in concentrating and poor decision making. A student who must give a speech may worry about it but be unable to prepare for it. Another type of cognitive stress reaction is suspicion or distrust of others for no real reason.

Frustration that lasts a long time can lead to burnout. People feel *burned out* when they feel unable to do their job well, physically worn out, and emotionally exhausted. Too much stress may not cause mental illness but can make it more severe.

Post-traumatic stress disorder is a condition in which someone who has experienced a terrible trauma feels the stressful effects long after the event. This disorder is common among combat veterans, survivors of disasters, and victims of violence. The event that caused the disorder overwhelmed the person's ability to cope.

13. If someone were really stressed over an upcoming test, how might she react when she cannot find her car keys to go to the library?

_____

_____

_____

_____

Behavioral Reactions (page 424)

A person's behavior may change as a result of stress. For example, someone may develop nervous habits, such as biting fingernails or pacing. The person may gulp meals or develop a shaky voice. The person's posture may change. Acting aggressively toward family members is another behavioral reaction to stress. Some behavioral reactions are positive. For example, in a tornado some people will risk their lives to help others. Escape is a behavioral reaction that is often the best way to deal with frustration. For example, if you are on a bus stuck in traffic, you may get off and walk to where you are going.

Many people can handle great amounts of stress without major changes in behavior. Others may be seriously affected. They may attempt to escape reality through alcoholism or drug addiction. They may be unable to hold a job, and they may attempt suicide. Stress may also contribute to violent and criminal behavior.

14. Give an example of a nervous habit that you have seen in yourself or someone else.

_____

_____

_____

Physical Reactions (page 425)

Your thoughts and emotions can produce physical changes in your body. For example, some people develop *psychosomatic symptoms* from stress. These are real physical problems caused by stress or tension. For example, stress can cause headaches, stomach aches, and muscle pains. The fight-or-flight response is a physical reaction. If this state of physical arousal continues for too long, the person could develop breathing difficulty, difficulty sleeping, migraine headaches, or other physical problems. Emotional stress is also related to such illnesses as ulcers, high blood pressure, asthma, and heart disease. People in high-stress jobs pay a high price. Air-traffic controllers have the lives of hundreds of people in their hands every day. People in these jobs have more ulcers than people in any other type of job.

Stress can be the direct cause of illness. It also contributes indirectly by hindering the *immune system*. This is your body's natural defense system against infection.

15. Give another example of a job that is so stressful that the people doing it might be at risk for stress-related illnesses.

_____

_____

_____

Factors Influencing Reactions to Stress (page 427)

Some people's personalities make them more likely than other people to get stress-related illnesses. People with extreme "Type A" personalities are always prepared for fight-or-flight. Their bodies are always in a state of stress. Their adrenaline flows constantly. These people are likely to have heart attacks as early as their thirties or forties. Type A people are very competitive. They are often angry and impatient. They often eat fast and do two or three things at once. On the other hand, Type B people are usually relaxed, patient, and not easily angered. These people are at less risk for stress-related illnesses.

Another personality trait that can affect the strength of a stress reaction is a person's ability to express emotion. Some research suggests that people who do not express strong feelings or even admit to having them are more likely to develop cancer. Physical problems are more likely when we do not have control over stressors. Research with rats showed that rats who could avoid a shock by touching their noses to a panel developed fewer ulcers than the rats who had no control over when they would be shocked. Feedback about our performance is also important. We feel less stress if we know how well we did.

In general, people prefer to have stress they can predict rather than stress they cannot predict. People who feel a sense of control over their lives are likely to be physically and psychologically healthier than those who do not.

Social support is information that leads someone to believe that he or she is cared for, loved, respected, and part of a group that helps each other. People with social support are less likely to develop stress-related diseases or the diseases will be milder.

Social groups offer four kinds of support. *Emotional* support involves listening with concern and offering affection. This helps the stressed person's self-confidence. In *appraisal* support, the listener helps the stressed person sort out the sources of stress by asking questions and giving feedback. In *informational* support, the stressed person responds to what he or she has learned from the appraisal support. The person then evaluates how he or she is dealing with the stressors. Finally, *instrumental* support is direct help such as money or a place to live.

16. Think of someone who has a Type A personality. Describe the Type A behaviors you see in this person.

_____

_____

_____

_____

_____

_____

Study Guide 15-3

For use with textbook pages 430–435

Coping With Stress

Key Terms

cognitive appraisal the interpretation of an event that helps to determine its stress impact (page 431)

denial a coping mechanism in which a person decides that the event is not really a stressor (page 431)

intellectualization a coping mechanism in which the person analyzes a situation from an emotionally detached viewpoint (page 431)

progressive relaxation lying down comfortably and tensing and releasing the tension in each major muscle group in turn (page 434)

meditation a focusing of attention with the goal of clearing one's mind and producing an "inner peace" (page 434)

biofeedback the process of learning to control bodily states by monitoring the states to be controlled (page 434)

Drawing From Experience

Think about what you do when you feel stressed. Do your behaviors help reduce the stress? Do you try to solve the problem, or just pretend it isn't there?

The last section described different reactions to stress. In this section, you will learn methods for managing your stress.

Organizing Your Thoughts

Use the diagram below to help you take notes as you read the summaries that follow. Think about ways you can actively reduce stress. Describe how each coping strategy listed below helps to reduce stress.

Coping Strategy	Reduces stress by...
Hardiness	1.
Escape	2.
Timing	3.
Problem Solving	4.
Thinking Style	5.
Progressive Relaxation	6.
Humor	7.

Reading Essentials and Study Guide

Read to Learn

Introduction (page 430)

Stress can smother your enjoyment of life and make you unhappy. If you focus on the positive, though, stress may be simply a roadblock to overcome. Coping with stress is an attempt to gain control over part of your life. People cope with stress in many ways. There is no one best way. People use the coping styles that work best for them. Some ways of coping are not healthy. Under stress, we may act in ways that harm ourselves or others.

8. Describe a stressful situation you faced. What is a positive side to this situation?

_____

_____

_____

Psychological Coping Strategies (page 431)

Cognitive appraisal is your evaluation of an event that helps determine how stressful it will be for you. For example, if you see the upcoming test as a challenge you can meet, it will not cause you much stress. If you see it as a threat, however, your stress will be high.

Two defensive coping strategies are denial and intellectualization. In **denial**, you decide that the event is not really stressful. **Intellectualization** is a way of coping in which you size up the situation without getting your emotions involved. Both of these coping strategies can prevent physical reactions to stress. However, in both cases, you are not really dealing with the problem.

By seeing the situation as a challenge and not a threat, you can deal with the stress actively rather than simply defend against it. Active coping strategies involve changing the environment or situation to remove the stressor or reduce the stress you feel.

Hardiness is a personality trait that can act as an active coping strategy. Hardy people feel they have the ability to do something about the situation. They actively try to achieve goals and solve problems, instead of feeling threatened or powerless by them. For example, suppose you must give a speech. You are being hardy if you approach the assignment as a positive experience, believe you can do it well, and prepare for and practice your speech.

You can also actively reduce stress by controlling the number of stressful events you face. Escape is one way to do this. If a social event becomes stressful for you, you can leave. Another way is to control the timing of stressful events, when possible. This way, you can avoid having them hit you all at once. For example, if you are going to have a baby soon, you may want to put off looking for a new home.

Sometimes you can't escape or change the timing of stressful events. For example, you may have an exam on the same day that a big project is due. In cases like this, problem solving, or facing the matter head-on, can be the best way to cope. Viewing frustrations as problems to be solved turns the situation into a challenge rather than a setback. Problem solving means thinking through the situation in a way that leads to a reasonable decision. For example, you could map out your time so that you worked on the project at some times and studied for the exam at others. You could decide that giving up social activities the weekend before the due date would solve the problem.

Your thinking style can also affect your ability to cope. *Optimists* usually put the best face on any event. If they lose a game, they might say, "I'll do better next week." *Pessimists* always see the dark side. If they fail at something, they might say, "That always happens to me." Research shows that pessimists are more likely to die at a young age.

Using a relaxation technique can help you cope with stress. **Progressive relaxation** is a method for reducing muscle tension. You lie down comfortably. Then you tense and relax each major muscle group in turn. **Meditation** is a mental relaxation method. You focus your mind on something and then let it go. The purpose is to clear your mind and produce an inner peace.

As you learned in Chapter 7, **biofeedback** is a way to bring certain body processes, such as blood pressure and muscle tension, under your conscious control. You are hooked up to a machine that gives feedback on your body's responses. In this way, you can, for example, train yourself to relax.

Keeping a sense of humor will help you get through stressful times. Laughing actually releases tension. Physical exercise is another way. It provides an outlet for the body's fight-or-flight responses. It may even help burn off stress hormones.

Support groups beyond your personal network can also help—Alcoholics Anonymous, Weight Watchers, crisis intervention centers, and so on. You can also seek help from professionals, such as psychologists, doctors, social workers, and ministers.

A situation can be stressful if it is new to you. Training to prepare can ease the stress. For example, if you are nervous about playing tennis at a friend's club, you might take tennis lessons first.

Much of the stress we feel comes from relationships with other people. A good way to manage stress is to develop skill in dealing with others.

9. Suppose your family is moving to another state. What can you do to help deal with the stress of this major life change?

_____

_____

_____

_____

_____

_____

Study Guide 15-4

Stress in Your Life

For use with textbook pages 437–442

Key Terms

autonomy ability to take care of oneself and make one's own decisions (page 437)

developmental friendship the partners force one another to reexamine their basic assumptions and perhaps adopt new ideas and beliefs (page 438)

resynthesis combining old ideas with new ones and reorganizing feelings in order to renew one's identity (page 439)

career a vocation in which a person works at least a few years (page 440)

comparable worth the concept that women and men should receive equal pay for jobs calling for comparable skill and responsibility (page 441)

Drawing From Experience

Have you ever lived apart from your family for a long time? What was it like? If you have never done so, what do you expect it to be like? If you could have any job in the world, what would it be? Why?

In the last section, you learned ways of coping with stress. This section discusses some of the stresses involved in going to college and working in a job.

Organizing Your Thoughts

Use the diagram below to help you take notes as you read the summaries that follow. Think about the kinds of adjustments that students make when they go to college. List three sources of these changes in the diagram below.

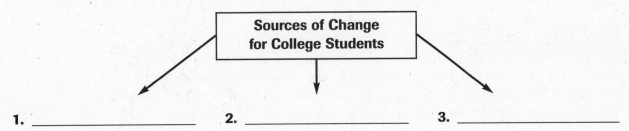

1. _____ 2. _____ 3. _____

Read to Learn

Introduction (page 437)

Children grow up and leave home to set up households of their own. This period of life is a major life change for both teens and parents. This life change involves dealing with stress. As you grow up, you gain a sense of **autonomy**.

This is the ability to take care of yourself and make your own decisions. You develop a value system and learn to be responsible. Growing up starts long before you leave home as an independent adult. In the end, growing up means separating from family, both physically and emotionally.

4. Why might separating from family cause stress?

_____

Choosing College (page 437)

For many Americans, college is one of the first big steps toward separation. Going to college can be exciting, but it also takes adjustment. Studies of first-year college students found that many students approach college with unrealistic goals. For example, Bridget wanted to be an astronomer. She liked the idea of being different. Plus, she thought it would be an adventure. She did not realize how many long, hard hours she would have to spend studying math to reach this goal. Keith wanted to be a doctor. But he never thought about what it would be like to watch people sicken and die. These students, like others, based their goals on fantasy. They did not have the experience to make realistic choices. They also did not have the maturity to evaluate their reasons for setting these goals.

College requires adjustment in many ways. First, college may challenge the identity a student built in high school. A top high school student may go to a top college. There, nearly everyone is as bright as she is. Within weeks, her identity as a star student is gone. She may have to struggle to get average grades.

Second, students are likely to find more diversity in college than they ever experienced before. They will meet people of different religions, ethnic backgrounds, family income levels, and attitudes. Suppose you form a close relationship with someone and then discover that the person holds beliefs that you consider immoral. Your choices are to adjust your deeply held belief or give up an important friendship. **Developmental friendships** are relationships in which the individuals force each other to examine their basic beliefs and perhaps adopt new ones.

These friendships can change students a lot, but so can class work. Keith found that he enjoyed his literature and philosophy classes better than his classes for medical school. He soon realized that his interest in medicine was shallow. He wanted to be a doctor because it was a respected profession. It would give him status and a good income. Yet it was not what he really wanted. The self-image Keith had brought to college was completely changed.

Students cope with the stress of going to college in different ways. Some stick to their initial goals and avoid people and situations that might bring doubt to the surface. For example, Troy stuck with his engineering program in spite of his growing interest in social science. He got an engineering degree, but left college with no idea where he was heading. Others avoid facing doubt by going through the motions of attending college without getting emotionally involved.

Still others manage to keep their options open until they have enough information and experience to make a choice. During a period of doubt and anxiety, the students try to combine the new and old. They may give up their original goal and go in a different direction. Sometimes they retreat and head in different directions several times. Finally, they reorganize their feelings and efforts into a new identity. This is **resynthesis**.

5. If you were to go to college, what field would you choose as your major? Why?

_____

Working (page 439)

Each person's work experience is different. People work in different settings—offices, stores, schools, mines, trucks, etc. Some jobs have strict time schedules. Others are more flexible. Some people work mostly for the money. Others get personal satisfaction from the work. Each person's personality affects how he or she will react to a job.

Most workers have both economic and personal goals. One study identified five major sources of job satisfaction. (1) *Resources*. People want to have enough help, supplies, and equipment to do the job well. (2) *Financial reward*. People want their jobs to pay well and offer good benefits and security. (3) *Challenge*. People want their jobs to be interesting and to use their special talents. (4) *Relations with coworkers*. People are more satisfied with their jobs if they get along well with their fellow workers. (5) *Comfort*. People want good working conditions—hours, work environment, reasonable closeness to home, and so on.

A **career** is a job field in which a person works for at least a few years. Some researchers predict that in the future, people will change careers several times in their lifetimes. People live longer now. It is fairly common for someone to retire from one job at age 60 and then start a new career. Many women split their careers by stepping out of the job market to raise children. Then they go back into the workforce in another career. To prepare for this kind of work world, you need many skills and interests. You should develop your skills in dealing with other people. Also, you should look at change as a challenge.

In theory, people in jobs that require about the same amount of training, skill, and responsibility should receive the same pay. This is the idea of **comparable worth**. In practice, however, jobs held mostly by women often pay lower than jobs with similar requirements held mostly by men. Overall, women face a large gap between their income and that of men. Groups like the National Organization for Women have been working to achieve equal pay for equal work. Congress has passed two laws to prevent discrimination and pay inequality. The Equal Pay Act of 1963 makes it illegal to discriminate in pay for jobs that require similar skills and responsibilities. The Civil Rights Act of 1964 makes discrimination illegal in all areas of employment on the basis of sex, race, color, religion, and national origin. This act also set up the Equal Employment Opportunity Commission (EEOC) to enforce this law.

6. Name the top three things that you would want in a job.

_____

Study Guide 16-1

For use with textbook pages 447–454

What Are Psychological Disorders?

Key Term

DSM-IV the fourth version of the American Psychiatric Association's *Diagnostic and Statistical Manual of Mental Disorders* (page 451)

Drawing From Experience

Have you ever been around someone who acted "odd?" Do you think this person is mentally ill or just different? How would you define abnormal behavior?

In this section, you will learn about the difficulty in judging normal from abnormal behavior. You will also learn about a system for classifying psychological problems.

Organizing Your Thoughts

Use the diagram below to help you take notes as you read the summaries that follow. Think about the different ways to define abnormal behavior. Give an example of behavior that would be considered "abnormal" according to each approach listed below.

Approach	Example
Deviation	1.
Adjustment	2.
Psychological Health	3.

Read to Learn

Introduction (page 447)

It is often difficult to draw a line between normal and abnormal behavior. Many people feel that having visions and hearing voices is an important part of a religious experience. Others believe these are signs of a psychological disorder (mental illness). The fact that someone is different does not always mean that the person is mentally ill.

4. Describe a time when you chose to be different in a healthy way.

_____

_____

_____

_____

_____

_____

Defining and Identifying Psychological Disorders (page 448)

There are several ways to define abnormality. There is no one correct definition, however. One approach is to say that whatever most people do is normal. Then abnormality would be anything that deviates or differs from what most people do. This is the deviation approach. For example, most people wear clothes out in the cold. According to the deviation approach, someone who wore a bathing suit in the snow would be abnormal. The deviation approach has serious problems. What most people do is not always right or best.

Another way to tell the difference between normal and abnormal is to say that normal people can get along in the world. They can take care of themselves, work, find friends, and live by the rules of society. By this definition, abnormal people are those who cannot adjust. According to this adjustment approach, people who are so unhappy that they refuse to eat or cannot hold a job would be abnormal. One problem with this approach is that some people with psychological disorders seem perfectly normal.

Some psychologists define normal and abnormal in terms of psychological health, similar to physical health or illness. They feel that a normal or healthy person is one who is making progress toward being the best they can be. As you learned earlier, this is the idea of self-actualization. One problem with this approach is that it is hard to tell if people are making progress toward their full potential.

Some psychologists believe that labeling someone as mentally ill simply because he or she is odd is wrong. Thomas Szasz argues that most people we call mentally ill are not ill at all. They just have "problems in living" that cause conflicts with the world around them. Rather than helping them deal with their problems, we often label them sick and shut them up in hospitals. This is an uncommon view. Most psychologists believe that some people do need hospitalization.

As you can see, abnormality is difficult to define. This means we should be careful not to judge someone as sick just because he or she acts in a way we cannot understand. Mild psychological problems are common. Only when the problems are big enough to get in the way of everyday life do they become illnesses.

5. Give an example of a behavior that would be considered abnormal according to the adjustment approach.

_____

_____

_____

_____

_____

The Problem of Classification (page 450)

For years psychiatrists have been trying to find a way to classify mental disorders. This task is difficult, because psychological problems are not as clear-cut as physical diseases. In 1952, the American Psychiatric Association agreed on a standard system for classifying abnormal symptoms. The most recent major revision is the *Diagnostic and Statistical Manual of Mental Disorders*, fourth version, or **DSM-IV**. It was published in 1994. Before 1980, the two major classes of illness were *neurosis* and *psychosis*. Now those terms have been replaced by more specific categories.

The DSM-IV includes the following descriptions within each category of illness. (1) *Essential features* are characteristics that define the disorder. (2) *Associated features* are additional characteristics that usually go with the essential ones. (3) *Differential diagnosis* describes ways to tell one disorder from another similar one. (4) *Diagnostic criteria* is a list of symptoms, taken from the essential and associated features, that must be present to say that a person has that illness.

Diagnosing mental disorders is complicated. People may have more than one illness. The DSM-IV overcomes this problem by looking at someone's mental functioning in five ways, or axes. *Axis I* classifies current symptoms. *Axis II* classifies long-standing disorders. *Axis III* describes related medical conditions. *Axis IV* measures the person's current stress level. *Axis V* describes how well the person is functioning in relationships with people, on the job, and in using leisure time.

6. How is classifying mental illnesses different from classifying physical diseases?

_____

_____

_____

_____

_____

Study Guide 16-2

Anxiety Disorders

For use with textbook pages 455–459

Key Terms

anxiety a vague, generalized apprehension or feeling that one is in danger (page 456)

phobia an intense and irrational fear of a particular object or situation (page 456)

panic disorder an extreme anxiety disorder that manifests itself in the form of panic attacks (page 457)

post-traumatic stress disorder disorder in which victims of traumatic events experience the original event in the form of dreams or flashbacks (page 459)

Drawing From Experience

Have you ever felt generally uneasy for no real reason? Have you ever been in love to the point that you had a hard time thinking about anything else? In this section, you will learn about the most common types of anxiety disorders.

Organizing Your Thoughts

Use the diagram below to help you take notes as you read the summaries that follow. Think about the symptoms of different anxiety disorders. For each example below, list the disorder that it describes.

Example	Disorder
Famous football announcer John Madden rides a bus to games around the country because he is afraid to fly in a plane.	1.
A store clerk who was robbed at gunpoint experiences the robbery over and over in her dreams.	2.
A student is so intent on writing a perfect paper that he can never finish one.	3.
A person feels a sudden anxiety so severe that he feels like he is choking and going to die.	4.
A person feels a vague worry all the time, so that she can't make decisions or keep up with friendships.	5.

Read to Learn

Introduction (page 455)

Anxiety is a general feeling of dread or uneasiness that you feel in response to a real or imagined danger. Everyone feels anxiety sometimes. People with anxiety disorders feel more than the normal amount. They feel very anxious over things that other people would see as minor problems. The anxiety gets in the way of their normal daily activities. Anxiety disorders may be expressed as constant worrying, mood swings, and physical symptoms like headaches, tense muscles, and fatigue.

6. Think of a time when you felt anxious. What was the "real or imagined danger" that caused this feeling?

_____

Generalized Anxiety Disorder (page 456)

Fear is a reaction to a real danger that you can identify. Yet anxiety can result from a vague feeling of danger for no reason that the person can identify. Some people feel an overall anxiety all the time. This is generalized anxiety disorder. They worry so much about unknown things that they cannot make decisions or enjoy life. They have trouble keeping relationships and fulfilling life's responsibilities. They are trapped in a cycle. The more they worry, the more difficulty they have. The more difficulty they have, the more they worry. People with this disorder often have tense muscles, trouble relaxing, poor appetites, indigestion, and trouble sleeping.

Some research suggests that this disorder may be learned. If a man feels very anxious on a date, even the thought of another date may make him nervous. So, he learns to avoid having dates. His anxiety may then spread as he learns to avoid other situations that make him anxious. Genes may play a role as well.

7. Give an example of a situation that involves fear. How is this different from anxiety?

_____

Phobic Disorder (page 456)

A **phobia** is an intense and unreasonable fear of a particular object or situation. It is anxiety that is out of proportion to the danger. For example, people with claustrophobia are afraid of enclosed spaces. They may be too afraid to get on an elevator. This is a *specific phobia*. People with *social phobias* fear that they will embarrass themselves in public. The most common social phobia is fear of speaking in public. People with *agoraphobia* fear being in public places. They may stop going to movies, shopping, and even leaving the house. Phobias can be mild or extreme. Most people deal with them by avoiding what they fear.

8. Suppose someone is so afraid of cats that he will not walk around his neighborhood for fear of seeing one. What type of phobia might this person have?

_____

Panic Disorder (page 457)

Panic disorder is extreme anxiety in the form of panic attacks. These attacks can involve choking feelings, chest pain, dizziness, trembling, and hot flashes. People may even feel that they are about to die. Attacks usually last just a few minutes but can last an hour or two. Panic disorder may be inherited, in part. Usually a stressful event sets off the first attack.

9. How is panic disorder different from generalized anxiety disorder?

_____

Obsessive-Compulsive Disorder (page 458)

An anxious person may keep thinking the same thoughts over and over again. Such an uncontrollable pattern of thoughts is called *obsession*. A person who repeats the same unreasonable actions over and over has a *compulsion*. These problems often occur together. This condition is called *obsessive-compulsive disorder*. A compulsive person may feel the uncontrollable urge to wash his hands 30 times a day. An obsessive person may be unable to stop thinking about death. An obsessive-compulsive person may do both.

Everyone has obsessions and compulsions. A hobby that occupies much of your time may be an obsession. People who become deeply involved in their hobby, enjoy it, and can still function well in life do not have a disorder. It only becomes a disorder when it prevents people from doing what they want and need to do.

People may develop obsessions or compulsions to take their attention away from their real fears. This would reduce their anxiety a bit. For example, a compulsion may make a person feel she is doing something well, even if it is only avoiding cracks in a sidewalk. Although most people with obsessive-compulsive disorder know that their thoughts and actions are unreasonable, they feel unable to stop them.

10. If someone checks his door locks every few minutes to make sure they are locked, is this an obsession or a compulsion? Explain.

_____

Post-Traumatic Stress Disorder (page 459)

Post-traumatic stress disorder is a condition in which a person who has experienced a terrible event feels the effects long afterwards. This disorder is common among combat veterans, survivors of disasters such as floods and plane crashes, and victims of violence, such as rape. Common symptoms include "flashbacks." These are nightmares during which the victim lives the experience over again. Following the flashbacks the person may be unable to sleep and may have feelings of guilt. This disorder can last for decades.

11. Why do you think a survivor of a Nazi concentration camp might feel guilty?

_____

Reading Essentials and Study Guide

Study Guide 16-3

For use with textbook pages 460–463

Somatoform and Dissociative Disorders

Key Terms

somatoform disorder physical symptoms for which there is no apparent physical cause (page 461)

conversion disorder changing emotional difficulties into a loss of a specific voluntary body function (page 461)

dissociative disorder a disorder in which a person experiences alterations in memory, identity, or consciousness (page 462)

dissociative amnesia the inability to recall important personal events or information, usually associated with stressful events (page 462)

dissociative fugue a dissociative disorder in which a person suddenly and unexpectedly travels away from home or work and is unable to recall the past (page 462)

dissociative identity disorder a person exhibits two or more personality states, each with its own patterns of thinking and behaving (page 462)

Drawing From Experience

What kinds of unusual psychological problems have you seen in television dramas? Have you seen shows about someone with multiple personalities? The last section discussed different types of anxiety disorders. In this section, you will learn about two other categories of disorders: somatoform and dissociative.

Organizing Your Thoughts

Use the diagram on the next page to help you take notes as you read the summaries that follow. Think about the differences between somatoform and dissociative disorders. Name the categories of disorders described in the diagram, and list the types in each category.

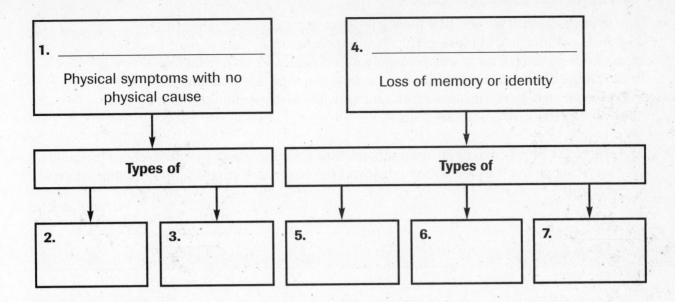

1. _____

Physical symptoms with no physical cause

4. _____

Loss of memory or identity

Types of

Types of

2.

3.

5.

6.

7.

Read to Learn

Introduction (page 460)

Sometimes psychological distress can bring on a variety of physical symptoms that have no physical cause. For example, a person may be unable to walk even though there is nothing wrong with his legs. This is called a **somatoform disorder**. Although nothing physical is wrong, the person is not faking. He really cannot move his legs.

8. How might suddenly being unable to walk actually help a person reduce stress?

_____

_____

_____

Somatoform Disorders (page 461)

Two types of somatoform disorders are conversion disorder and hypochondriasis. A person with a **conversion disorder** changes or "converts" emotional difficulties into a loss of a body function. The person might suddenly be unable to hear. Many people experience mild conversion reactions. For example, you might be so frightened that you cannot move. This brief loss of function is not a disorder. A conversion disorder can be a long-term disability. For example, a man might wake up one morning and find he is paralyzed. Most people would panic. However, he takes it calmly. This calmness is one sign that the problem is psychological rather than physical. People with conversion disorders invent physical symptoms to avoid some unbearable problem. For example, a woman who lives in terror of blurting out things she does not want to say may lose the power of speech. This "solves" the problem. Conversion disorders are rare.

Hypochondriasis is a disorder in which a person in good health becomes obsessed with imaginary illnesses. The person spends a lot of time looking for signs of serious illness. He or she thinks any minor pain is a sign of a fatal illness. In spite of medical reports showing nothing is wrong, a hypochondriac will continue to believe a disease exists. Like conversion, hypochondriasis is a physical expression of emotional distress.

9. Suppose a person makes an appointment with a doctor once a month to check for cancer, even though her tests are always negative. Which somatoform disorder does this behavior suggest?

_____

_____

_____

Dissociative Disorders (page 462)

A **dissociative disorder** is a breakdown in a person's normal conscious experience, such as a loss of memory or identity. Memory loss that has no physical explanation is **dissociative amnesia**. This may be an attempt to escape problems by blotting them out. People with amnesia may keep their other knowledge, but may not know who they are, where they work, or who their family is. It often results from a terrible event, such as witnessing a serious accident. Since it has no physical cause, amnesia is not the same as memory loss due to brain injury.

Dissociative fugue is a combination of memory loss and physical escape. The person may suddenly disappear and "wake up" three days later 200 miles away, not knowing who she is. She may establish a new identity—take a new name, get a job, and so forth—in the new place. The fugue state may last days or decades. When she wakes up, she will have no memory of what she did in the new location. Fugue is sort of a traveling amnesia. It serves as an escape from unbearable anxiety.

In **dissociative identity disorder**, a person seems to have two or more personalities, each with its own ways of thinking and behaving. These different personalities take control at different times. Some psychologists believe that dividing a personality is a person's attempt to escape from part of himself that he fears. People with this disorder usually suffered severe abuse as a child. This disorder is very rare.

10. Suppose a person saw someone murder her mother. She could remember nothing about herself from then on. Which type of dissociative disorder does this suggest?

_____

_____

_____

Reading Essentials and Study Guide

Study Guide 16-4

Schizophrenia and Mood Disorders

For use with textbook pages 465–473

Key Terms

schizophrenia a group of disorders characterized by confused and disconnected thoughts, emotions, and perceptions (page 466)

delusions false beliefs that a person maintains in the face of contrary evidence (page 466)

hallucinations perceptions that have no direct external cause (page 466)

major depressive disorder severe form of lowered mood in which a person experiences feelings of worthlessness and diminished pleasure or interest in activities (page 470)

bipolar disorder disorder in which an individual alternates between feelings of mania (euphoria) and depression (page 471)

Drawing From Experience

Do you feel a little down at times? Yet, in the back of your mind, do you know that the feelings will pass?

The last section described two rare types of disorders, somatoform and dissociative. In this section, you will learn about schizophrenia and mood disorders.

Organizing Your Thoughts

Use the diagram below to help you take notes as you read the summaries that follow. Think about mood disorders and their symptoms. List two major types of mood disorders and their symptoms in the diagram below.

Mood Disorder   **Symptoms**

1. _____   ➔   2. _____

                            Phases

                            4. _____ ➔ 5. _____
3. _____ ⟨
                            6. _____ ➔ 7. _____

Read to Learn

Introduction (page 465)

Schizophrenia is the most complex and severe psychological disorder. We have difficulty understanding it because it is so far outside our experience.

Reading Essentials and Study Guide   **175**

Most of us have felt depressed or anxious at times. However, a schizophrenic's perceptions and behavior are bizarre beyond most people's ability to imagine.

8. Give an example of a behavior you have seen on TV, in a movie, or in real life that was so strange that it seemed out of touch with reality.

_____

What Is Schizophrenia (page 466)

Disorders you have learned about to this point are emotional problems. Schizophrenia is a problem with the ability to reason and perceive reality. **Schizophrenia** is a group of disorders characterized by confused and disconnected thoughts and perceptions. The person lives in an unreal world. It is not a single problem. It has no single cure.

Many people with schizophrenia have **delusions**. These are false beliefs that they hold on to in spite of evidence that these beliefs are not true. Schizophrenics also have **hallucinations**. These are perceptions of things that are not there. For example, the person may hear voices when no one is speaking. Other symptoms include *incoherence* and showing emotions that are not appropriate to the situation.

9. Some people with schizophrenia believe that they are the Pope. Is this a delusion or a hallucination?

_____

Types of Schizophrenia (page 467)

Psychologists classify schizophrenia into several types. The *paranoid type* involves delusions and hallucinations. It includes delusions of *grandeur*: "I am the savior." It also includes delusions of *persecution*: "Someone is always watching me." The *catatonic type* may not move for long periods. Symptoms of the *disorganized type* include confused language, inappropriate emotions, and disorganized movements. The *remission type* is anyone whose symptoms have disappeared for now, but are likely to come back. The *undifferentiated type* includes all the basic symptoms of schizophrenia.

Treatment is long-term and usually requires hospitalization. Recovery is possible, but no real cure exists. Victims usually never escape from it.

10. "Aliens are trying to take over my brain!" Which type of schizophrenia does this statement suggest?

_____

Causes of Schizophrenia (page 468)

Schizophrenia is likely caused by a combination of genetic, physical, and environmental factors. Studies show that schizophrenia affects 1 percent of people. The odds increase to 5.5 percent if a parent or sibling is diagnosed.

To work properly, the brain needs the right amounts of different chemicals, from oxygen to proteins. Some psychologists believe that schizophrenia is caused by not having the right amounts of certain chemicals. The *dopamine hypothesis* suggests that too much of the chemical dopamine is to blame. Yet it is hard to tell if the chemical differences are the cause or the result of the condition. Also, CAT and MRI scans show loss of brain tissue in schizophrenics.

Being part of a *pathogenic*, or unhealthy, family does not cause schizophrenia but can make the problems worse later in life. The *diathesis-stress hypothesis* states that a person may inherit a tendency toward schizophrenia. However, for schizophrenia to develop, the person must be exposed to an environment with certain stressors, such as a bad family life.

11. According to the diathesis-stress hypothesis, will a person born with a tendency toward schizophrenia always get it? Explain.

_____

_____

Mood Disorders (page 470)

Feeling depressed sometimes is common. Most of us know the feelings will pass. In some people, moods like this are more intense and last longer. They feel as though their depression will last forever and they can do nothing about it. People with **major depressive disorder** spend at least two weeks feeling depressed, sad, anxious, tired, upset, and less able to function. Such feelings are normal when a person loses a loved one. If the symptoms occur at other times, however, they suggest major depressive disorder.

People with **bipolar disorder** go back and forth from feeling extremely happy (manic) to deeply depressed. In the *manic phase*, they feel extremely happy yet confused and easily distracted. They act at a frantic pace. They may do something irresponsible, like go on a shopping spree. In the *depressive phase*, they are overcome by feelings of failure, worthlessness, and despair. They become sluggish and not responsive. In this stage, the symptoms are the same as those of major depressive disorder.

Depression may result from the interaction of physical and psychological factors. Some researchers point to a combination of personality traits plus social support and the ability to deal with stressful situations as causes. Others believe depression is learned helplessness. Still others are studying brain chemicals for an answer.

Not all depressed people attempt suicide, and not all people who commit suicide are depressed. Many depressed people, though, think about suicide. People may take their lives to escape physical or emotional pain. Every year more than 30,000 Americans end their lives. It is most common among the elderly, but is also the second most common cause of death among college students. People who threaten suicide or make unsuccessful attempts usually *are* serious.

12. If you feel depressed for a couple of days, do you have major depressive disorder? Explain.

_____

_____

Study Guide 16-5

Personality Disorders and Drug Addiction

For use with textbook pages 474–478

Key Terms

personality disorders a wide array of psychological disturbances characterized by lifelong maladaptive patterns that are relatively free of anxiety and other emotional symptoms (page 475)

antisocial personality a personality disorder characterized by irresponsibility, shallow emotions, and lack of conscience (page 475)

psychological dependence use of a drug to such an extent that a person feels nervous and anxious without it (page 476)

addiction a pattern of drug abuse characterized by an overwhelming and compulsive desire to obtain and use the drug (page 476)

tolerance physical adaptation to a drug, so that a person needs an increased amount in order to produce the original effect (page 476)

withdrawal the symptoms that occur after a person discontinues the use of a drug to which he or she has become addicted (page 477)

Drawing From Experience

Have you ever been to a party where adults were drinking? How did they act at first? How did their behavior change when they drank too much?

The last section described schizophrenia and mood disorders. In this section, you will learn about personality disorders and the nature of drug addiction.

Organizing Your Thoughts

Use the diagram below to help you take notes as you read the summaries that follow. Think about the stages of alcoholism. Describe each stage below.

Stage	Description
Stage 1	1.
Stage 2	2.
Stage 3	3.

Read to Learn

Introduction (page 474)

Some people commit crimes for no reason we can understand. They may shoot someone because they want to. Emotions and social rules do not hold back their behavior. This lack of emotion and concern for the rules of society is a sign of an antisocial personality disorder.

4. What might life be like if no one felt emotion for others or the need to obey laws?

_____

_____

_____

_____

Personality Disorders (page 475)

People with **personality disorders** do not feel anxiety. They do not feel much of any emotion. Most of the time, they behave normally. Yet they can't form meaningful relationships or act responsibly in society. This broad class of disorders includes a wide variety of personality patterns, from painfully shy, lonely people to pushy show-offs.

One type of personality disorder is **antisocial personality**. People with this disorder act irresponsibly, have shallow emotions, and lack a conscience. They have no concern for the rights of others. They treat people as objects—things to be used to get what they want and then discarded. They are thrill-seekers living for the moment. If they injure someone along the way, they do not feel shame or guilt about it. Getting caught does not bother them either. Many such people get away with their behavior because they are smart and can fake emotion they do not feel. They win people's confidence and then take advantage of them. Some researchers think antisocial behavior is learned from antisocial parents. Others point to a lack of discipline during childhood. Still others are studying genes to look for a cause.

5. How might someone with antisocial personality disorder react when sentenced to prison?

_____

_____

_____

_____

Drug Addiction (page 476)

Drug abuse involves **psychological dependence**. This is the use of a drug to the point that people feel nervous and anxious without it. They come to depend on the feeling of well-being that they get from the drug, so they feel the need to continue using it. People can become psychologically dependent on many drugs, including alcohol, caffeine, nicotine (in cigarettes), marijuana, and cocaine. Without it, people feel restless.

Drugs can also lead to physical **addiction**. This is an overwhelming desire to use the drug. The drugged state has become normal for the body. When the drug is not in the body, people feel extreme discomfort. The physical need is as great as the need for oxygen or water. Once people are addicted, they develop **tolerance**. Their bodies become used to the drug, so they need more and more of it to get the same effect. When they do not get it, they go into **withdrawal**. This is physical and psychological pain as the body and mind try to get used to being without the drug. Symptoms can range from nausea and the shakes to hallucinations, convulsions, coma, and death.

Alcohol is involved in half of deaths from car accidents and murders. In small doses, alcohol makes people relaxed and playful. This is why people think it is a stimulant, but it is really a depressant. With more drinks, the senses become distorted, reactions slow, and speech slurs. After even more drinks, people pass out. In some cases, they die.

Alcohol can produce psychological dependence, tolerance, and addiction. In the first stage, alcohol makes people feel confident and less tense. In the second stage, people drink so heavily that they feel they have to hide their habit. They sneak drinks. In this stage, they may black out and not be able to recall what they did during that period. In the final stage, they drink constantly. They can no longer function well in life. They may go on drinking sprees for weeks. Their health goes down hill quickly. Alcohol has a violent withdrawal, called *delirium tremens*.

6. How is psychological dependence different from addiction?

_____

_____

_____

_____

_____

_____

_____

Study Guide 17-1

What Is Psychotherapy?

For use with textbook pages 485–492

Key Terms

psychotherapy any treatment used by therapists to help troubled individuals overcome their problems (page 486)

eclectic approach method that combines various kinds of therapy or combinations of therapies (page 487)

placebo effect the influence that a patient's hopes and expectations have on his or her improvement during therapy (page 488)

empathy capacity for warmth and understanding (page 489)

group therapy patients work together with the aid of a leader to resolve interpersonal problems (page 489)

Drawing From Experience

Think about someone you like to talk to when you are troubled. What qualities does this person have that cause you to go to him or her? Would you want these same qualities in a therapist if you needed professional help?

In this section, you will learn what psychotherapy is and how it works. You will also learn about different kinds of therapy and the people who provide it.

Organizing Your Thoughts

Use the diagram below to help you take notes as you read the summaries that follow. Think about the three things involved in psychotherapy. List them in the diagram below.

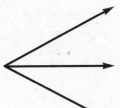

Psychotherapy involves . . .

1. _____

2. _____

3. _____

Read to Learn

Introduction (page 485)

At times of crisis in life, we all need to talk to someone we trust. Often a parent, relative, or close friend can fill this role. Sometimes the problems are too complex or confusing to be solved this way, however. When people become unhappy with life and think the reason lies within themselves, they need professional help. Mental health professionals trained to deal with psychological problems are psychologists, psychiatrists, and social workers. **Psychotherapy** is any treatment used by these therapists to help people overcome their problems. It includes three things: (1) conversation between the therapist and client, (2) developing a trusting relationship between the two, and (3) the therapist's analysis of the client's problems and suggestions for overcoming them.

4. How can a trusted friend or relative help you overcome problems?

_____

The Nature of Psychotherapy (page 486)

In early times, people with psychological problems were thought to have demons inside them. They were treated with exorcism—religious ceremonies to drive out the demons. Later people began to look at these problems as diseases or *mental illness* that required treatment. Now this label may do more harm than good. It causes people to think of themselves as helpless victims with no control over their problems. By thinking of themselves this way, they may avoid taking an active role in helping themselves change. One function of psychotherapy is to help people realize that they are the only ones who can solve their problems. The therapist is a guide that helps clients find the source of their problems and possible solutions.

There are many kinds of therapy. Each is based on different theories about how personality works. Each has its own style. Some therapists use an **eclectic approach**. They use combinations of different kinds of therapy.

Over the years, people may develop certain feelings about themselves. Their behavior supports these feelings, making them hard to change. These behaviors and feelings get in the way of reaching their goals. To change, people must believe that they can change. The influence of people's beliefs on their improvement is called the **placebo effect**. Patients who believe they have the power to change will find a way, with hard work and the help of a therapist.

5. Why might the label "mental illness" get in the way of someone's ability to recover?

_____

Who Are Therapists? (page 488)

Good therapists have three characteristics. First, they must be psychologically healthy. Second, they must have **empathy**. This is the ability to give warmth and understanding. Troubled people are usually fearful and confused.

The therapist must give them confidence that he or she understands and cares. Third, good therapists must have experience dealing with people and understanding their complex problems.

6. Why is empathy so important in a therapist?

_____

_____

Group Therapies (page 489)

In some forms of therapy, the patient is alone with the therapist. In **group therapy**, patients work together with the aid of a leader to solve problems. One advantage is that patients can see how other people are struggling with problems like their own. Also, they can discover what others think of them and can express what they think of other people. This way, people can see their mistakes in their views of themselves and of other people. In group therapy, people can also see others recovering, giving them hope.

Sometimes therapists suggest that the whole family work together in group therapy. In *family therapy*, family members can untangle the twisted web of relationships that led to emotional problems for one or more members. Often family members mistreat each other or are mistreated in ways they do not understand or want to talk about. The therapist can point out what is happening and suggest ways to improve communication and fairness in the family.

Self-help groups are voluntary groups of people who share a particular problem. These groups often operate without a professional therapist. At meetings, members discuss their difficulties and support each other. Self-help groups exist for alcoholism, overeating, child abuse, gambling, and many other problems. Alcoholics Anonymous (AA) serves as a model for other self-help groups. According to AA, the only way for alcoholics to change is to first admit that they can't control their drinking and that they can no longer manage their lives.

7. If one family member is having emotional problems, why might family therapy help?

_____

_____

Does Psychotherapy Work? (page 491)

Hans Eysenck reviewed five studies about the effectiveness of psychotherapy. He concluded that therapy is no more effective than no treatment at all. Others disagreed with his conclusions. One problem with trying to determine the success of therapy is to define improvement. In a later analysis of nearly 400 studies, using statistical tools, Mary Lee Smith and Gene V. Glass estimated the effects of psychotherapy. They concluded that therapy is helpful. Most forms of therapy improved the quality of life for patients. Some kinds of therapy work better in some situations than others, however. The patient and therapist must determine the type that will work best for them.

8. Based on this summary, how did Smith and Glass define improvement in therapy?

_____

_____

Study Guide 17-2

Psychoanalysis and Humanistic Therapy

For use with textbook pages 493–497

Key Terms

psychoanalysis therapy aimed at making patients aware of their unconscious motives so that they can gain control over their behavior (page 494)

insight the apparent sudden realization of the solution to a problem (page 494)

free association a method used to examine the unconscious; the patient is instructed to say whatever comes into his or her mind (page 494)

resistance the reluctance of a patient either to reveal painful feelings or to examine long-standing behavior patterns (page 494)

dream analysis a technique used by psychoanalysts to interpret the content of patients' dreams (page 495)

transference the process, experienced by the patient, of feeling toward an analyst or therapist the way he or she feels or felt toward some other important figure in his or her life (page 495)

humanistic therapy focuses on the value, dignity, and worth of each person; holds that healthy living is the result of realizing one's full potential (page 496)

client-centered therapy reflects the belief that the client and therapist are partners in therapy (page 496)

nondirective therapy the free flow of images and ideas, with no particular direction (page 496)

active listening empathetic listening; a listener acknowledges, restates, and clarifies the speaker's thoughts and concerns (page 497)

unconditional positive regard a therapist's consistent expression of acceptance for the patient, no matter what the patient says and does (page 497)

Drawing From Experience

Do you sometimes have the same dream over and over? Did you ever try to make sense out of the dream? In this section, you will learn about two types of therapy: psychoanalysis and humanistic.

Organizing Your Thoughts

Use the diagram on the next page to help you take notes as you read the summaries that follow. Psychoanalysis and humanistic therapy approach psychological problems and their solutions in different ways. In the diagram, write about how each approach views the source of problems and the goal of therapy in solving them.

	Psychoanalysis	Humanistic Therapy
Psychological problems occur because . . .	1.	2.
Goal of therapy is . . .	3.	4.

Read to Learn

Introduction (page 493)

Sigmund Freud believed that dreams are a window into the unconscious mind. Therapists who follow Freud's approach look for meaning in patients' dreams to help them understand their problems. For example, suppose a patient dreamed about herself as a child riding a bicycle. The bicycle could represent the freedom from illness that the patient longed for.

5. Think about a dream you had recently. Identify something in it that could represent something you think or feel.

_____

What Is Psychoanalysis? (page 494)

Psychoanalysis is therapy based on Freud's theories. Freud believed that psychological problems come from anxiety about hidden conflicts among the unconscious parts of one's personality. The psychoanalyst's job is to help patients become aware of their unconscious desires and fears. Once they understand their unconscious motives, they can gain control over their behavior. This will free them from their problems. Suddenly understanding the solution to a problem is called **insight**.

Psychoanalysis can take years of weekly sessions to accomplish change. The process starts with the analyst telling patients to relax and talk about everything that comes to mind. This method is called **free association**. Patients may describe dreams, private thoughts, or long-forgotten experiences. Patients usually do not want to talk about painful feelings or old patterns of behavior that need to be changed. So, they hold back information. This is called **resistance**. When resistance occurs, the analyst may point out what is happening and suggest ways to approach the area of resistance.

In **dream analysis**, the analyst tries to explain the meaning of clients' dreams to find out about their unconscious thoughts and feelings. Freud believed that dreams contain manifest and latent content. *Manifest content* is what you remember about your dream. For example, you may dream that your house fell apart, brick by brick. *Latent content* is the hidden meanings represented as symbols in the dream. For example, the analyst might suggest that your house falling apart was a symbol of your worry over your current health problems.

The analyst may begin to appear in patients' free association and dreams. Patients begin feeling toward the analyst the way that they feel toward some important person in their lives, such as a parent. This process is called **transference**. Patients may start acting toward the analyst the way they act toward the important person. For example, the analyst might ask, "What do you see when you imagine my face?" The patient might reply that she sees an angry, frowning person. The therapist then might say, "What does this make you think of?" Gradually, the patient may come to understand that she is reacting to the neutral therapist as though he were a threatening father. This helps her become aware of her true feelings toward her father.

Short-term dynamic psychotherapy is a shortened version of psychoanalysis. The therapist takes a more direct, active role in this type of therapy. It works well for people able to gain insight into their behavior. It does not work well for schizophrenics.

6. How might free association help bring problems to the surface?

_____

_____

Humanistic Therapy (page 496)

The goal of **humanistic therapy** is to help people reach their full potential. **Client-centered therapy** refers to several humanistic approaches. All reflect the belief that the client and therapist are partners in therapy. Client-centered therapy is based on the theories of Carl Rogers. Success of this therapy depends on the strength of the client's desire for growth and self-actualization. Client-centered therapists must have three qualities: positive regard, empathy, and genuiness. Positive regard is the therapist's ability to show caring and respect for the client. Empathy is the therapist's ability to understand what the client is feeling. Genuiness is the therapist's ability to act toward the client in a real and not defensive manner.

Client-centered therapists believe that people are basically good and capable of handling their own lives. Psychological problems happen when the true self becomes lost. A goal of therapy is to help clients learn to be true to their own standards and ideas about how to live.

The therapists encourage clients to speak freely about what is bothering them. This method is called **nondirective therapy** because the therapist does not direct it. Clients talk about whatever they want. The therapist tries to echo back the feelings the clients have expressed. This technique is called **active listening**.

Client-centered therapy takes place in an atmosphere of emotional support called **unconditional positive regard**. This means that the therapist always expresses acceptance of clients, no matter what they say. The therapist does not judge clients' thoughts. The therapist creates a warm and accepting relationship with the clients. This acceptance makes it easier for clients to explore thoughts about themselves. Clients gain courage to accept parts of their personality they used to think were bad. They begin to feel their self-worth. They set up realistic goals and plan steps to reach them.

7. Why is unconditional positive regard important in client-centered therapy?

Study Guide 17-3

Cognitive and Behavior Therapies

For use with textbook pages 499–505

Key Terms

behavior modification a systematic method of changing the way a person acts and feels (page 499)

cognitive therapy using thoughts to control emotions and behaviors (page 499)

rational-emotive therapy (RET) aimed at changing unrealistic assumptions about oneself and other people (page 500)

behavior therapy changing undesirable behavior through conditioning techniques (page 502)

systematic desensitization a technique to help a patient overcome irrational fears and anxieties (page 503)

aversive conditioning links an unpleasant state with an unwanted behavior in an attempt to eliminate the behavior (page 504)

contingency management undesirable behavior is not reinforced, while desirable behavior is reinforced (page 504)

token economy desirable behavior is reinforced with valueless objects or points, which can be accumulated and exchanged for various rewards (page 505)

cognitive-behavior therapy based on a combination of substituting healthy thoughts for negative thoughts and beliefs and changing disruptive behaviors in favor of healthy behaviors (page 505)

Drawing From Experience

Do you ever promise yourself a reward if you do something? Are you more likely to actually do it then? What happens when you take part in some activity several times but never get much pleasure from it? Do you keep doing it?

The last section described the psychoanalytical and humanistic approaches to therapy. In this section, you will learn about the cognitive and behavior approaches.

Organizing Your Thoughts

Use the diagram below to help you take notes as you read the summaries that follow. Think about how behavior modification works. In the diagram, describe the three steps in counterconditioning.

Counterconditioning

■ 1. _____

　　■ 2. _____

　　　　■ 3. _____

Reading Essentials and Study Guide

Read to Learn

Introduction (page 499)

Behavior modification, or behavior therapy, is a step-by-step method for changing the way a person acts. For example, Brooks Workman wanted to cut down on the number of soft drinks she consumed. To get rid of this undesired behavior, she used behavior modification. She imagined herself putting a soft drink to her mouth and roaches suddenly coming out of the can.

4. If you imagined Brooks's scene a number of times, how do you think you would feel about consuming a soft drink?

_____

Cognitive Therapy (page 499)

Cognitive therapies focus on the way people think. The idea is that our thoughts can control our emotions and behaviors. False beliefs and flawed thinking can lead to emotional and behavioral problems. To improve our lives, we need to change our thinking patterns.

Albert Ellis developed **rational-emotive therapy (RET)**. He believed that people act reasonably, based on their way of thinking about life. Emotional problems happen when a person's way of thinking is not realistic. For example, a man seeks therapy because a woman left him. His life is empty without her. He must get her back. The problem, in the therapist's view, is the man's thinking. He defined his feelings for the woman as a need rather than a desire. By convincing himself that he needed her, he was in fact unable to go on without her. This faulty thinking, not the woman, was causing his depression. The goal of rational-emotive therapy is to correct such false, self-defeating beliefs. Rejection is unpleasant, but it is not unbearable.

Ellis said that behavior is like ABC. *A* is the *Activating* event. *B* is the *Belief* about it. *C* is the *Consequences*. A does not cause C. B causes C. So the therapist and client work to change B, the belief. To cure himself, the client must (1) realize his thinking is false, (2) see that he is causing himself problems by acting on false thinking, and (3) break the old false way of thinking.

Aaron Beck introduced a similar cognitive therapy that focuses on illogical thought processes. He believed in having clients test their own beliefs. For example, if a client believes that "I never have a good time," the therapist should point out that this is an assumption, not a fact. The client should look at the evidence and note times when she did have a good time. Beck's approach works well with depressed people. He believed that they focus on the negative and ignore the positive. They come to negative conclusions about their own worth. Therapists help clients recognize their negative thoughts. They help clients use more reasonable standards for evaluating themselves.

5. According to cognitive therapists, what might cause a person to be very depressed if she did not get the job she wanted?

_____

Behavior Therapies (page 502)

Behavior therapy emphasizes behavior rather than thoughts. It uses rewards and punishments to change unwanted behaviors. Behavior therapy assumes that the troubled person has learned to behave in an undesirable way. Whatever can be learned can be unlearned. The reasons for the behavior are not important. The focus is on changing the behavior. When people change their behavior, their thoughts change as well.

Counterconditioning is a method that puts the unwanted behavior (fear of snakes) together with a new, more desirable behavior (relaxation). This method has 3 steps. (1) The person ranks fears from least at the bottom to most feared at the top. (2) The person learns muscle relaxation techniques. (3) The person imagines or experiences each step up the list while learning to relax at each step. **Systematic desensitization** is a counterconditioning method used to overcome unreasonable fear.

Aversive conditioning links an unpleasant state with an unwanted behavior in an attempt to get rid of the behavior. For example, alcoholics can take medicine that makes them sick when they drink alcohol.

Behavior that is not reinforced tends to go away. In **contingency management**, client and therapist decide what behavior to reward to replace an unwanted behavior that they will not reward. For example, a student might say to himself, "If I get a good grade on the exam, I'll treat myself to ice cream." The reward is contingent (depends) on the behavior (getting a good grade). **Token economies** are reward systems in which desirable behavior earns an object or points. These things can then be exchanged for rewards.

6. If a student studies hard for exams but keeps getting poor grades, how is the student's behavior likely to change?

   _____

   _____

Cognitive-Behavior Therapy (page 505)

Cognitive-behavior therapy uses parts of both cognitive and behavior therapies. It tries to change clients' behavior and then tries to change their thoughts about the situation. The therapist may help the client identify her behaviors and thought patterns. They would work to replace negative thoughts with positive thoughts and practice new behaviors. Many self-help programs use this technique.

7. How is cognitive-behavior therapy different from behavior therapy?

   _____

   _____

   _____

Study Guide 17-4

Biological Approaches to Treatment

For use with textbook pages 506–510

Key Terms

drug therapy biological therapy that uses medications (page 507)

antipsychotic drugs medication to reduce agitation, delusions, and hallucinations by blocking the activity of dopamine in the brain; tranquilizers (page 507)

antidepressants medication to treat major depression by increasing the amount of one or both of the neurotransmitters noradrenaline and serotonin (page 508)

lithium carbonate a chemical used to counteract mood swings of bipolar disorder (page 508)

antianxiety drugs medication that relieves anxiety and panic disorders by depressing the activity of the central nervous system (page 508)

electroconvulsive therapy (ECT) an electric shock is sent through the brain to try to reduce symptoms of mental disturbance (page 509)

psychosurgery a medical operation that destroys part of the brain to make the patient calmer and freer of symptoms (page 510)

prefrontal lobotomy a radical form of psychosurgery in which a section of the frontal lobe of the brain is severed or destroyed (page 510)

Drawing From Experience

If you were depressed, would you be willing to take a pill to reduce it, even if it caused you to gain a lot of weight? The last section discussed different cognitive and behavior therapies. In this section, you will learn about therapies applied to the physical body.

Organizing Your Thoughts

Use the diagram below to help you take notes as you read the summaries that follow. Think about the different categories of drugs used to treat psychological problems. List the four types below and describe the types of disorders they treat.

Main Types of Drugs	Used to Treat
1.	5.
2.	6.
3.	7.
4.	8.

Read to Learn

Introduction (page 506)

Antibiotics can clear up ear infections. Is it possible that medicines might cure psychological problems? Some experts think that biological therapies, such as medicines, should be used only when psychotherapy fails. Others believe a combination of psychotherapy and biological therapy is the answer for many patients.

9. From what you know about psychological problems, why do you think medicine might help in some cases?

_____

Biological Therapy (page 507)

Biological approaches assume that there is a physical reason for mental problems. Biological methods include medicine, electric shock, and surgery. These treatments must be done by medical doctors, such as psychiatrists. Psychologists can help decide if a biological approach might work for a patient.

Drug therapy is the use of medicines. There are four main types of drugs used for psychological problems: antipsychotic drugs, antidepressants, lithium, and antianxiety drugs. Drugs treat symptoms, not causes of disorders. When patients stop taking the drug, their symptoms come back.

Antipsychotic drugs are tranquilizers. They can calm schizophrenics and reduce their delusions and hallucinations. Antipsychotic drugs block the activity of dopamine. These strong drugs have serious side effects, including shaking, lack of coordination, and very stiff muscles.

Antidepressants relieve depression by adjusting levels of noradrenaline and serotonin in the body. They also help cases of anxiety, phobias, and obsessive-compulsive disorders. Side effects may include dizziness, tiredness, and weight gain.

Lithium carbonate counteracts the wide mood swings of bipolar disorder. It controls the body's norepinephrine levels.

Antianxiety drugs are sedatives or mild tranquilizers. They relieve anxiety and panic disorders by slowing the activity of the central nervous system. The main side effect is drowsiness. However, use over a long time can cause dependence.

Electroconvulsive therapy (ECT) commonly called shock treatment, involves sending an electric shock through the brain to relieve severe depression and some types of schizophrenia. The shock causes a convulsion or seizure that lasts up to a minute. As applied today, this treatment causes little discomfort to the patient. Still, this therapy is controversial and must be applied with great caution.

Psychosurgery is brain surgery done to treat psychological problems. It destroys part of the brain. The most common type is **prefrontal lobotomy**. This surgery destroys the brain's frontal lobe, which controls emotions. This surgery is used to treat extremely violent behavior. It is a very serious treatment that is seldom used now, as new drugs offer other options.

10. Why might someone taking lithium decide to stop taking it?

Study Guide 18-1

For use with textbook pages 519–525

Interpersonal Attraction

Key Terms

social psychology seeks to explain how our thoughts, feelings, perceptions, and behaviors are influenced by interactions with others (page 519)

social cognition focuses on how we perceive, store, and retrieve information about social interactions (page 519)

physical proximity the distance of one person to another (page 522)

stimulation value the ability of a person to interest you in or to expose you to new ideas and experiences (page 523)

utility value the ability of a person to help another achieve his or her goals (page 523)

ego-support value the ability of a person to provide another person with sympathy, encouragement, and approval (page 523)

complementarity the attraction that often develops between opposite types of people because of the ability of one to supply what the other lacks (page 525)

Drawing From Experience

Think about your closest friends. Are they like you in many ways? Do you live close to each other and participate in many of the same activities? What do you like about them?

In this section, you will learn about why friends are important. You will also learn some reasons why we choose the friends we do.

Organizing Your Thoughts

Use the diagram below to help you take notes as you read the summaries that follow. Think about the rewards people get from friendships. List the three rewards below and give an example of each.

Rewards of Friendship	Examples
1.	4.
2.	5.
3.	6.

Copyright © by The McGraw-Hill Companies, Inc.

Reading Essentials and Study Guide

Read to Learn

Introduction (page 519)

People need to interact with other people. That is, we need to talk to and do things with other people. **Social psychology** is the study of how our interactions with others influence our thoughts, feelings, and behaviors. Every day we make judgments about others based on who we think they are. When we interact with them, we must adjust our judgments to explain their behavior and ours. **Social cognition** is the study of how we perceive, store, and retrieve information about our interactions with others.

7. What do you think life would be like if you lived on an island by yourself?

_____

Why You Need Friends (page 520)

As infants, we depend on others to meet our needs. Later, we seek personal contact for the same reason, even though we can care for ourselves. We have developed needs for praise, respect, love, the sense of achievement, and other rewarding experiences. Only other human beings can satisfy these needs.

Social psychologists have found that we need company most when we are afraid or anxious. Stanley Schachter designed an experiment to test the old saying "Misery loves company." He arranged to have college women come to his laboratory. He told one group that they would receive painful shocks to study the effect of electricity on the body. This produced high anxiety in that group. He told the other group that the shocks would produce a tingling feeling that they might even find pleasant. He told both groups to wait. He handed out a questionnaire that asked each woman if she would like to wait alone or with others. Most of the high-anxiety group chose to wait with others. Most of the low-anxiety group chose to wait alone. This experiment showed that high anxiety produces a need to be around others.

We also need company when we are unsure of ourselves and want to compare feelings or performance with others. For example, when you get tests back, you probably ask your friends how they did. Many people evaluate themselves based on how well they performed compared to others. In a similar experiment, Schachter made all the women anxious. Then he gave one group the choice of waiting alone or with others taking part in the same experiment. He gave the other group the chance to wait alone or in a room where students were waiting to see their advisers. The women who had the chance to be with others in the same difficult situation grabbed the chance. Most in the other group chose to wait alone rather than with unconcerned students.

Friends offer support in trying times. You can bounce ideas off them. They can act as a go-between when you have problems with other people. However, predicting the effects of friendships can be complex. Studies show that friends can help reduce high stress. Yet friends do not help much with average stress. They may even make low levels of stress worse.

8. Think about a recent conversation with a friend. What were you actually doing for each other in the interaction?

_____

How You Choose Friends (page 522)

One of the most important things that determines whether two people will become friends is **physical proximity**. This is how close to each other the people live or work. Being close together provides opportunity to interact. Psychologists studied people living in a small apartment building. Even though everyone was close to everyone else, the residents were more likely to become friends with the person next door than with anyone else. Psychologists think this is a result of the fear of meeting strangers. When two people live next door, go to the same class, or work in the same place, they find reasons to talk to each other without risking rejection.

You get three kinds of rewards from friendship. One is stimulation. Friends have **stimulation value** if they are interesting and can introduce you to new ideas or experiences. Another reward is utility. Friends have **utility value** if they are willing to give you their time and resources to help you achieve your goals. For example, a friend may help you with your homework so you can pass the course. A third reward is ego support. Friends have **ego-support value** when they can give you sympathy and encouragement when things go badly and approval when things go well. You consciously or unconsciously evaluate these three rewards in every friendship. A woman may like a man because he values her opinions (ego-support value) and she enjoys his company (stimulation value).

Physical appearance also plays a role in our choice of friends. People feel better about themselves when they associate with people that others consider desirable. In one study, participants viewed more physically attractive people as having more positive personality traits than unattractive people. Psychologists found that physical appearance is less important in choosing a marriage partner or close friend than when inviting someone to the movies. Both men and women seek out others whom they consider their equal in attractiveness.

Approval also influences our choice of friends. We all like people who agree with us. Yet studies suggest that we choose friends who give a mix of praise and criticism rather than all of one or the other. We take people more seriously if they see both sides.

We tend to choose friends whose backgrounds, attitudes, and interests are like ours. There are several explanations for this. First, agreement on what is exciting, worthwhile, and fun provides the opportunity for shared activities. Second, we feel uneasy around people who are constantly challenging our views. Third, people who agree on things find it easier to communicate.

Sometimes opposites attract because one person can supply something the other lacks. This is called **complementarity**. Still, being more alike than different seems to be more important to friendship.

9. Why do we seek friendships with people more like us rather than different from us?

_____

Study Guide 18-2

Social Perception

For use with textbook pages 527–532

Key Terms

primacy effect the tendency to form opinions on others based on first impressions (page 528)

stereotype a set of assumptions about people in a given category often based on half-truths and nontruths (page 530)

attribution theory a collection of principles based on our explanations of the causes of events, other people's behaviors, and our own behaviors (page 530)

fundamental attribution error inclination to over attribute others' behavior to internal causes (dispositional factors) and discount the situational factors contributing to their behavior (situational factors) (page 531)

actor-observer bias tendency to attribute one's own behavior to outside causes but attribute the behavior of others to internal causes (page 531)

self-serving bias tendency to claim success is due to our efforts, while failure is due to circumstances beyond our control (page 531)

nonverbal communication the process of communication through the use of space, body language, and facial expression (page 531)

Drawing From Experience

Have you ever judged what a stranger is like after seeing that person across the room? How does this first impression cause you to act toward that person? In this section, you will learn how you form first impressions about people. You will also learn about how you attach meaning to your behavior and that of others.

Organizing Your Thoughts

Use the diagram below to help you take notes as you read the summaries that follow. Think about how you form first impressions of people. Give an example of each key word below.

Key Word	Example
primacy effect	1.
schema	2.
stereotype	3.

Read to Learn

Introduction (page 527)

We often make judgments about people from a brief conversation. Or, we may think we know what people are like from looking at them across the room. From these first impressions, we decide whether or not to get to know the person better. You might judge a stranger to be "boring." Someone else might judge him to be "mysterious." First impressions depend on the person making the judgment.

4. Describe a time when you formed a really negative first impression of someone. Then later you discovered that the person wasn't like that at all.

_____

First Impressions (page 528)

The **primacy effect** is the tendency to form opinions of others based on first impressions. For example, a researcher invited a guest speaker to class. Before the lecture, students were given descriptions of the speaker. The descriptions were the same, except that some said the speaker was cold and the others said he was warm. After the lecture, students filled out evaluations. Students who were told the speaker was cold evaluated him as self-centered and without humor. Students who were told the speaker was warm described him as friendly and concerned. The change in one adjective in the description made a big difference in the way the students perceived the speaker.

First impressions can become self-fulfilling prophecies. That is, you act toward someone based on your first impression. This in turn affects how the person acts toward you. For example, you may have been in a bad mood the first day of class. You did not pay attention and made a few jokes. Your teacher labeled you a troublemaker. Then your teacher treated you like a troublemaker, so you lost interest in the class and stopped studying. In reality, you might be a great student who just had a bad day.

Forming impressions helps us put people into categories. The set of assumptions about a person or event is a *schema*. We develop a schema for every person we know. For example, your schema about intelligent people may be that they are active, motivated, and responsible. John's schema about intelligent people may be that they are boring, big-headed, and unfriendly. You both meet someone who seems intelligent. You are impressed with the person's enthusiasm as she talks about her work. John applies his schema and thinks the woman is boasting about her work. Schemas about people are judgments about their personality traits.

Sometimes we develop schemas for whole groups of people. You may have schemas for men, women, Asian Americans, African Americans, or certain religious groups. Such schemas are **stereotypes**. They are assumptions about a group of people based on half-truths or untrue information. The assumptions that males are independent and females are emotional are examples. Stereotypes can cause our first impressions to be prejudiced.

5. When you think of professional athletes, what descriptive words come to mind? These are part of your stereotype for this group of people.

_____

Attribution Theory (page 530)

You are waiting at a traffic light. Somebody behind you honks and motions frantically for you to get out of the way. Not sure what's happening, you move your car slowly over. You do not want him to think you are a pushover. The driver pulls even with you. He rolls down his window and says, "Thanks. My wife is in labor." **Attribution theory** is a set of principles about how we interpret other people's behavior. When you first heard the horn, you probably believed the man was a jerk. Attributing or relating a behavior to a personal characteristic is called *internal attribution*. After the man gave a good reason, you changed your conclusion. You attributed or related the behavior to an outside cause, the needs of the man's wife. This is called *external attribution*.

We often explain the cause of others' behavior as being inside them (internal attribution). We reject the external factors (external attribution) contributing to their behavior. This is **fundamental attribution error.** While we tend to focus on internal factors when explaining the behavior of others, we focus more on external factors when explaining our own behavior. This is **actor-observer bias.**

When there is glory to be claimed, we often show another form of error called a **self-serving bias.** In victory, we are quick to claim personal responsibility (internal attribution). In defeat, we blame events beyond our control (external attribution).

6. Suppose a softball player struck out three times in the game. Afterward she said, "That umpire wouldn't know a strike if it came with a label." What form of error would this person be displaying?

_____

Nonverbal Communication (page 531)

Communication requires a sender and a receiver. The message includes an idea plus an emotion. We can send messages verbally (with words). Or, we can send them as **nonverbal communication** (without words). We express nonverbal messages through body language, facial expressions, and use of space. For example, a friend says in a low voice, "It doesn't matter," and turns away. The nonverbal message is that his feelings are hurt. We often are not aware of the nonverbal messages we send. We are more aware of those we receive.

The way you carry your body communicates information about you. This is your *body language.* If you sit with your arms folded and legs crossed, you are protecting yourself. If you unfold your arms and stretch out, you are saying you are open to people. *Social rules* determine some body language, such as whom you can touch and where.

7. Describe the body language you see when you are having a disagreement with someone.

Study Guide 18-3

For use with textbook pages 533–540

Personal Relationships

Key Term

generational identity theory that people of different ages tend to think differently about certain issues because of different formative experiences (page 534)

Drawing From Experience

Have you ever loved a boyfriend or girlfriend? How did this love feel? Did you want to be with that person all the time? Did you think about him or her constantly?

The last section discussed first impressions and the ways you perceive behavior. In this section, you will learn about what makes love relationships healthy and lasting. You will also learn about adjusting to divorce.

Organizing Your Thoughts

Use the diagram below to help you take notes as you read the summaries that follow. Think about the three main parts of romantic love. List and describe each part below.

Parts of Romantic Love	Description
1.	4.
2.	5.
3.	6.

Read to Learn

Introduction (page 533)

Your personal relationships with family and others enrich your life and bring meaning to everyday experiences.

7. Think about someone you care about deeply. How has this person made your life richer?

_____

_____

Parent-Child Relationships (page 533)

Erik Erikson believed that the ways children interact with their parents early in life influence the ways they deal with people important to them in their adult lives. If an infant's first relationship with a caregiver is loving and responsive to his needs, he will develop trust in other people. This trust encourages him to be open to others. Children also learn what behavior will get what they want from their parents. They may learn to get what they want by being well-behaved. Or, pouting or throwing a temper tantrum may work. As children develop and form relationships with people outside their family, they apply what they learned in their family interactions. For example, from childhood experiences, a person might believe the only way to hold onto a friendship is to always say what pleases the other person rather than speak the truth.

Your parents also serve as your first model of a love relationship. As you watch your father and mother relate to each other, you form conclusions about what relationships should be like. Later, you might use this model as a guide in selecting and relating to a mate. Evidence suggests that people who grow up in a violent family are likely to continue that model of behavior against their own mate or children.

Parents often clash with their adolescent children. Each generation has a **generational identity**. This means that adolescents and their parents (different generations) tend to think differently about some things. Your generation has shared experiences that are different from the shared experiences of your parents' generation. For example, the Vietnam War and civil rights movement shaped the ideas of people growing up at that time. Increases in divorce, households in which both parents work, and computers and the Internet have influenced the way a younger generation thinks.

8. People who are now elderly grew up during the Great Depression. How might this shared experience influence the way their generation deals with money?

_____

Love Relationships (page 535)

Love means different things. You love a boyfriend or girlfriend differently than parents or friends. Sometimes couples do not adjust well to love and marriage because their expectations of love are too high. *Passionate love* is very exciting and intense. This intensity usually fades in any romance. When it does, it may turn into *compassionate love*. This kind of love includes friendship, trusting each other, and wanting to be with each other. Compassionate love is a more lasting love. It includes commitment and intimacy (deep closeness).

Zick Ruben studied the difference between liking and loving. Liking is based mostly on respect for another person and the feeling that he or she is similar to you. Romantic love has three main parts: (1) *need* or *attachment*, (2) *caring* or *the desire to give*, and (3) *intimacy*. The need part involves a strong desire to be with each other, to touch, to receive praise, and to fulfill and be fulfilled. The need part is the reason people describe love as a longing, hunger, or desire to possess someone. The caring part means that the couple is as concerned for their partner's happiness as they are for their own. It is a very giving side of love. Finally, all people in love share intimacy. This is a special knowledge of each other that they gain by openly sharing their inner thoughts and feelings. It comes from "exposing your true self" to the other person. This is very risky. Rejection of your "inner self" can be very hurtful.

Rubin found that most couples were equal on his "love scale." The woman expressed the same amount of love for her partner as he did for her. However, women tended to *like* their boyfriends more than their boyfriends *liked* them. Ruben's studies also showed that women and men are now equally romantic. Also, when both the man and woman express their interest in each other, the relationship deepens. So, love is not something that happens *to* you. You must create it.

According to Robert Sternberg's triangular theory, love has three parts: intimacy, passion, and commitment. The various combinations of these parts explains why people experience love in different ways. "Love at first sight" has a lot of passion but little commitment. In contrast, the love between people who have been married 50 years has much intimacy but probably less passion.

Two types of behavior help marriages succeed. *Endogamy* is our tendency to marry someone from our own social group. Marriages are more likely to succeed with someone similar to you. *Homogamy* is our tendency to marry someone who has similar characteristics to our own. These characteristics include physical attractiveness, age, and physical build.

In general, three things go into a healthy adjustment to marriage. (1) The couple's needs must go well together rather than conflict. (2) The husband and wife's image of themselves must be the same as their images of each other. (3) They should agree on the husband's and wife's roles in the marriage.

Adjusting to divorce is like adjusting to death. It is the death of a relationship. Divorce releases strong emotions: anger, fear, loneliness, and a feeling of failure. Both people must learn to cope with unfamiliar situations. The man may now have to cook for himself. The woman may have to fix a leaky faucet. Plus, they may not know what to do with the free time they suddenly have.

Most divorced people go through a period of mourning until they realize they survived. This is the first step in adjusting to divorce. They become less angry at their former partner. The pain of the past no longer dominates their lives. They begin calling old friends and making new ones. They construct a new identity as a single person.

Adjusting to divorce is more difficult for children than for their parents. First, children rarely want the divorce. Second, while the parents may have good reasons to divorce, the children do not understand them. Third, the children have no control over the outcome of divorce. They do not decide with whom they will live and how often they will see the other parent. Finally, young children do not have the emotional maturity to deal with the overwhelming experience.

9.   What is "intimacy" and why is it important in marriage?

_____

Study Guide 19-1

Group Behavior

For use with textbook pages 545–554

Key Terms

group a collection of people who have shared goals, a degree of interdependence, and some amount of communication (page 545)

task functions activities directed toward getting a job done (page 547)

social functions responses directed toward satisfying the emotional needs of members (page 547)

norms shared standards of behavior accepted by and expected from group members (page 547)

ideology the set of principles, attitudes, and defined objectives for which a group stands (page 548)

social facilitation an increase in performance in front of a crowd (page 549)

social inhibition a decrease in performance in front of a crowd (page 549)

group polarization theory that group discussion reinforces the majority's point of view and shifts group members' opinions to a more extreme position (page 550)

groupthink poor group decision making that occurs as a result of a group emphasizing unity over critical thinking (page 551)

sociogram a diagram that represents relationships within a group, especially likes and dislikes of members for other members (page 552)

Drawing From Experience

How many groups do you belong to? Try to list them. Do not forget groups such as family, school class, ethnic group, and country in which you are a citizen. You might be surprised at the number of hats you wear!

In this section, you will learn about the nature of groups and your role in them. You will also learn about group decision making and leadership.

Organizing Your Thoughts

Use the diagram below to help you take notes as you read the summaries that follow. Think about what makes a group hold together, or cohesive. List these things below.

Group Cohesion

1. _____

2. _____

3. _____

Read to Learn

Introduction (page 545)

A **group** is a collection of people who communicate with each other, share common goals, and influence how each other thinks and acts. People who come together but do not interact are not a group. For example, people waiting for a bus are simply a bunch of people. But if the bus almost hits them, they become a group, as they talk to each other about the near miss. *Interaction* is what makes them a group.

4. What groups influence your life?

_____

_____

What Are Groups? (page 545)

To be a group, a collection of people must show interdependence. Interdependence occurs when any action by one member affects the other members. For example, in groups of athletes and roommates, each member has a certain responsibility to the rest of the group. If he or she does not fulfill it, the other members will be affected. For athletes, the result may be losing the game. For roommates, it may be a messy apartment. In small groups, members directly influence each other. One member communicates directly with another. In larger groups, the influence is indirect. The interdependence between you and the president of the United States does not come from direct contact. Yet the president's actions affect you, and your actions, together with those of other Americans, affect the president.

Communication is another key feature of a group. Communication with each other helps members feel like part of the group. Through communication, they set group goals and commit to them.

Group members become interdependent because they share common goals. Groups usually form to carry out activities that no individual could do alone. For example, a band forms a group to create music that members alone could not create.

Groups serve two purposes. (1) **Task functions** are activities directed toward getting some job done. (2) **Social functions** are activities directed toward filling the emotional needs of members. All groups serve both functions. However, one function may be more important than the other in a particular group. For example, groups like construction crews are more task oriented. Social interactions occur within the group, but getting the job done is the most important purpose. People who take walks together have formed a group more for the social rewards than for completing the walk.

5. What kinds of things make your friends a group?

_____

_____

How Groups Are Held Together (page 547)

Things that hold groups together (make them *cohesive*) are norms and ideology and members' commitment to them. **Norms** are standards of behavior expected of group members. They are unwritten rules accepted by the group. For example, you follow unwritten rules about how you should talk to parents and friends. Would you use the same words with both your parents and your friends? Probably not. Members who go against group norms are punished in some way. For example, a norm among your friends may be that you wear a certain kind of athletic shoe. If you wear the "wrong" kind, the group may express disapproval. If you go against a norm that is very important to the group, the punishment may be worse. You may be thrown out of the group.

Ideology is the set of attitudes and goals shared by the group. For a group to be cohesive, members must have these values in common. For example, members of the National Organization for Women share a goal of ending discrimination against women.

For groups to be cohesive, members must feel a commitment to group norms and ideology. Requiring some personal sacrifice increases commitment. For example, if you have to pay money or undergo some initiation to join, you will be more loyal to the group. Participation also strengthens group commitment. When you actively participate in group decisions and share in the rewards, you will feel more like you belong to the group. Commitment works both ways. Members must commit to the norms and ideology of the group. The group must respond to the needs of its members.

6. Describe some norms in a group you belong to.

_____

_____

_____

Types of Groups (page 549)

Members who identify with a group are the *in-group*. The *out-group* is everyone who is not in the in-group. A *primary* group is a group of people who interact daily face-to-face. Because you interact so often with a primary group, the exchanges can get emotional. For example, you see your family every day. You eat, sleep, and have fun with them. You probably also fight with them. A *secondary* group is a larger group with whom you have looser ties. For example, your psychology class is a secondary group.

7. Give another example of a primary group and a secondary group in your life.

_____

_____

_____

Social Facilitation Versus Social Inhibition (page 549)

Social facilitation is the tendency to perform better in front of a crowd. **Social inhibition** is a tendency to perform less well in front of a crowd. Both may occur because the presence of a crowd increases your physical excitement. Studies show that your level of performance is likely to increase in front of others if the task is simple and well-learned. A crowd is likely to reduce your performance on more complex or unfamiliar tasks. For example, suppose you are an expert tennis player but a beginner at the piano. A crowd will likely drive you to play tennis at top form. However, a crowd will probably cause your piano playing to be worse than usual.

8. Describe something that you did well in front of others. Were you doing something that you know well?

_____

_____

_____

_____

_____

_____

Interactions Within Groups (page 550)

Groups provide members with values and an identity. Each person has a role to play in the group's activities. The different roles and how the roles work together in the group are *group structure*. Group structure includes personal relationships among members. It includes each person's rank in the group in such areas as power, status, and popularity. Also, it includes each person's role. A *role* is behavior the group expects of a member. When your class meets, someone has the role of teacher and others have the role of students. Each of us has *multiple roles* because we belong to many groups. You may play the role of student at school and the role of organizer in your friendship group.

Groups make decisions. For example, you and your friends discuss what to do Saturday night and make a decision. **Group polarization** is a theory that group discussion strengthens the view of the majority. It shifts members' opinions to a more extreme position. During the discussion, the view most members hold gets repeated many times. This repetition causes people to feel more strongly about that view than they did before the discussion.

Groupthink is poor group decision making that occurs when groups emphasize sticking together over critical thinking. Groups stuck in groupthink fail to evaluate their options. Group members do not criticize each other because they want to please other members. When no one expresses opposing views, the group does not think critically about its options. The result is a bad decision. To avoid groupthink, leaders should not promote their views too strongly. Instead, they should encourage open discussion. Members should hear all opinions and challenge one another's views.

When studying groups, psychologists use a diagram called a **sociogram**. This diagram shows the relationships within the group, especially who likes or dislikes whom. Psychologists ask members questions like with whom they would like to go to a party, vacation, or do a task. Psychologists use these responses to create a sociogram to help them examine communication patterns in the group. In one experiment, researchers learned that groups with a central leader can make decisions more quickly than groups without a clear leader, but group members were less satisfied with the process. So, task-oriented groups will work best with a central leader to make decisions. Social groups will work best when members have more say in decisions.

All groups have a leader. This person has a lot of influence on the members. Most of us think of leadership as a *personality trait*. This is partly true. Leadership is the ability to get people to go along with you. Studies show that leaders tend to be more confident, high energy, outgoing, and intelligent than other group members. Other researchers say that leaders have concern for both getting the job done and the welfare of group members. Some leaders are more focused on the job. Others are more concerned with keeping group members happy.

Different types of leaders may be needed in different situations. Groups with internal conflict need a leader who is good with people. Groups with a serious task at hand need a task-oriented leader. A group needs a *transformational leader* if it needs large-scale organizational change. Transformational leaders are charismatic. This means that they have a stronger than usual ability to persuade people to follow them.

The three leadership styles are authoritarian, laissez-faire, and democratic. An *authoritarian* leader makes all the decisions and assigns tasks to group members. A *laissez-faire* leader takes only a small role in group decision making. A *democratic* leader encourages members to come to a decision by agreement.

9. Why is it important to express opposing views in group decision making?

_____

_____

_____

_____

_____

_____

_____

Study Guide 19-2

For use with textbook pages 555–562

Conformity and Obedience

Key Terms

conformity acting in accord with group norms or customs (page 556)

obedience a change in attitude or behavior brought about by social pressure to comply with people perceived to be authorities (page 558)

Drawing From Experience

Have you ever been the only one in a group with a particular opinion? Did you stick to your opinion or give in to the views of the rest of the group?

The last section discussed groups and group roles, decision making, and leadership. In this section, you will learn about the pressures on people to conform to a group and to obey orders.

Organizing Your Thoughts

Use the diagram below to help you take notes as you read the summaries that follow. Think about the famous experiments by Stanley Milgram and Philip Zimbardo. Briefly describe the results of each experiment.

Experiment	Results
Milgram	1.
Zimbardo	2.

Read to Learn

Introduction (page 555)

Sometimes we do not make decisions based on our own reasoning. We just do what everybody else is doing. The pressure to conform can be strong.

3. Give an example of something you do just because "everybody else does it."

_____

Group Pressure to Conform (page 556)

Conformity is anything you do because of direct or indirect group pressure. For example, you probably dress the way your friends dress.

In one experiment, Solomon Asch found that many people will conform to other people's ideas of truth, even when they disagree. If you had participated in the experiment, this is what you would have experienced. You and six other students sit in a room. A line is projected on a screen in front of all seven of you. You are then shown another view of three lines and are asked to pick the one that is the same length as the first one. One of the three is exactly the same length. The other two are different. Answers are given in order. You are the sixth person to answer. Everyone agrees on the right answer the first few trials. But on the next one, the first person gives an answer that you are sure is wrong. The next four people answer the same as the first person. After a number of such trials, almost a third of the people in your position begin to answer the same way as the first five people do, even though they know the answer is wrong. In the experiment, the other people are actors who were told to give the wrong answer. When researchers asked participants why they went along, the participants said they did not want to appear different from the others. Why the conformity? According to one theory, children are taught that being liked and accepted is extremely important. Conformity is one way to gain this approval.

Studies show that it is hardest to stand alone. Sometimes the view of a few can win over the larger group. When someone expresses an opposing view, this reduces the pressure on the rest of the members to conform. Then people are more likely to really examine their views rather than just go along. *Compliance* occurs when we outwardly give in to pressure to conform, but we do not change our private beliefs.

Several things make a person more likely to conform. These include (1) belonging to a group that considers the group more important than individuals, (2) a desire to be liked, (3) low self-esteem, (4) shyness, and (5) lack of knowledge of the task.

4. What are some reasons why people conform, even when they know the others are wrong?

_____

_____

Obedience to Authority (page 558)

Many people serve as authorities—parents, teachers, police officers, and the boss at work. People with authority give orders and expect you to obey. **Obedience** is doing what people in authority tell you to do. Obedience can be good or bad. For example, obeying the orders of a firefighter in an emergency is a good idea. But history shows that sometimes people obey unreasonable orders. For example, Nazis during World War II committed terrible acts in obedience to their leader, even though those acts went against their conscience.

In a famous experiment, Stanley Milgram told participants that they were testing the effects of punishment on memory. One participant was to be the "teacher" and the other, the "learner." In reality, the learner was Milgram's assistant. The teacher was to read into a microphone a list of words that the learner was to memorize. The learner was in another room. If the learner did not say the list correctly, the teacher was to give an electric shock. Milgram wanted to see how far the teacher would follow his instructions to give increasing amounts of shock to a fellow human being. The teacher saw the learner being strapped into a chair and the electrodes attached, so the teacher really believed the learner was receiving the shocks. In reality, the learner received no shocks. The "generator" dial that the teacher saw showed amounts of shock from mild to "Danger: Severe Shock." As the experiment continued, the learner kept making mistakes. The researcher told the teacher to keep increasing the shock. At 300 volts, the learner pounded the wall and refused to continue answering. The researcher told the teacher to count no answer as wrong. In the end, 65 percent of participants gave the full range of shocks. These were not bad people. Many showed signs of extreme tension and said they wanted to stop. Yet, they kept obeying the authority figure.

Why did people obey? Participants considered the researcher a real authority. They assumed he knew what he was doing, even when the instructions went against their own standards of moral behavior. Also, society teaches people to obey authority. Getting up and leaving would have gone against the unwritten rules of acceptable social behavior.

Philip Zimbardo ran another experiment that caused ordinary people to act against their normal standards of behavior. Zimbardo divided male volunteers into two groups: "prisoners" and "prison guards." He sent both groups to live in a "prison" set up in the basement of a university building. He gave the guards instructions to keep order. Within two days, most guards became drunk with power. They acted cruelly toward prisoners, often without reason. They expected prisoners to follow the rules without question. If they did not, they lost the privilege to read or write letters. Sometimes the guards made the prisoners do embarrassing things, like washing toilets with their bare hands.

Prisoners began to show signs of extreme stress. They acted depressed, yelled at guards, and later became passive from defeat. Some developed psychological illnesses and rashes. The emotional reactions were so strong that researchers ended the experiment early. The roles these people adopted changed the way they acted. This experiment showed the power that situations can have in changing how we feel, think, and behave.

Both Milgram's and Zimbardo's experiments raised questions about the ethics of psychological experiments. How would you feel if you had been a participant in either of these experiments? Since these experiments, new standards have been set to protect experiment participants from harm.

Why did the Germans obey Adolf Hitler's commands to kill many thousands of people? Why do cult members sometimes obey their leader's command to commit suicide? These orders are unreasonable, so why do people obey them? We are taught to obey authority figures. We obey parents, doctors, and teachers. We also learn to follow orders. We follow traffic rules, school rules, and family rules.

5. Why do you think these two experiments raised ethical questions?

_____

Study Guide 19-3

Conflict and Cooperation

For use with textbook pages 564–570

Key Terms

aggression behavior intended to do physical or psychological harm to others (page 565)

catharsis releasing anger or aggression by letting out powerful negative emotions (page 566)

altruism helping others, often at a cost or risk, for reasons other than rewards (page 568)

diffusion of responsibility the presence of others lessens an individual's feelings of responsibility for his or her actions or failure to act (page 569)

bystander effect an individual does not take action because of the presence of others (page 569)

social loafing the tendency to work less hard when sharing the workload with others (page 569)

deindividuation individuals behave irrationally when there is less chance of being personally identified (page 570)

Drawing From Experience

Think about all the violence you see on TV and in movies and video games. Has seeing these scenes all the time made violence seem "normal" to you? Do you think it has added to violent behavior in our society? In this section, you will learn about aggression, group conflict, and altruism.

Organizing Your Thoughts

Use the diagram below to help you take notes as you read the summaries that follow. Think about ways to control aggression. List four of them in the diagram below.

1. _____   2. _____

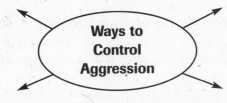

Ways to Control Aggression

3. _____   4. _____

Read to Learn

Introduction (page 564)

Aggression is behavior intended to do physical or psychological harm to others. Violence and aggression seem to be increasing in our society. What causes humans to act in ways that harm others? Psychologists have proposed that biology, learning, personality, and the person's environment all influence aggressive behavior.

5. Describe a violent act you have seen or heard about. Why do you think the person acted that way?

_____

_____

_____

Aggression (page 565)

Some animals are naturally aggressive. For example, when injured, a usually friendly dog can become mean. This is an inborn biological reaction. Humans may also have things in their biological make-up that cause aggression. Too much of the chemical serotonin in the brain can cause violent behavior. But biology is not the only reason.

Albert Bandura's social learning theory proposes that children learn aggressive behavior by watching their parents. Parents who use aggression to discipline their children may be teaching them to be aggressive. Television, movies, video games, and music may also teach aggressive behavior to children. Children see so much violence in the media that they become numb to the horror of it.

Some personality traits are common among aggressive people. Examples are a tendency to act without thinking, not having much feeling for others, and being self-centered. Aggressive children usually become aggressive adults.

Sometimes events in the environment lead to violent behavior. The *frustration-aggression hypothesis* suggests that failure to get something expected leads to aggression. But Berkowitz proposed that frustration leads to aggression only in certain instances. For example, a stranger bumps you. You may hit the person if you have hit someone and the results were good for you. But you probably would not hit the person if you have never been in a fight or have had bad results from fighting.

6. Describe the personality traits of someone you think is a "bully."

_____

_____

_____

Controlling Aggression (page 566)

One method to control aggression is through **catharsis**. This involves releasing anger or aggression by expressing powerful negative emotions. For example, when you are angry you might find an outlet by talking to a friend, playing hard in a soccer game, or kicking a toy around. Opponents of catharsis think that expressing aggression may lead to more aggression. Another way to control aggression is to punish children for violent behavior, within reason. Too much punishment can cause violence. We can also teach people to accept frustrations and move on or react to them in ways other than violence. If people do not view violence as an option, they will not use it.

7. How might hitting a punching bag when angry cause more rather than less aggression?

_____

_____

_____

Group Conflict Versus Cooperation (page 566)

Conflict between groups happens all the time. Some amount of tension can exist between women and men, workers and bosses, young and old. To study relations among groups, psychologists set up a boys' camp. The boys did not know they were part of an experiment. The boys were divided into two groups. Each group did the usual camp activities together. Friendships and group spirit developed. Then the researchers brought the groups together for a tournament. As expected, tension and aggressive behavior developed between the groups. Next, the researchers brought the groups together for fun activities, like a movie. This did not end the conflict. Next, researchers set up "emergencies" that required the boys to work together. They told the boys that the water line was broken. If they did not work together to find and fix the problem, they would all have to leave camp. As the boys from both groups cooperated to solve these emergencies, conflict decreased. Friendships developed among boys of opposing groups. Psychologists learned that groups can develop hostility toward each other just from competition. The key factor in getting rid of group conflict was cooperation. A *social trap* occurs when individuals in a group decide not to cooperate.

8. Give a real-life example of groups that are sometimes in conflict coming together to solve a problem.

_____

_____

_____

Altruism (page 568)

Altruism is helping others for reasons other than rewards. Often, altruism involves a cost or risk to the helper. For example, if you saw a man trying to steal a woman's purse, would you help or stay out of it? Often people feel less responsibility to act when other people who could help are present. This idea of spreading the responsibility around is called **diffusion of responsibility**. Someone seeing the purse snatching would be less likely to help the woman if other people are nearby. Everyone tends to think someone else will do it. Also, bystanders assure each other that getting involved is not a good idea. This is the **bystander effect**. Another influence that keeps individuals from acting is the tendency to play down the need to respond.

Social loafing is the tendency to work less hard when sharing the workload with others. When a large group is working on something together, the contributions of individual members are not as obvious. Some people may feel that no one will notice if they do not do their share.

When people act according to what they think is right, they are being *individualistic*. **Deindividuation** occurs when people lose their sense of self and just go along with the group. Why did normally pleasant people throw rocks at innocent people during the Los Angeles riots? Being in a crowd may reduce the awareness of self. People in crowds are anonymous. Probably no one can identify who threw the rocks.

Social pressure can be positive, too. Most people want others to like them. This is a powerful source of pressure for people to behave in a socially acceptable way.

9. If people give money to a charity because they can take the amount off their taxes, are they being altruistic? Explain.

_____

_____

_____

_____

_____

_____

_____

_____

_____

_____

Study Guide 20-1

Attitude Formation

For use with textbook pages 577–581

Key Terms

attitude predisposition to act, think, and feel in particular ways toward a class of people, objects, or an idea (page 577)

self-concept how we see or describe ourselves; our self-perception (page 580)

Drawing From Experience

If someone asked you to describe yourself, what would you say? What parts of your description are really your attitudes about things? How do you think you developed your attitudes? This section describes what attitudes are, where they come from, and what they do for us.

Organizing Your Thoughts

Use the diagram below to help you take notes as you read the summaries that follow. Think about how we develop attitudes. Briefly describe how each method below shapes attitudes.

Where Attitudes Come From	Description
Classical Conditioning	1.
Operant Conditioning	2.
Cognitive Evaluation	3.
Observational Learning	4.

Read to Learn

Introduction (page 577)

An **attitude** is the tendency to respond in certain ways toward people, things, or ideas. It has three main parts: (1) a belief about something, (2) a feeling about that thing, and (3) a tendency to act toward that thing in certain ways. For example, what is your attitude toward the president of the United States? Do you *believe* he is doing a good job? Do you *feel* you trust him? Would you *act* to vote for him?

5. What is your attitude toward homework? Describe your attitude in terms of the three main parts.

_____

_____

Where Attitudes Come From (page 578)

Classical conditioning can create attitudes by pairing two stimuli. For example, a dog likes to eat meat, so it wags its tail when given meat. When the first stimulus is put together with a second one, the individual begins to show the same attitude toward the second stimulus. For example, if the dog hears the tone of a tuning fork whenever it receives meat, it will begin to wag its tail when it hears the sound alone. The dog learned a positive attitude toward the sound of the tuning fork.

Operant conditioning can also create attitudes. We receive praise and approval for expressing certain attitudes. We may be punished for expressing others. We learn to express the attitudes that bring rewards.

We also form attitudes by thinking things through. This is cognitive evaluation. Suppose you are not sure if you want to go to college. You may make a list of the pros and cons. From this evaluation, you form your attitude about going to college.

You may also develop your attitudes by watching and imitating others. For example, you probably formed your attitudes about dress by seeing what your friends wear. Your culture, parents or guardians, and friends or peers all shape your attitudes.

Culture influences everything from our taste in food to our attitudes about relationships. Most Americans consider eating worms disgusting. Yet in some parts of the world, worms are a favorite food.

6. Give an example of an attitude that you and your best friend share.

_____

_____

Functions of Attitudes (page 580)

Attitudes help us define ourselves. Ask a friend to describe herself. Along with a physical description, she may include her attitudes about some things. For example, she may say that she tries to be a good student and is a strong supporter of equal rights for women. These attitudes help her define who she is. They make up her self-concept. Our **self-concept** is how we see ourselves. If you have a positive self-concept, you will tend to act and feel positively. If you have a negative self-concept, you will tend to act and feel negatively.

Our attitudes serve as guidelines for understanding and categorizing people, objects, and events. For example, you may link negative feelings to walking in dark alleys. You may link positive feelings with friendly people. These attitudes tell you to avoid dark alleys and seek out friendly people.

7. What are some attitudes that define you?

_____

_____

Study Guide 20-2

Attitude Change and Prejudice

For use with textbook pages 582–588

Key Terms

compliance a change of behavior to avoid discomfort or rejection and gain approval (page 583)

identification seeing oneself as similar to another person or group and accepting the attitudes of another person or group as one's own (page 583)

internalization incorporating the values, ideas, and standards of others as a part of oneself (page 584)

cognitive dissonance the uncomfortable feeling when a person experiences contradictory or conflicting thoughts, attitudes, beliefs, feelings, or behaviors (page 584)

counterattitudinal behavior the process of taking a public position that contradicts one's private attitude (page 585)

self-justification the need to rationalize one's attitude and behavior (page 586)

self-fulfilling prophecy a belief, prediction, or expectation that operates to bring about its own fulfillment (page 586)

prejudice preconceived attitudes toward a person or group that have been formed without sufficient evidence and are not easily changed (page 587)

discrimination the unequal treatment of individuals on the basis of their race, ethnic group, age, gender, or membership in another category rather than on the basis of individual characteristics (page 588)

Drawing From Experience

Is there someone in your life that you really admire? Do you tend to adopt that person's views? Do you have a little brother or sister who tries to act like you?

The last section discussed the nature of attitudes, how they form, and how they become part of your self-concept. In this section, you will learn about changing attitudes, how actions affect attitudes, and prejudice.

Organizing Your Thoughts

Use the diagram on the next page to help you take notes as you read the summaries that follow. Think of ways people use to reduce cognitive dissonance. List them on the diagram.

1. _____

| Ways People Reduce Cognitive Dissonance |

2. _____

3. _____

Read to Learn

Introduction (page 582)

Three main processes involved in forming and changing attitudes are compliance, identification, and internalization. If you praise a recording artist because everyone else does, you are complying. If you agree with everything an admired friend says about the artist, you are identifying with your friend's attitudes. If you really like the artist's songs, no matter what other people think, you are expressing an internalized attitude.

4. Suppose your friends think Nikes are the best shoes on the market. You actually like Adidas better, but you wear Nikes anyway. Are you complying, identifying, or internalizing?

_____

_____

_____

Attitude Change (page 582)

People's behavior reveals their attitudes. For example, suppose a man settles in his chair after dinner and launches into a discussion of his support of women's rights. Then he yells at his wife in the kitchen to bring him more coffee. Which would you believe—his words or his actions? Actions speak louder than words. Yet the same man may hire women for jobs he considers "men's work" because the people at work expect him to. People often adapt their actions to the wishes of others to avoid discomfort or rejection. This is **compliance**. The social pressure caused the man to adapt his behavior, but his attitudes did not really change.

Identification can actually change attitudes. **Identification** occurs when people want to define themselves in terms of a person or group. Therefore, they adopt that person's or group's attitudes and way of behaving. Suppose your favorite uncle is everything you hope to be. He is fun, smart, and successful. You identify with him and copy his behavior. One night, you argue about why you do not vote. As you listen to your uncle, you begin to agree with him. If someone as smart as your uncle votes, then maybe you should, too. You have adopted a new attitude.

Identification is different from compliance because the person actually believes the newly adopted views. However, these attitudes are based on emotional attachment to another person or group. They are not based on the person's own judgment. If the person's attachment to the person or group fades, the attitudes may also weaken.

The wholehearted acceptance of an attitude is **internalization**. The attitude becomes part of the person. Internalization is most likely to occur if the attitude fits well with the person's basic beliefs and self-image. Internalization is the most lasting of the three sources of attitude formation or change. Your internalized attitudes resist pressure from other people because your reasons for holding these views have nothing to do with others. They are based on your own evaluation of the issues.

5. When someone identifies with a gang, how do the person's attitudes and behavior change?

_____

_____

_____

Cognitive Consistency (page 584)

Many psychologists believe that people's attitudes change because they are always trying to get things to fit together logically inside their heads. This is called *cognitive consistency*. Holding two opposing attitudes can create inner conflict. **Cognitive dissonance** is the uncomfortable feeling that occurs when a person's behavior conflicts with thought, beliefs, or feelings. To reduce the dissonance, one or both of the attitudes must change. One way people reduce dissonance is to pretend the conflict is not there. For example, when faced with information on the hazards of smoking, smokers often treat it as nonsense spread by anti-smoking groups. Another way is to avoid the information that would cause conflict. For example, people may subscribe only to magazines that support their political views. Finally, some people reevaluate their attitude. If they think the new information is better, they revise their attitude.

6. Suppose someone chooses to be friends only with people who share his view on gun control. What method is this person using to reduce cognitive dissonance?

_____

_____

_____

Attitudes and Actions (page 585)

Clearly, your attitudes affect your actions. If you like Fords, you buy a Ford. But actions also affect attitudes. If you decided to buy a Chevy because you got a better deal, you will end up liking Fords less. Often, if you act and speak as though you have certain beliefs, you may begin to really believe this way. This is called **counterattitudinal behavior**. You take a public position that goes against your personal beliefs. Then you end up believing what you say. For example, people have given in to pressure and confessed to crimes they didn't commit. Then they begin to believe they *are* guilty. One explanation is that a person who acts one way and thinks another will experience dissonance. To reduce the dissonance, the person has to change the behavior or the attitude. A similar explanation is that people have a need to explain or justify their behavior. This is **self-justification**. In one experiment, participants were led to believe that they had injured other participants. Researchers then asked them how they felt about their victims. They found that the aggressors talked themselves into believing that their defenseless victims had deserved their injury.

It is also possible to act in a way that makes your belief come true. This is called a **self-fulfilling prophecy**. For example, suppose that you believe people are basically cold. Because of your negative attitude, you look away from others and act unfriendly. People think your actions are unfriendly, so they act coldly toward you. Your belief has produced the kind of behavior that makes the attitude come true.

7. Suppose you studied hard for a test but failed anyway. To protect your self-esteem, you tell several friends that you did not study. Soon you really believe that you did not study. What behavior are you displaying?

_____

_____

Prejudice (page 587)

Prejudice means prejudging, deciding beforehand what someone will be like instead of getting to know the person first. Believing stereotypes of people is prejudice. Patricia Devine proposed that when we encounter someone from a particular group, it sets off our stereotype process. For example, if you see an old person, you immediately think about your stereotyped characteristics of old people. Thomas Pettigrew suggested that group members may act in ways that uphold the stereotype. For example, members of a dominant group may act dominant. They speak first, interrupt more, and talk louder. Members of the less dominant group may listen more and show more courtesy.

Prejudice is an attitude. **Discrimination** is an action. It is the unequal treatment of members of certain groups based on group membership rather than on individual characteristics. It is possible to be prejudiced but not discriminate. The person must recognize the prejudice and not act on it.

8. Why is stereotyping a form of prejudice?

_____

_____

Study Guide 20-3

Persuasion

For use with textbook pages 590–596

Key Terms

persuasion the direct attempt to influence attitudes (page 590)

boomerang effect a change in attitude or behavior opposite of the one desired by the persuader (page 592)

sleeper effect the delayed impact on attitude change of a persuasive communication (page 594)

inoculation effect developing resistance to persuasion by exposing a person to arguments that challenge his or her beliefs so that he or she can practice defending them (page 595)

brainwashing the most extreme form of attitude change; uses peer pressure, physical suffering, threats, rewards for compliance, manipulation of guilt, and intensive indoctrination (page 595)

Drawing From Experience

Think of an advertisement you have seen recently. What was the ad trying to make you believe? How did the ad try to persuade you to believe this way? What kinds of things make one ad more persuasive to you than another? In this section, you will learn about how persuasion works to change attitudes and behaviors.

Organizing Your Thoughts

Use the diagram below to help you take notes as you read the summaries that follow. Think about three methods of persuasion, two common ones and one extreme. Give an example of each method listed below.

Method of Persuasion	Example
Foot-in-the-Door Technique	1.
Door-in-the-Face Technique	2.
Brainwashing	3.

Read to Learn

Introduction (page 590)

Advertisers use persuasion to encourage consumers to buy their products. **Persuasion** is a direct attempt to influence attitudes. Everyone uses persuasion. Parents try to persuade their children to conform to their values. Young people try to persuade their parents that they need a video game. In each case, the persuader hopes that changing the other person's attitudes will also change the person's behavior.

4. Why does McDonalds advertise?

_____

Persuasion (page 590)

The communication process has four parts. The *message* is only one part. The *source* of the message, the *channel* through which it is delivered, and the *audience* that receives it all play a role in the success of the message.

How the audience sees the source of a message is key to accepting or rejecting it. People are more likely to accept the message if they trust the source and think the source knows the subject. For example, if you want to know the best way to hit a baseball, you are more likely to accept instructions from a major league baseball player than from someone who never played the game. People are also more likely to go along with the message if they admire the source and want to be like him or her. This identification process explains why advertisers often use athletes in their ads.

Identification can also backfire. If you dislike the person delivering the message, you will likely take the opposite view. A change in attitude or behavior that is opposite the one desired by the persuader is the **boomerang effect**. For example, sales of a product may go down if the spokesperson gets arrested for beating his wife.

The channel (where, when, and how the message is delivered) also plays a key role in audience response. In general, personal contact is most persuasive. For this reason, candidates for office get out and meet the people. Evidence also suggests that television and movies are more effective media for persuasion than is printed matter. People tend to believe what they see and hear with their own senses.

The audience includes all people whose attitudes the communicator is trying to change. To persuade an audience to change its views, the communicator must understand who the audience is and why its members hold the views they do. Suppose you were trying to persuade people in a country where food is in short supply to use birth control. You provide all the needed information, but their behavior does not change. You need to know why they value large families. Perhaps children in that country begin working for pay at a young age. So having many children helps the family earn money. If this is the reason, then you might persuade them if you can offer financial rewards to families that limit their size.

One common strategy for persuading an audience is the *foot-in-the-door technique*. This involves making a small request that people are likely to agree to. Then you make a more demanding request. In one experiment, researchers

Reading Essentials and Study Guide

asked residents for permission to put a small sign reading "Be a Safe Driver" in a window of their homes. Later, another researcher asked people to put a large "Drive Carefully" sign in their front yard. Most of the people who agreed to the first request also agreed to the second. But few people who heard only the second request agreed to the sign.

Another strategy, the *door-in-the-face technique*, works like this. When you want people to agree to a request that they might otherwise reject, you first ask for something big. Then when they reject this request, as expected, you follow up with the smaller request. For example, you might ask a friend, "I'm helping someone move. Would you come over and help all weekend?" "No? Well, how about just stopping by Saturday morning to help move the big stuff?"

People think about messages at different depths. If they are very interested in the topic, they may thoughtfully consider each of your arguments. This is central route processing. If they are not interested in the topic, they may use *heuristics*. These are rules of thumb or shortcuts to arrive at a decision about the message. Rather than think deeply about it, people tune in to the peripheral or less important aspects of the message. For example, they may consider how much they like the source and the tone of voice. Advertisers take advantage of their audience's heuristic processing. They make sure to include nice-sounding words such as "fresh" or "natural" in their ads.

Attitude changes from persuasive messages usually fade away in a short time. Sometimes a persuasive message causes an attitude change after a period of time has passed. This is the **sleeper effect**. One explanation is that people tend to remember the message but forget the source. If the audience sees the source as negative, they may come to accept the message after their memory of the source fades. It may also be that sometimes it takes time for a message to "sink in."

You can learn to resist persuasion. One way to learn resistance is similar to an inoculation or vaccination against disease. The vaccine causes your body to produce defenses that make you immune to the disease. The **inoculation effect** is developing resistance to persuasion by being exposed to arguments that challenge your beliefs, so you can practice defending them. The attitudes that persuasion can most likely change are those you have not defended.

The most extreme form of attitude change is **brainwashing**. It involves psychological and physical torture. Studies on prisoners taken by the Chinese during the Korean War revealed brainwashing methods. The first step was to strip away the person's identity. In prison, the captors would isolate the prisoners, give them a number to replace their names, and surround them with people whose thoughts had been "reformed." As long as the prisoners held out, they were questioned and humiliated. Cooperation involved confessing to crimes against the people. When prisoners cooperated in any way, their captors rewarded them by making prison life a little easier. Eventually, after enduring extreme psychological and physical stress, prisoners often began to believe their confessions. Some cults also use forms of brainwashing to gain control over their members. A cult is a group of people who organize around a strong authority figure.

5. Advertisers are very careful about whom they select to promote their products. Why?

_____

Study Guide 21-1

For use with textbook pages 603–608

Careers in Psychology

Key Term

crisis intervention program short-term psychological first aid that helps individuals and families deal with emergencies or highly stressful situations (page 604)

Drawing From Experience

Do you wonder what kind of job would make you happy? Do the many choices sometimes overwhelm you? Do you think a job in some area of psychology might interest you?

The last section described some of the contributions that psychology has made to our lives. It also discussed the challenges ahead for the field. In this section, you will learn about several career opportunities in the field of psychology.

Organizing Your Thoughts

Use the diagram below to help you take notes as you read the summaries that follow. Think about the different jobs in psychology available to you. Also think about the school degrees needed for each one.

Careers in Psychology

High School	⟶	1._____	2._____
Associate Degree	⟶	3._____	
Bachelor's Degree	⟶	4._____	
Master's Degree	⟶	5._____	
Doctorate Degree	⟶	6._____	7._____

Read to Learn

Introduction (page 603)

You have many career options from which to choose. The field of psychology applies to many jobs, as you will learn in this section.

8. If you could work in the field of psychology, what kinds of things would you like to do?

_____

_____

_____

_____

_____

Careers in Psychology (page 603)

Employers want to hire people who offer special skills. Some jobs are open to high school graduates. But higher education opens more options. A Ph.D. in psychology would make you a specialist in an area. A bachelor's degree in psychology would give you choices among a variety of employers. This degree is also a good starting point for graduate work in sociology, social work, law, medicine, and education. Human behavior plays a role in all of these areas.

Psychology is both a science and a profession. As a science, psychologists study how people perceive, think, feel, and act. Professional psychologists use psychological principles to predict how people will act. They help people change their behavior. They also help businesses and communities change. Some jobs available in the field of psychology are described below.

Large hospitals and other agencies employ crisis hotline advisers. High school graduates and even high school seniors can hold this position. After completing a training program, these advisers work in **crisis intervention programs**. These programs offer short-term psychological first aid. They help mostly with two kinds of problems. One kind involves sudden crisis situations that are possibly life-threatening. These situations can come from a personal or family crisis, such as an argument or unexpected death of a loved one. The other kind of problem is a crisis that comes out of long-term stress over family or job problems. Hotline advisers have a list of mental health professionals and treatment programs in the area. They must calm the caller and identify the problem. Then they provide information about the right agency to contact for long-term care.

People who like psychology probably have an interest in behavior. This interest, with just a high school diploma, can help you become a successful salesperson. Good salespeople need to understand what motivates people. You must have good language skills. Also, you must be able to ask customers good questions to find out their needs. Then, you can identify the products that best meet their needs.

A mental health assistant is a new career field. It requires at least an associate degree. You can get this degree by completing a two-year course. The course prepares you for working in nursing homes, community mental health centers, centers for the mentally retarded, and special-education centers in public schools. Mental health assistants help with admission interviews. With supervision, they may give various psychological tests.

A personnel director in a business requires a bachelor's degree in psychology. It also requires courses in interviewing, testing, statistics, and law. A minor in management helps. This is not an entry-level job. Personnel directors make decisions about hiring and firing. They also develop worker training programs.

To be a school psychologist, you need a master's degree. An undergraduate major in psychology is helpful. You must also pass a test to be licensed in your state. School psychologists work with children who have problems in school. They give reading, aptitude, interest, and intelligence tests. They must also be able to understand the meaning of test scores.

Clinical psychologists must have a Ph.D. (a Doctor of Philosophy) or a Psy.D. (a Doctor of Psychology). In a Psy.D. program, students gain skills in psychotherapy. They learn testing, interviewing, and therapy work. Clinical psychologists are often self-employed. So, they also need skill in running a small business. They must develop working relationships with other mental health professionals in the area as well as with hospitals and care facilities. These contacts refer clients to them. Clinical psychologists spend most of their time doing individual and group therapy with their clients. It is not a 9-to-5 job. They must offer times when clients are free to visit. Clinical psychologists can also find employment in mental hospitals, Veterans Administration hospitals, and community mental health centers.

To be a consulting psychologist with a management consulting firm, you must have a Ph.D. In an industrial/organizational psychology program, you would learn management practices, testing, and strategies for working with people. Consultants must offer skills that companies do not normally have among their employees. Consultants work with companies for a short time, advising top management. For example, they might help a company design a control panel that takes human performance limits into account.

New areas of psychology often form to meet new challenges. Health psychology is a new area that focuses on the role of psychological processes in a person's health. Health psychologists might research obesity and try to find good treatments. They might also deal with how stress relates to illness.

9. Which job described above most appeals to you? Why?

_____

_____

_____

_____

_____

_____

_____

Study Guide 21-2

Psychology's Contributions

For use with textbook pages 610–616

Key Terms

ACT a standardized test that consists of four assessment tests that measure academic development (page 611)

SAT a standardized test that is an admission requirement at some colleges; the test measures verbal and mathematical reasoning abilities (page 611)

forensic psychology deals with diagnosis, evaluation, treatment, and testimony regarding the law and criminal behavior (page 615)

industrial/organizational psychology deals with the psychology of the workplace (page 615)

sports psychology studies athletics and athletic performance (page 615)

visualization mentally rehearsing the steps involved in a successful performance or process (page 615)

gerontology the study of aging (page 615)

Drawing From Experience

In what ways do you think psychologists have touched your life? Did you watch "Sesame Street" as a child? Did you know that this show was designed around principles discovered by psychologists?

In this section, you will learn what different types of psychologists do. You will also learn about the challenges facing the field of psychology today.

Organizing Your Thoughts

Use the diagram below to help you take notes as you read the summaries that follow. Think about the many contributions that psychology has made to everyday living.

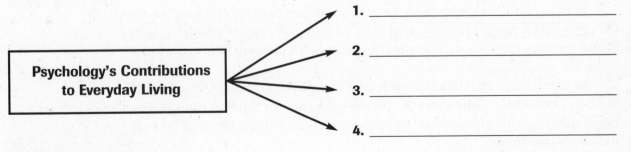

| Psychology's Contributions to Everyday Living |

1. _____
2. _____
3. _____
4. _____

Read to Learn

Introduction (page 610)

Many people do not know what psychologists do for a living. But psychology has made many contributions to life.

5. Name one thing that psychologists do that you did not know before you took this course.

_____

Psychology's Role in Mental Health (page 610)

One of psychology's greatest contributions is the development of forms of professional help. One form is psychotherapy. French doctor Philippe Pinel was a founder of psychiatry. In the 1790s, he unchained patients in mental wards. Pinel argued against the belief at that time that the mentally ill were possessed by demons. It took over 50 years for the U.S. to make the same progress. In the 1840s, teacher Dorothea Dix pushed for reform. Her efforts led to more reasonable treatment of the mentally ill. Former mental patient Clifford Beers was the guiding force behind the modern mental health movement. In the early 1900s, he published a book about his own illness and recovery called *A Mind That Found Itself*. In 1908, Beers started the Connecticut Society for Mental Hygiene to improve care for mental problems. It also provided information on mental illness to the public.

6. Why might giving information on mental illness to the public help improve care of the mentally ill?

_____

_____

Psychology's Role in Testing (page 611)

Psychologists created IQ (intelligence) tests that children take in elementary school. They also developed skills tests that colleges use for accepting students.

7. Why do you think the SAT stresses thinking skills more than recall of facts?

_____

_____

Psychology's Role in Everyday Living (page 612)

In many families today, both parents work. Day care for children is a major concern. Psychologists have studied the effects of day care on children. They found that day care is not a bad experience. It helps develop children's social skills.

In another study, Harry Harlow found that physical contact strengthens the bond between children and the people who care for them. It does not matter whether mothers breast-feed or bottle-feed their babies. Holding them is the important thing.

Psychologists have also helped design learning tools. For example, the PBS series "Sesame Street" was designed around the principles of learning. Studies show that this program educates young children in skills they will need in school.

Computer software uses some of B.F. Skinner's ideas on learning. Feedback, knowledge of results, and reinforcement are part of computer games as well as educational software. The work of many psychologists has also led to a clearer understanding about the challenges of aging.

8. Think about a video game you play. What kinds of "feedback" tell you that you did the right or wrong thing?

_____

Psychology Today (page 612)

Psychology can be grouped into two fields: experimental and applied. Experimental psychologists use scientific methods to study psychological processes and look for long-range answers. Applied psychologists put knowledge of psychology to work solving human problems.

The American Psychological Association (APA) is the world's largest scientific and professional organization for psychologists. Recently, the American Psychological Society (APS) was formed for educators and science-oriented psychologists. Many colleges have chapters of Psi Chi, an honor society for psychology students.

According to an APA survey, 43 percent of psychology students get master's degrees in counseling. Thirty-two percent major in clinical psychology. Fifteen percent major in school psychology. The remaining students get degrees in a research field. U.S. statistics place psychology among the fastest-growing fields in the twenty-first century. Also, the number of women in the field has increased rapidly. Ethnic minorities are still a minority in the field, but their numbers are increasing.

Forensic psychology is a type of applied psychology. It involves psychology and the law. Some of these psychologists study criminal behavior. Others study the effects on children who appear in court, counsel victims, and study jury selection. Forensic psychologists often have law as well as psychology degrees.

Industrial/organizational psychology deals with work and the workplace. Some psychologists in this field help businesses operate efficiently and provide a good work environment. Others work on union relations, harassment, job satisfaction, and worker motivation.

Sports psychology applies psychology to sports activities. Some sports psychologists help athletes improve performance through **visualization**. This is mentally reviewing steps in successfully performing the skill. Others study the benefits of sports participation and ethics in sports.

Challenges in psychology today include social change, psychology and minorities, and violence. Also, the aging of the population opens new challenges in **gerontology**, the study of aging. Today, the top killers of children are accidents, violence, and drugs. These are psychological, not physical, problems. They need to be solved by changing attitudes and behavior.

9. Are psychotherapists experimental or applied psychologists? Why?

_____

Answer Key

Chapter 1, Section 1

1. description of behavior
2. explanation of behavior
3. prediction about behavior
4. influence of behavior
5. Students' answers will vary. An example of a physiological need is the need to eat. An example of a cognitive need is the need to be motivated.
6. Students' answers will vary. Examples of behaviors that students want to understand may include love and anger.
7. Students' answers will vary. Examples of things students would like to learn about include why people fall in love, why we dream, and how people form groups.
8. Students who want to discover how human behavior works may cite a desire to make a contribution to improving the human condition. Students who want to help people solve their problems may cite the desire to see the immediate results of helping people.
9. Students' answers will vary. Encourage creative ways to remember the facts presented in Chapter 1 of the text.

Chapter 1, Section 2

1. structuralism
2. functionalism
3. inheritable traits
4. Gestalt psychology
5. psychoanalytic psychology
6. behavioral psychology
7. humanistic psychology
8. cognitive psychology
9. biological psychology
10. sociocultural psychology
11. Psychologists would be able to study the shape of people's heads and the bumps on it to predict behavior.
12. They knew that blood was warm and believed that the heart was the source of feelings.
13. Students' answers will vary. They should recognize that thinking about their thought patterns affects their thoughts. This is actually an altered state of consciousness.
14. Students' answers will vary. An example could be the use of reinforcement to encourage two different ethnic groups to work together.

Chapter 1, Section 3

1. private offices, mental hospitals, clinics, and prisons
2. schools or industrial firms
3. schools or research laboratories
4. schools or research laboratories
5. business firms and government agencies
6. business firms or government agencies
7. legal, court, and correctional systems
8. hospitals, clinics, or government agencies
9. research laboratories
10. Experimental psychologists practice basic science. Clinical and counseling psychologists practice applied science. The other fields listed including developmental, educational, industrial/organizational, and forensic may practice both basic and applied science.

Chapter 2, Section 1

1. Naturalistic observation involves observing participants in their everyday environments.
2. Case studies involve intensive study of an individual or group.
3. Surveys are questionnaires or polls used to learn about the attitudes or behaviors of many people.
4. Longitudinal studies are conducted with the same participants over a period of time.
5. Cross-sectional studies use participants from various age groups to measure such things as behavioral changes that occur over time.
6. Correlations compare two sets of data to see if there is a relationship.
7. Experiments test hypotheses using experimental and control groups to test variables and develop theories.
8. Jane Goodall studied chimpanzees in their native habitats to learn about their behavior.
9. Jean Piaget based his theory of intellectual development partly on case studies of his own children.
10. Opinion polls about political candidates are surveys.
11. The New York Longitudinal Study followed 133 infants as they grew to adulthood.
12. A study showing children of different ages the picture of a woman and asking the children to explain what the woman was thinking about is an example of a cross-sectional study designed to show the cognitive development at different ages.
13. An example of a correlation is the relationship between grades in school and IQ.
14. An experiment could be conducted using the amount of time spent studying as the independent variable and the grade on a test as the dependent variable and eighth-grade students as the participants.
15. Psychologists use similar methods to gather information but their procedures are more formal to ensure that the data gathered are reliable.
16. The sample is a random sample.
17. A survey is the method best suited to gather this information.

Chapter 2, Section 2

1. Self-fulfilling prophecies can be avoided by using double-blind studies.
2. Deceiving participants can be avoided by designing experiments that do not use deception.
3. Single- and double-blind studies can avoid the placebo effect.
4. Students' answers will vary. Common examples of influence include encouraging a friend to avoid a dangerous situation or helping a sibling learn a new skill.
5. A participant's expectations can result in an effect simply from the expectations themselves, not from the actual independent variable.
6. His experiment has been considered unethical because the participants were deceived into believing that they had harmed another person.
7. The placebo effect works because a person's expectations influence his or her reaction. There is no actual treatment.

Chapter 2, Section 3

1. frequency distribution
2. normal curve
3. mean
4. median
5. mode
6. standard deviation
7. correlation coefficient
8. range
9. Statistics help you compile and analyze the data you have gathered.
10. The mean is the mathematical average. The median is the middle score. The mode is the most frequent score. The correlation coefficient describes the strength and direction of the relationship between two sets of data. The range is the difference between the highest and lowest scores.
11. Past results indicate nothing about the future results when the results are due to chance. The results in this case are due to chance.

Chapter 3, Section 1

1. 2 to 3 months
2. 3 months
3. 4 months
4. 4 months
5. 5 to 6 months
6. 5 to 6 months
7. 7 to 8 months
8. 9 to 10 months
9. 8 to 10 months
10. 11 to 12 months
11. 12 to 13 months
12. They study an individual's physical, social, emotional, moral, and intellectual growth.
13. Students' answers will vary. Students should be able to identify some traits that are inherited and some that are not.
14. Students' answers will vary. The infant may be showing his or her feelings of pleasure, but if the child does not reach for the cookie, the smile may be an unrelated event to seeing the cookie.
15. Unless you notice other developmental problems, walking at 14 months should not cause great concern. The child simply had not reached maturational readiness for walking until this point.
16. Researchers have found a difference in perceptual maturity between young infants and crawling infants that allows the older infant to recognize danger.
17. It indicates that the child is applying the rules of grammar, even though this verb form is an exception to the rule.

Chapter 3, Section 2

1. E
2. C
3. D
4. B
5. A
6. Students' answers will vary. An example would be thinking that you could dig a hole deep enough to reach the other side of the earth.
7. The child has demonstrated the principle of conservation.
8. Imprinting is important for basic survival needs so the goslings stay close to their mother and imitate her behaviors.

Chapter 3, Section 3

1. Freud's theory of psychosexual development
2. Erikson's theory of psychosocial development
3. learning theories of development
4. cognitive-developmental approach
5. Students' answers will vary. Some examples include learning not to touch a hot stove, learning that hitting someone makes them sad, or learning that giving a gift to someone makes the giver and the receiver feel good.
6. An authoritarian parent would announce the curfew. A democratic/authoritative parent would discuss the curfew and allow the teen to have input into the decision. The permissive/laissez-faire parent may suggest a curfew, but allow the teen to come home whenever he or she would like. The uninvolved parent would not set a curfew and may not even be aware when the teen is at home.
7. Students' answers will vary. Reasons include society discouraging reporting such incidents, fear of the abuser, and not recognizing that the abuse is wrong.

Answer Key

8. Role taking allows children to explore everyday situations from different points of view.

Chapter 4, Section 1
Possible answers:
1. growth spurt
2. increased fat tissue
3. breasts and hips fill out
4. pubic hair develops
5. experience menarche
6. growth spurt
7. pubic hair and larger genitals develop
8. experience spermarche
9. shoulders broaden and trunk thickens
10. voice deepens
11. Student answers will vary. An example would be seeing teens engaged in conversation, rather than playing games.
12. Student answers will vary. An example would be the stress of increasing freedom and responsibility.
13. Teens need to learn to feel good about their bodies because it increases their self-esteem and gives them confidence in social situations.
14. Teenagers can choose abstinence, or avoiding harmful behaviors.

Chapter 4, Section 2
Possible answers:
1. Most adolescents go through a crisis of identity formation versus identity confusion.
2. Adolescents begin to see the future as reality, not as a game.
3. Identity crises arise because adolescents must make commitments on important matters such as occupation, religion, and political orientation.
4. Adolescents may experience four different attempts to achieve a sense of identity: identity moratorium, identity foreclosure, identity confused or diffused, and identity achievement.
5. Crisis is not the normal state for adolescents.
6. Human development, including adolescence, is a continuous process in which people learn by interacting with others.
7. Student answers will vary. An example is that children often spend money as soon as they get it, while adults realize the benefit of saving some of the money.
8. The person must be in Piaget's formal operations stage since they are able to think abstractly.
9. An example would be a person who is kind to people even when he or she is treated unkindly and a person who ignores a law to save a human life.
10. Adolescents must make decisions about occupation, religion, politics, sexual behavior, and other important life issues.

Chapter 4, Section 3
Possible answers:
1. attitudes toward marriage
2. choice of religion
3. future educational choices
4. basic values
5. social support
6. establishing an identity
7. choice of clothing
8. taste in music
9. depression
10. drug use
11. eating disorders
12. attempts at suicide
13. Student answers will vary, but should clearly show the relationship of social equals.
14. Parents may have set up their lives around their children and fear the changes that allowing the children to leave will bring in their own lives. Parents may also fear that children are not ready for the responsibilities of life on their own.
15. Student answers will vary. Common answers include choice of clothing, choice of friends, and attitudes about school and parents.
16. Teens may appear angry and rebellious. Their behavior may include truancy, running away, drinking, using drugs, or sexual promiscuity.

Chapter 4, Section 4
1. dominant
2. competitive
3. emotionally reserved
4. submissive
5. cooperative
6. emotionally responsive
7. Student answers will vary. Often boys choose to play with mechanical equipment or engage in physical play. Often girls enjoy playing with dolls or pretending to be mothers.
8. Student answers will vary. As a class discuss these examples and what they communicate to us about society's expectations for males and females.
9. Student answers will vary. Often boys are encouraged to mock fight or wrestle.
10. This would support the social learning theory.
11. Student answers will vary. Some will say that they work outside the home to help support their families. Others will say that the dominant reason is to allow women to reach their full potential.

Chapter 5, Section 1
1. slow decline in physical strength, speed, and reflexes
2. decline in the speed of processing information, but continued growth in acquiring information and expanding vocabularies

3. Levinson's stages of social development show ongoing development is marked by crisis or transitions about every 10 years.
4. Menopause occurs between 45 and 50 years of age.
5. decline in the speed of processing information, but continued growth in acquiring information and expanding vocabularies
6. Women may experience the "empty nest" syndrome when their last child leaves home. They may also experience midlife depression as her roles as wife, lover, mother, and daughter change.
7. A positive outlook on life during early adulthood has been shown to result in a better quality of life during old age.
8. Experience can compensate for slower reflexes by allowing the person to anticipate what is coming next. For example, in volleyball, an older person may anticipate the direction of a spike and react before the spike is even struck.
9. Student answers will vary. The environment should allow for creativity and a wide variety of experiences and challenges.
10. Men during midlife often choose to share their wisdom with those who are younger or they can long for the past. Those who experience generativity often experience a relative stability in midlife. Those who stagnate often experience extreme frustration and dissatisfaction in midlife. Women may experience the "empty nest" syndrome when the last child leaves home. They may also experience depression as their major functions in life—daughter, mother, wife, lover, and wage earner—change. This may be a time of freedom and redirection or a time of depression.

Chapter 5, Section 2
1. physical and mental decline are inevitable with age
2. Although physical decline may occur, it is not strictly a result of chronological age. Mental decline does not necessarily occur with age.
3. Older people do not engage in sex or have sexual desires.
4. If physical health is good and the person has a healthy partner, normal sexual activity may continue into old age.
5. All older people are senile.
6. Senile dementia does not occur in most older adults. Although fluid intelligence declines as the nervous system declines, crystallized intelligence shows little decline with age.
7. Student answers will vary. Older adults may be shown as physically disabled, senile, or set in their ways.
8. Student answers will vary. Examples include

Charles Schultz, George Burns, and Ronald Reagan.
9. Reasons include not having the resources to get proper care, an unwillingness of doctors to treat chronic illnesses, and stereotypical views held by healthcare workers.
10. People face the loss of friends, spouses, and loved ones; changes in living situation; loss of income; and loss of purpose.
11. Student answers will vary. A healthy sex life can benefit an older person physically, mentally, and emotionally.
12. Student answers should reflect the loss of independence experienced when a person must give up driving.
13. Signs include frequent forgetting, poor judgment, increased irritability, and social withdrawal.

Chapter 5, Section 3
1. The person does not accept the seriousness of the illness.
2. The person expresses anger toward any perceived cause of the illness.
3. The person bargains with God to let him or her live until a specific event, such as the birth of a grandchild, occurs.
4. As the person becomes aware of the losses, they become sad and depressed. They may detach themselves from others.
5. The person resigns himself or herself to death and may experience a calm and peace.
6. Student answers will vary. It may be interesting to allow students to share their different family customs surrounding death.
7. The dying person may be comforted by being in his or her own home surrounded by the things and people that he or she loves.

Chapter 6, Section 1
1. nucleus
2. cell body
3. axon
4. myelin sheath
5. dendrites
6. axon terminals
7. synapse
8. It increases the level of endorphins, which are neurotransmitters, in the bloodstream.
9. The autonomic nervous system control involuntary activities like breathing.

Chapter 6, Section 2
1. spinal cord
2. cerebellum
3. corpus callosum
4. cerebral cortex

Answer Key

5. thalamus
6. hypothalamus
7. pons
8. medulla
9. He observed the effect of head injuries on people's behavior and concluded that the brain was the source of thought.
10. If the left hemisphere of the brain is damaged, the person may lose feeling on the right side of his body.
11. A researcher may use a PET scan to observe which areas of the brain show activity when a person is reading a book or watching a video.

Chapter 6, Section 3

1. Too little thyroxine makes you feel lazy and lethargic. Too much thyroxine may cause weight loss and sleeplessness.
2. Epinephrine or adrenaline cause the heartbeat and breathing to increase and can heighten emotions such as fear.
3. Cortical steroids are responsible for muscle development and the release of stored sugar in the liver to provide extra energy.
4. Testosterone is a male hormone that helps decide the sex of the fetus and promotes growth during adolescence.
5. Estrogen and progesterone are female hormones responsible for the development of female sex characteristics and regulation of reproductive cycles.
6. Answers may include any act of daring such as bungee jumping, sky diving, and hang gliding.
7. The endocrine system releases hormones that travel through the bloodstream.
8. Norepinephrine would work as a neurotransmitter when it is released by a neuron to provide a quick response to a fearful situation. It would work as a hormone when it is released by the adrenal gland into the bloodstream to keep your heart beating faster when you a performing an athletic activity.

Chapter 6, Section 4

1. nature
2. nature
3. nurture
4. Genes provide the basic material that makes us who we are. Who we actually become depends on how the experiences we have and the people we learn from.
5. Nature is our genetic makeup that is inherited from our parents. It accounts for many of our traits and behaviors. Nurture refers to the what we learn from our environment.

Chapter 7, Section 1

1. Insomnia is characterized by an inability to get enough sleep over a prolonged period.
2. Sleep apnea involves frequent interruptions of breathing during sleep, snoring that lasts 10 to 15 seconds and ends suddenly, blockage of the air pathways.
3. Narcolepsy is characterized by a permanent and overwhelming feeling of sleepiness and fatigue during the day, unusual sleep and dream patterns, and dreamlike hallucinations or the feeling of temporary paralysis.
4. Nightmares are frightening dreams that occur during REM sleep.
5. Night terrors occur during Stage IV sleep, may last from five to twenty minutes, and may involve screaming, sweating, confusion, and a rapid heart rate.
6. Sleepwalking is walking or carrying out other behaviors while asleep with no memory of doing it.
7. Consciousness is a state of awareness. An altered state of consciousness is simply a different level of awareness such as sleep.
8. Sleeping allowed them to be in a sheltered area, out of harm's way, at night when it was dark.
9. During REM sleep your face and fingers may twitch, your eyes move rapidly from side to side, and your brain waves are similar to a person who is awake.
10. Since babies are growing and undergoing major developmental changes they need more sleep than older people who are no longer developing.
11. A person with narcolepsy may have difficulty holding a job, problems with interpersonal relationships, and be prone to accidents.
12. Student answers will vary. Students should be able to identify the common events like exams that may appear in dreams mixed with fantasies.

Chapter 7, Section 2

1. Student answers will vary. An example would be using posthypnotic suggestion to help someone forget a past poor performance at a music recital. This would be done to help the person overcome the fear of performing.
2. Student answers will vary. An example would be an athlete who uses biofeedback to monitor his heart rate and breathing while training for a marathon.
3. Student answers will vary. An example would be a figure skater who uses breathing meditation to focus on the upcoming performance.
4. Researchers have found that hypnosis, an altered state of consciousness, can help people with physical problems such as overeating.

Reading Essentials and Study Guide

5. A person may want to be hypnotized to help him or her remember the details of a crime that he or she has witnessed.

6. Student answers will vary. Although biofeedback is more systematic than feedback from a human, the result, learning, is the same.

7. Meditation helps people relax, which lowers their heart rate.

Chapter 7, Section 3

1. Marijuana distorts perception, disrupts memory formation, may increase the strength of negative emotions, and may lead to dependence.

2. LSD impairs thinking, creates panic reactions, and results in flashbacks.

3. Opiates are physically addictive and may cause death from respiratory failure.

4. Alcohol use may result in slurred speech, blurred vision, impaired judgment and memory, and damages a person's liver and brain.

5. Psychoactive drugs alter the chemical makeup of the body. In the short-term, effects such as hallucinations may endanger a person. Long-term effects may include permanent brain damage and damage to other organs and the central nervous system.

6. He may blow the worry out of proportion and experience an anxiety or panic attack.

7. They can cause you to act or react in ways that are dangerous. For example, you could walk into the path of an oncoming training thinking that you are walking toward a light.

8. Many people think they will only experience the pleasant experiences; they do not think bad things will happen to them. Others who consider the possibility of the terror may decide not to risk taking the drug.

9. Physical addiction is the body's need for continued use of the drug. If the body does not receive it, withdrawal symptoms may result.

10. Alcohol is socially acceptable and its use is encouraged in traditions, advertisements, and movies.

11. Drug addiction may lead to illegal actions, loss of a job, and alienation from friends and family.

Chapter 8, Section 1

1. The person is placed in a soundproof room.

2. She is instructed to say "I hear it" when she hears a sound.

3. The psychologist uses a very precise machine to send sound into the room, starting a the faintest levels.

4. The psychologist repeats the process with many different participants to establish the threshold.

5. We combine sounds and letters to make words. We combine words into meaningful sentences. We speak in specific languages that can only be understood by members of our language group.

6. Answers will vary. Sights may include friends or the weather outside. Sound may include music or the general noise that many conversations in the same room make. Smells will include the various foods available. You will taste and touch the food that you are eating.

7. Answers will vary. Many pets can detect light and sound before humans can.

8. You would perceive a greater increase in your car because the sound in the car is a weaker stimulus than the sound at a rock concert.

9. Answers will vary. Once you have adjusted to being in a noisy room, you may be able to hear your name called out.

10. Answers will vary. You may be talking to your friends or listening to music. You may be watching for cars or for pedestrians.

Chapter 8, Section 2

1. Light enters through the pupil.

2. It is focused by the lens.

3. It is sensed by the rods and cones in the retina.

4. The rods and cones change the light energy into neuronal impulses.

5. The optic nerve transmits the impulses to the brain.

6. The sense organs are eye, ears, nose, mouth (the tastebuds on the tongue), and the skin.

7. The object when it is held close creates more retinal disparity.

8. You are hearing sounds from a low frequency.

9. Answers will vary. Good examples include riding roller coasters and other amusement park rides.

10. The sense of smell is better in dogs. An example would be a hunting dog trained to smell a rabbit that cannot be detected by humans.

11. The gate control theory explains that an athlete can shift his attention away from the pain by concentrating on the competition. The pain will not be felt until after the game is over.

12. Answers will vary. You need to know where you are on the court in order to be able to respond to the right or left to receive the serve.

Chapter 8, Section 3

1. An example would be the ability to distinguish pictures (figures) hanging on the wall (background).

2. You hear your cat meowing when you walk in your house even though you cannot see the cat who is in another room.

3. When driving down the road, you know that the larger vehicle is closer to you.

Answer Key

4. An object such as a pencil, close to your face has a larger retinal disparity and is perceived as being closer than an object that is held farther away.

5. You know that the door to your house is large enough for you to enter your home even when it is viewed from a distance.

6. It would seem like a jumble of noises and make no sense.

7. Answers will vary. Another example would be when have a handful of change, you group the quarters together.

8. The words are the figures and the paper is the background.

9. It tells you that there is a dog in the house or yard even if you do not see it.

10. He might describe the dog as mean or ferocious because of his frightening experience.

11. You can see all of your friend, but part of the building is blocked from view by your friend. From that you know that your friend is closer than the building.

12. The five-foot person standing three feet away would appear taller.

13. Answers will vary. Examples include card tricks, pulling a rabbit out of a hat, and viewing yourself in a mirror that makes you appear very tall and thin or very short and fat.

14. Many fortune-tellers use generalities and allow people to attach their own interpretation to things. For example, telling someone that you will get a surprise at school can be interpreted in many ways.

Chapter 9, Section 1

1. no response
2. unconditioned response
3. neutral stimulus
4. conditioned response
5. conditioned response
6. extinction
7. Ivan Pavlov first explained classical conditioning.
8. You will likely react negatively to being served peas because you have generalized your dislike for green vegetables.
9. You could use classical conditioning to pair the food you dislike with something enjoyable or rewarding. If the food is paired with something enjoyable, you can eventually learn to overcome your distaste for the particular food.

Chapter 9, Section 2

1. rewards
2. the removal of pain
3. punishment
4. fear
5. pain

6. Answers will vary. Examples include receiving praise for being helpful and getting a good grade on a test you took.

7. You would use a primary reinforcer, at least at first, to get the dog to comply with your request.

8. Variable schedules have a more long-lasting effect because you do not know when the reinforcement will be received and so you keep trying at something.

9. Students can defend either choice. Most students will choose chaining because cheers involve numerous steps that can be learned sequentially.

10. She might whine or cry hoping that her parent's will give in and not punish her.

Chapter 9, Section 3

1. An example of cognitive learning is making a mental map of the route to a friend's house so that you can return to it in the future.

2. An example of modeling is clapping at the end of a speech because everyone else begins to clap.

3. An example of behavior modification is using a systems of rewards to quit biting your fingernails.

4. An example would be the mental image that skiers make of the best routes down a slope.

5. Simple modeling involves repeating someone else's action just to fit in. No real learning occurs. Observational learning allows a person to watch a behavior or skill and is later able to repeat it. Children may learn how to hold a baseball bat by observing baseball players.

6. Answers will vary. Examples include a snack after finishing studying or watching a movie if you do well on a test.

Chapter 10, Section 1

1. An example of maintenance rehearsal is a football player who repeats the play and play count over and over in his head so that he runs the right play.

2. An example of chunking would be learning your Social Security number by grouping the digits between the hyphens (three digits, two digits, and four digits).

3. An example of the primacy-recency effect is asking someone for directions and only remembering the first two turns and the name of the street on which the person lives.

4. An example of semantic memory is the fact that a question mark is placed at the end of a sentence that asks a question.

5. An example of episodic memory is your memory of your first day of high school.

6. An example may be a line from a movie that impressed you at the time, but that you had forgotten. Some event or someone brings the line back into your memory.

7. Answers will vary. Make sure that the memory described matches the method of encoding.

8. Answers will vary. An example of semantic memory is the fact that the word red and read are pronounced the same, but understood as different words because of the context in which they are used.

9. If we clearly understand how learning occurs, we may be able to find ways to stimulate the parts of the brain responsible for learning.

Chapter 10, Section 2

1. Confabulation affects recall by filling in gaps in memory with things that never occurred.

2. Our schemas act like a filter to influence the way we make sense of the world. We recall events and people through this filter.

3. Interference blocks our recall of events because other memories get in the way.

4. Repression affects our ability to bring a memory to the conscious mind, but the memory still exists.

5. Amnesia is the inability to recall memories that should be accessible.

6. Answers will vary. Some students maintain calendars, planners, or write notes. Other students try to keep the information in their heads.

7. Items of information are stored in memory in categories. An item may be stored under various categories just like a book may be located in a cataloging system by author, title, and subject.

8. Memories are not like snapshots of events. They are influenced by our schemas and altered by confabulation.

9. An example would be the list of state capitals that you learned in elementary school. The relearning process should be easier than the initial learning process.

10. The person may be repressing the painful details of the accident.

11. You would be using elaborative rehearsal since you are linking the friend's phone number (new information) to your phone number (existing information).

Chapter 11, Section 1

1. image
2. symbol
3. concept
4. prototype
5. rule
6. a shoe
7. the word shoe
8. footwear
9. an athletic shoe
10. Women's dress shoes do not have shoe laces.
11. Answers will vary. The invention of the Internet solved a problem of making information immediately available worldwide.

12. You are using directed thinking.

13. It is an algorithm because it is a consistent procedure used to "solve the problem" of starting the car.

14. Many problems cannot be solved using a fixed set of rules or procedures. Creativity allows you to discover unique solutions to problems.

Chapter 11, Section 2

1. phoneme
2. syntax
3. semantics
4. morpheme
5. It would be like random noise since it would not have meaning.
6. The phonemes are f, ea, r, l, e, ss, n, e, and ss.
7. An infant moves from cooing and babbling during her first months of life to saying single words like mama. Children learn by listening and by practicing. When certain sounds are reinforced, they are likely to be repeated.
8. It would represent Stage 3 in which the child puts two words together and is beginning to learn the rules of grammar.
9. Answers will vary. Many students will give examples of communication between pets. Most of the examples will involve forms of communication other than verbalizations. For example, one cat pouncing on another may indicate a desire to play or an act of aggression.
10. She may believe that only men can become doctors and only women can become nurses.

Chapter 12, Section 1

1. An example would be the annual north-south migration of geese.
2. When we are hungry, we seek food.
3. Adults go to work each day to earn money.
4. A person may spend years in school and training to become a psychologist because he finds great personal value in helping other people.
5. The internal state may motivate you to seek homeostasis, or to bring your body back into balance by eating.
6. Yes, this is instinctive behavior because it is a behavior that occurs at the same time each year by all deer.
7. The elephant would seek any source of water to quench its thirst.
8. The drive is to learn how to solve the problem. The incentive may be an upcoming test.
9. Answers will vary. An extrinsic motivator may be the desire to improve one's grade point average. An intrinsic motivator may be the desire to learn more about an area of interest.

Answer Key

Chapter 12, Section 2

1. has a fear of failure
2. avoid extreme challenges
3. avoid success
4. seek a place to belong and give and receive love
5. Answers will vary. Examples include academic challenges and physical challenges.
6. Your brain would not signal you to stop eating and you would gain weight.
7. Answers will vary. Women may not fear success in the medical profession as much now as then because more women have become doctors. Other fields dominated by one gender may cause a fear of success in people of the opposite gender.

Chapter 12, Section 3

1. interpretation of stimulus
2. experience of a subjective feeling about the stimulus
3. experience a physiological response to the feeling
4. display an observable behavior
5. Examples will vary. Encourage students to consider both positive and negative decisions made based on emotions.
6. Physically, you may fall to the floor or seek shelter. Behaviorally, you may scream or freeze. Cognitively, you may begin to think about how to avoid being hurt or how to keep the person with the gun from firing it.

Chapter 13, Section 1

1. reliable
2. valid
3. standardized
4. Answers will vary. A test may help you understand things about yourself more clearly.
5. Yes, the two scores have a very small variance.
6. The validity of a test can be measured only if the purpose of the test is absolutely clear. In this instance, the test may measure only talent for improving productivity, not general management ability.
7. A score at the 60th percentile means that you scored higher than 60 percent and lower than 40 percent of others taking the test.

Chapter 13, Section 2

1. general intelligence
2. specific mental abilities or skills
3. verbal comprehension
4. numerical ability
5. spatial ability
6. musical ability
7. creative thinking
8. practical thinking
9. perceive and express emotions
10. use emotions while thinking
11. Answers will vary. A person may have a high degree of math reasoning and spatial ability but have poor verbal skills. If a majority of assignments and tests rely heavily on the ability to use words, the student may do poorly.
12. ability with words, math reasoning
13. It would mean that you were slightly below the average for test takers of your age. It would place you in the low-average category.
14. Your intelligence would be classified as high average.
15. Answers will vary. A question that presupposes that only immediate family members live in the same dwelling may be culturally biased for a Hispanic student. It is not uncommon for extended families to live together in Hispanic culture.

Chapter 13, Section 3

1. achievement
2. aptitude
3. interest
4. Answers will vary. An interest inventory may indicate your preferences, attitudes, and interests that correspond to the work done in a certain profession or occupation.
5. Answers will vary. You would more likely enjoy your work and succeed in a career that matches your talents.
6. Achievement tests often predict job talents as well as measure how much a student already knows.
7. Interest tests try to find out what a person likes, not what a person knows.

Chapter 13, Section 4

1. objective test designed to reveal psychiatric illnesses
2. objective test developed for general use
3. objective test designed to help individuals understand their own personalities in order to understand better how they relate to others and how others relate to them
4. an open-ended examination that interprets not only the person's responses to 10 ink blots, but also the style of the responses
5. an open-ended examination that assesses personality problems of individuals by interpreting the story the test taker tells about each of 20 cards with pictures of vague situations
6. Answers will vary. A reserved person may display less emotion when confronted with a crisis than a person who is very demonstrative.

7. Answers will vary. The test identifies extravert and introvert personalities. An extravert may make a better salesperson than an introvert.

8. The Rorschach tests asks the person to examine ink blots and say what he sees.

Chapter 14, Section 1

1. psychoanalytic theory
2. behaviorists
3. social learning theory
4. cognitive theory
5. humanistic theory
6. trait theory
7. importance of motives hidden in the unconscious mind
8. the way rewards and punishments shape our actions
9. the impact of observational learning on personality
10. how our thoughts, perceptions, and feelings shape our personalities
11. one's potential for growth, such as creativity and spontaneity
12. the importance of understanding basic personality characteristics, such as friendliness and aggression
13. Answers will vary. Optimism is an example.
14. Theories present ideas of why people are different in systematic and scientific forms that allow objective testing to determine the validity of these ideas.
15. Answers will vary. Example: I look for practical solutions when problems arise, a behavior I learned from my mother.

Chapter 14, Section 2

1. Answers will vary. Example: A person is rationalizing when he says, "I didn't pass my driver's license test because the examiner didn't like me."
2. Answers will vary. Example: A girl who is rejected by a boy she likes may repress her hurt feelings and replace them with feelings of apathy.
3. Answers will vary. Example: A person may deny her obesity and refuse to alter eating and exercise habits to address health problems associated with being overweight.
4. Answers will vary. Example: If a person feels that others dislike him, when in reality he dislikes himself, he is said to be projecting.
5. Answers will vary. Example: A person who acts strong and confident when she is really scared is an example of reaction formation.
6. Answers will vary. Example: A person is displaying regression if he throws a temper tantrum when he does not get his way.

7. Answers will vary. Example: if you wanted to kick your brother but knew you would get in trouble, you might kick the wall.
8. Answers will vary. For example, you may be so upset by your friend's arrogant attitude that you work extra hard at soccer practice.
9. Answers will vary. Reactions will vary with the type of inadvertent remark. Often we assign more meaning to other people's "Freudian slips" than we do to our own.
10. The adult may be confident to attempt new or difficult tasks in his career.
11. The superego would be behind this behavior.
12. You would be using denial.
13. Answers will vary. The person may engage in behavior that is socially unacceptable or morally wrong.
14. Answers will vary. Example: A child might take lessons to learn how to play a musical instrument.

Chapter 14, Section 3

1. Reinforcement includes the occurrences of a reward or punishment following a particular behavior.
2. Observational learning occurs when a new behavior is acquired by watching the actions of another person.
3. Reciprocal determinism is the interaction that occurs among the observing individual, the behavior of that individual, and the environment in which the behavior occurs.
4. This school of thought is called behaviorism because it focuses on observable behavior rather than influences, unconscious forces, and irrational thoughts.
5. Answers will vary. Example: If a person likes to take the dog on walks, the reinforcing behavior may be that the dog is very happy when we are walking.
6. Answers will vary. Example: I learned to fold towels by watching my mother.

Chapter 14, Section 4

1. realistically oriented
2. have a great deal of spontaneity
3. have an air of detachment and a need for privacy
4. identify with humanity
5. resist conformity to the culture
6. Answers will vary. An excellent example is Helen Keller who succeed despite being deaf and blind.
7. Answers will vary. Humanistic psychology recognizes the potential and uniqueness of human beings.
8. Answers will vary. Example: This person has a great fund of creativeness. He transcends the environment rather than just coping with it. He is realistically oriented.

Answer Key

9. Unconditional positive regard allows a person to accept himself and become fully functioning.
10. Answers will vary. You can change your behavior upon gaining a new understanding of a situation.

Chapter 14, Section 5

1. extraversion
2. agreeableness
3. conscientiousness
4. openness to experience
5. emotional stability
6. introversion
7. cruelty
8. carelessness
9. fearfulness
10. neuroticism
11. Answers will vary. Some examples may include conscientiousness, agreeableness, and emotional stability.
12. Answers will vary. This person might stand against the wall waiting for others to approach her.
13. Answers will vary. Examples may include any of the traits discussed in this section.
14. Source traits are at the core of personality while surface traits are characteristics that can be observed in certain situations.
15. Answers will vary. Example: I would rate myself as a 5 because I am equally comfortable with people and by myself.
16. This person would be neurotic.

Chapter 15, Section 1

1. stressor
2. stress reaction
3. distress
4. eustress
5. how a person perceives and evaluates an event
6. Answers will vary. Example: I feel like I'm in danger of some kind.
7. Answers will vary. Example: A person might experience eustress while performing well at a piano recital.
8. Answers will vary. Example: I wanted to ask my dad for an increase in my monthly allowance, but was afraid he would blow up at me if I asked.
9. Answers will vary. Example: I needed to leave the house to be on time but couldn't find my other shoe. Then I missed every green light from my house to the highway.

Chapter 15, Section 2

1. increased rate of heartbeat
2. increased rate of breathing
3. increased amount of blood sugar
4. anxiety
5. anger
6. fear
7. nervous habits
8. changes in posture
9. escape
10. Answers will vary. Example: Laughing calms me by giving me an outlet for my discomfort in a situation.
11. Answers will vary. Example: My muscles tense and my breathing becomes shallow.
12. In the resistance stage a person finds a way to cope with the stressor.
13. Answers will vary. Example: She might burst into tears.
14. Answers will vary. Example: I know a girl who continually twirls several strands of her hair around her finger.
15. Answers will vary. Example: A heart surgeon may be at risk for a stress-related illness.
16. Answers will vary. Example: He is impatient, easily angered, and very competitive.

Chapter 15, Section 3

1. actively confronting and solving problems
2. taking the person out of the stressful situation or circumstance
3. postponing the stressor to a time when the person is able to cope more effectively
4. determining a rational analysis of the situation that will lead to an appropriate decision
5. optimistic thinking about events in a positive perspective
6. reducing muscle tension
7. laughing to help keep a proper perspective on the situation
8. Answers will vary. Example: My cousins were coming to visit, and they would be sleeping in my room, which was a mess. The positive side to this situation was that I have a lot of fun with my cousins and got my room cleaned up.
9. Answers will vary. Example: I can find out if my new school has a Web site to give me information about the extracurricular activities that interest me.

Chapter 15, Section 4

1. challenge to personal identity
2. greater diversity among students than in high school
3. developmental friendships
4. Answers will vary. Example: While in high school you may not have had total responsibility for all aspects of living that you have in college, such as doing your own laundry and maintaining a checking account.
5. Answers will vary. Example: I might choose music education because I enjoy teaching and music.

6. Answers will vary. Example: I would want challenge, financial reward, and flexibility.

Chapter 16, Section 1
1. not expressing grief at the death of one's parent
2. refusing to eat
3. hearing voices
4. Answers will vary. Example: My friends thought it was cool not to wear winter coats when the temperature was near zero degrees. I chose to wear my coat.
5. Answers will vary. Example: A person who is unable to hold a job would be considered abnormal according to the adjustment approach.
6. Mental illnesses are not as clear-cut as physical diseases.

Chapter 16, Section 2
1. phobic disorder
2. post-traumatic stress disorder
3. obsessive-compulsive disorder
4. panic disorder
5. generalized anxiety disorder
6. Answers will vary. Example: I planned an event for my friends and was anxious that everyone would have a good time. The "danger" was imagined.
7. Answers will vary. Being in a bank during a robbery would be an example of a situation that involves fear. The danger is real, not imagined.
8. This person has a specific phobia.
9. A panic disorder is extreme anxiety characterized by panic attacks that involve choking feelings, chest pain, dizziness, trembling, and hot flashes.
10. This is a compulsion. Uncontrollable patterns of thoughts are called obsessions. Repeatedly performed irrational actions are called compulsions.
11. Answers will vary. A survivor of a Nazi concentration camp might feel guilty because he survived, while many others died.

Chapter 16, Section 3
1. somatoform disorders
2. conversion disorder
3. hypochondriasis
4. dissociative disorders
5. dissociative amnesia
6. dissociative fugue
7. dissociative identity disorder
8. Answers will vary. Example: Being unable to walk might give a person a real way to avoid a responsibility that he finds stressful.
9. The behavior suggests hypochondriasis.
10. The behavior suggests dissociative amnesia.

Chapter 16, Section 4
1. major depressive disorder
2. problems with eating, sleeping, thinking, concentrating, or decision making
3. bipolar disorder
4. manic phase
5. elation, extreme confusion, distractibility, and racing thoughts
6. depressive phase
7. feelings of failure, sinfulness, worthlessness, and despair
8. Answers will vary. I watched a movie about a person who hears voices.
9. This is a delusion.
10. This statement suggests the paranoid type of schizophrenia.
11. No, because this hypothesis states that for schizophrenia to develop, the person must be exposed to an environment with certain stressors.
12. No, in order to be diagnosed as having major depressive disorder, the symptoms must be present for at least two weeks.

Chapter 16, Section 5
1. The individual discovers that alcohol reduces her tensions, gives her self-confidence, and reduces social pressures.
2. The beverage becomes a drug, and the individual feels she has to hide her habit.
3. The individual drinks compulsively, beginning in the morning.
4. Answers will vary. Example: Life would be dangerous because people would do whatever they felt like with no regard for the lives of others.
5. Answers will vary. Example: The person would show little or no emotion.
6. Psychological dependence does not involve physical dependence on the drug. Addiction involves a physical need for the substance.

Chapter 17, Section 1
1. verbal interaction between a therapist and client
2. the development of a supportive and trusting relationship
3. an analysis by the therapist of the client's problems
4. Answers will vary. Sometimes a friend or relative can give a new perspective to a problem while offering comfort and understanding.
5. Answers will vary. Sometimes the label of mental illness leads people to see themselves in a passive, helpless position.
6. Answers will vary. Empathy in the therapist gives the patient confidence that he is capable of caring and understanding.
7. Answers will vary. A therapist can help family

Answer Key

members recognize behaviors and attitudes within the family that contribute to the emotional problems of one family member.

8. Smith and Glass defined "improvement" as improvement in the quality of life for patients.

Chapter 17, Section 2

1. Psychological problems are due to anxiety about hidden conflicts between the unconscious components of one's personality.
2. Psychological problems arise when the true self becomes lost and the individual comes to view himself according to the standards of others.
3. The goal is to help clients understand their unconscious motives in order to gain control over their behavior and to free themselves of their problems.
4. The goal is to help people fulfill their human potential.
5. Answers will vary. Example: I dreamed I was driving a car and couldn't get my foot to reach the brakes. My life feels out of control, and I am powerless to change the situation.
6. Answers will vary. Passing thoughts may offer insight into the unconscious.
7. This acceptance makes it easier for the client to explore thoughts about himself and begin to see himself, his situation, and his relationships with others with new confidence.

Chapter 17, Section 3

1. The person builds an anxiety hierarchy with the least feared situation on the bottom and the most feared situation on top.
2. The person learns deep muscle relaxation.
3. The person imagines each step in the hierarchy while learning to be relaxed.
4. Answers will vary. Example: I would not want to drink a soft drink.
5. Cognitive therapists believe that it is not the event (in this case, not getting the job that was desired) that causes depression, but the way the person thinks about the event.
6. Answers will vary. The student may stop studying at all because the behavior did not produce the desired reward.
7. Cognitive-behavior therapy, like behavior therapy, tries to change clients' behavior, but cognitive-behavior therapy also tries to change their thoughts about the situation.

Chapter 17, Section 4

1. antipsychotic drugs
2. antidepressant drugs
3. lithium carbonate
4. antianxiety drugs

5. schizophrenia
6. major depression
7. mood swings of bipolar disorder
8. anxiety and panic disorders
9. Answers will vary. There are physiological factors to some psychological disorders that medicine helps manage.
10. Answers will vary. During the manic phase, the person may not feel that he or she needs it.

Chapter 18, Section 1

1. stimulation
2. utility
3. ego-support
4. A friend took you skiing, a new experience for you.
5. A friend helped you refinish an antique table.
6. A friend listened to you tell about your new job.
7. Answers will vary. Example: I think it would be very lonely and boring.
8. Answers will vary. Example: My friend sympathized with me when I told her about a problem I was having.
9. There is more opportunity for shared activities. We feel uneasy around people who are always challenging our views. It makes it easier to communicate with those who agree with us on things.

Chapter 18, Section 2

1. Example: A teacher forms a negative impression about a student based on an incident the first day of class and interprets all subsequent behavior during the semester in light of that first impression.
2. Example: We can yell at a basketball game. We should be subdued and quiet at a funeral.
3. Example: Female blondes are clueless.
4. Answers will vary. Example: I met a person who seemed to talk nonstop. As it turned out, she had just found out her family was going skiing during spring break, and her excitement caused her to talk more than usual.
5. Answers will vary. Words may include egocentric, overpaid, and spoiled.
6. They would be displaying a self-serving bias.
7. Answers will vary. Example: The person folds his arms in front of his chest. He scowls.

Chapter 18, Section 3

1. need or attachment
2. caring or the desire to give
3. intimacy
4. a strong desire to be with each other, to touch, to receive praise
5. as much concern for their partner's happiness as their own
6. special knowledge of each other that is gained by

openly sharing inner thoughts and feelings

7. Answers will vary. Example: This person believes in me and gives me the courage to tackle challenges.
8. Answers will vary. Example: The generation who grew up during the Great Depression lived with great deprivation that gives them a mentality of scarcity. They are likely to save their money and live frugally.
9. Answers will vary. Intimacy is a special knowledge of each other. This special knowledge enables each person to meet the other's needs and thus provide a solid foundation for commitment.

Chapter 19, Section 1

1. norms
2. ideology
3. commitment
4. Answers will vary. Example: I am part of a study group, and I am on the volleyball team.
5. Answers will vary. Example: When we work on the homecoming float together we are a group.
6. Answers will vary. Example: We all like the same kinds of music and styles of clothing.
7. Answers will vary. Example: My close friends are a primary group. My fellow classmates are a secondary group.
8. Answers will vary. Example: I played a flute solo. Yes, I have taken private lessons for 3 years.
9. Opposing views help a group think critically about its options and may enable the group to make a wise decision.

Chapter 19, Section 2

1. Despite feelings of extreme tension and discomfort, 65 percent of the participants continued to obey the experimenter's commands to administer ever-increasing voltages of electric shocks to the "learner."
2. The roles the individuals adopted (prison guards and prisoners) changed the way they acted. Those in the role of prison guards became intoxicated with the power of their positions and were cruel and harsh. Those in the role of prisoners had extreme emotional reactions; some became angry, while others developed psychological illnesses.
3. Answers will vary. Examples may include going to a party, hanging out at the mall, or buying a certain brand and style of shoes.
4. People do not want to appear different from others. There is a high value for being liked and accepted.
5. The participants were put in unpleasant and even temporarily harmful circumstances without their prior consent.

Chapter 19, Section 3

1. catharsis
2. punishment
3. teaching people to accept frustrations and move on
4. teaching people to react to disappointments in ways other than violence
5. Answers will vary. Example: Four police officers shot a suspect 41 times. They shot him because they thought he was getting ready to shoot them.
6. Answers will vary. Examples may include aggressive, hot-tempered, and arrogant.
7. Expressing aggression may lead to more aggression.
8. Answers will vary. Example: Police and residents may come together to get rid of drugs in the neighborhood.
9. No. These people are giving to get the reward of lower tax payments. Altruism is giving for reasons other than rewards.

Chapter 20, Section 1

1. Attitudes are shaped automatically through pairing a new stimulus with a stimulus that already causes a certain reaction.
2. Attitudes are acquired when we receive praise, approval, or acceptance for expressing certain attitudes or punishment for expressing other attitudes.
3. Attitudes are acquired by systematically thinking about an issue.
4. Attitudes are shaped by watching and imitating others.
5. Answers will vary. Example: I believe homework helps me learn. I feel obligated to complete homework. I almost always complete my assignments.
6. Answers will vary. Example: We both admire our parents.
7. Answers will vary. Example: I think hard work pays off. I believe it is important to be loyal to my friends.

Chapter 20, Section 2

1. People deny the dissonance.
2. People evade dissonance by avoiding exposure to information that would create conflict.
3. People change their attitude and/or reevaluate the event.
4. complying
5. The person adopts the attitudes and behavior of the gang.
6. This person is reducing cognitive dissonance by avoiding information that would cause conflict.
7. self-justification
8. Stereotyping prejudges people based on their membership in a certain group rather than on individual characteristics.

Answer Key

Chapter 20, Section 3

1. Example: People were asked to put a small sign in a window in their house. Two weeks later, another person asked these people for permission to stake a large sign in the front yard.
2. Example: You ask your friend to help you and your family move all day Saturday and Sunday until the task is done. Upon refusal of that request, you ask him to help move the grand piano on Saturday.
3. Example: A cult may use brainwashing to gain control over its members.
4. McDonalds advertises to attract people to their restaurants. They especially focus on getting children interested in eating their food, knowing that their parents will likely agree.
5. Advertisers are careful about whom they select to promote their products because they realize that many people are likely to rely on heuristic processing, a very casual, low-attention form of analyzing evidence. In this processing, the recipient tunes in to the peripheral aspects of the message—the likability of the source and the tone of voice.

Chapter 21, Section 1

1. crisis hotline adviser
2. word processor salesperson
3. mental health assistant
4. personnel director
5. school psychologist
6. clinical psychologist
7. consulting psychologist
8. Answers will vary. Examples should include tasks such as helping people or conducting research, not job titles.
9. Answers will vary. Encourage students to use their answer to question 8 to help make a choice.

Chapter 21, Section 2

1. Researchers explore the effect of day care on childhood development.
2. Being held is more important to forming secure attachment than being breast-fed or bottle-fed.
3. The role of play in development led to the PBS series "Sesame Street."
4. Computer software designers use some of B.F. Skinner's ideas on reinforcement.
5. Answers will vary. Areas of research such as sports or forensic psychology would be an example.
6. Knowledge leads to understanding. It helps to know that most psychological disorders have identifiable causes and useful treatments.
7. The test designers believe that the results will better predict success in college.
8. Answers will vary. Clues include sounds and visual clues like "Game Over."
9. Psychotherapists are applied psychologists because they use psychological methods to help people resolve their problems.

Reading Essentials and Study Guide